INDIA'S ECONOMY FROM NEHRU TO MODI

PULAPRE BALAKRISHNAN

India's Economy from Nehru to Modi

∽ A Brief History ∽

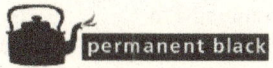 and

Published by
PERMANENT BLACK
'Himalayana', Mall Road, Ranikhet Cantt,
Ranikhet 263645
perblack@gmail.com
and

Distributed by
ORIENT BLACKSWAN PRIVATE LTD
Bangalore Bhopal Bhubaneshwar Chandigarh Chennai
Ernakulam Guwahati Hyderabad Jaipur Kolkata
Lucknow Mumbai New Delhi Patna
www.orientblackswan.com

COPYRIGHT © 2022 PULAPRE BALAKRISHNAN

ISBN 978-81-7824-667-3

First published in hardback 2022
First paperback printing 2023

Typeset in Adobe Garamond Pro
by Guru Typograph Technology, Crossings Republic, Ghaziabad
Printed and bound by Manipal Technologies Limited, Manipal

Whither do we go and what shall be our endeavour? To bring freedom and opportunity to the common man, to the peasants and workers of India. To fight and end poverty and ignorance and disease. To build up a prosperous, democratic and progressive nation, and to create social, economic and political institutions that will ensure justice and fullness of life to every man and woman.

Jawaharlal Nehru
Message to the Nation, Independence Day, 1947

*For my compatriots
who await the promised freedom*

Contents

Preface		ix
Introduction		1
1	Breakout	11
2	Watershed	57
3	Return to the World	94
4	Momentum Lost	141
5	An Unfinished Journey	204
	Bibliography	241
	Index	251

TABLES

1.1	Economic Performance in the Nehru Era	31
1.2	Economic Growth in the Nehru Era in Comparative Perspective	43
1.3	The Allocation of Public Expenditure on Education, 1951–1966	47
3.1	Financing External Payments	120
3.2	Manufacturing's Share of the Economy	133

4.1 Inflation and the Fiscal Deficit Since 2014 152
4.2 Gross Fixed Capital Formation (GFCF) 158
4.3 Foreign Direct Investment 165
4.4 Making in India 166
4.5 A Contractionary Macroeconomic Policy 181
4.6 Expenditure Priorities of the Modi Government 185
4.7 The Macroeconomic Policy Response to COVID-19 199
5.1 Human Development in India and the World 214
5.2 Public Spending and Educational Outcomes Across the World 216
5.3 Regional Variation of Development in India 218
5.4 Gender in Development 220
5.5 The Imprint of Caste 222

CHARTS

1.1 A Century of Economic Growth in India 18
2.1 A Growth Cycle 58
4.1 Economic Growth since 2014 155
4.2 Unemployment 156
4.3 The Inter-state Variation in COVID-19 Mortality 193

Preface

To be able to reflect and write at leisure on the topic of India's economic journey at seventy-five – the content of this book – is a great privilege. This opportunity came to me due to the generosity of Ashoka University, where I teach. I was not only granted a sabbatical to pursue my work but was granted it a year earlier than I was formally entitled to. The Vice Chancellor, Malabika Sarkar, the Dean of Faculty and Research at the time, Upinder Singh, and the Head of the Department of Economics, Ratul Lahkar, all played a role in this decision. It made it possible for me to write this book in time for the completion of India's seventy-five years on 15 August 2022. The Chancellor, Rudrangshu Mukherjee, enabled its publication in the University's series "Hedgehog and Fox" of which he is the editor.

For the past six years I have been at the Indian Institute of Management Kozhikode for six months every year. Its magnificent campus and comfortable buildings have inspired me to try and give of my best while I worked on this book. The Senior Fellowship that I have enjoyed at the IIMK is a somewhat rare position. For my election to it, I thank A.C. Muthiah, former Chairman of the institute, and K.C. Mohan, former member of its Board of Governors. Since then, Debashish Chatterjee, the Director, and Anandakuttan Unnithan, the Dean of Faculty, have ensured my continuation in the same position. This work owes in the largest part to the two institutions named above.

My book is the outcome of discussions I have had with professional colleagues and fellow citizens over a long period, perhaps running into decades. Among them are Bharat Ramaswami, Arunava Sen, Dipankar Dasgupta, Aditya Bhattacharjea, Mausumi Das, Ramachandra Guha, J.V. Meenakshi, the late Amitava Bose, Ajit Kumar Ghose, Dilip Mookherjee, the late Bhaskar "Gopu" Kumar, Balaram Menon, Venugopal Menon, N.R. Nanda Kishore, C.T. Kurien, C. Selvaraj, Amit Basole, Ravi Kanbur, Madhavan Palat, and Pranabes Dutta. Two persons deserve particular mention in relation to the present work. M. Parameswaran and Manalaya Suresh Babu not only served as my interlocutors over a long period but have actively assisted this book's birthing by assisting me with everything from acquiring the data to its analysis and the mounting of the empirical findings. In addition, my research assistants at the IIM, namely Ankita Kurur, S. Kabilan, Sreenath Namboodhiry, Marzouk Muhammed, and, above all, Rohith Unnikrishnan, have all cheerfully pursued my requirements, often at short notice. I gratefully acknowledge the inputs of all those mentioned above while absolving them of any errors that may have crept into this study.

The Library staff of Ashoka University, IIM Kozhikode, and the Centre for Development Studies at Thiruvananthapuram have assisted me with material. Nisar Kizhakkayil, then of the Nehru Memorial Museum and Library, New Delhi, and Amrit Tandon assisted me with the references. Raghunath Nageswaran compiled the index. I thank them all.

Finally, I must mention my editor at Permanent Black. I chose to publish my book with this relatively secluded house in anticipation of working with Rukun Advani, who had published my first book over three decades ago. That rewarding experience has only been enhanced now when his quick reading, deft editing, and sound advice left me with the sense that my manuscript was in the most assured of hands. As part of the editorial process I also received the comments of an anonymous reader, which led me to sharpen my argument.

This book was written at Klari, my ancestral village in Kerala. The combination here of a pastoral setting, plain-speaking folk, and distance from the uncongenial political climate in the world today provided the right environment for a writer to reflect. I hope that I have done justice to this bequest.

Though I have refrained from the academic economist's penchant for policy recommendation, each chapter points to what public policy has missed in the past, showing us how we can improve the present. The intention is that this work will serve as an input into a meaningful discussion of how India's economy should be structured to enable a better life for its citizen. I believe that it brings the perspective and contains the evidence necessary for this.

PULAPRE BALAKRISHNAN
Klari, 1 April 2022

Introduction

On 15 august 2022 India completed seventy-five years as an independent political entity. There have been reasons to celebrate this event, not least because over this period India has shown a better record of survival than the other national units of what in 1947 was Britain's South Asian empire. Since then, what was once Pakistan has broken into two, what was once Burma is ruled by its army, and what was once Ceylon ended a civil war only to remain mired in mutual distrust between its principal ethnic groups. Rocked though it has been by occasional strife and endless controversy, India has largely maintained its identity as a secular democratic republic, though this character has come under strain today.

My book is a reflection on India's economic journey since 1947 with a view to assessing how much the country has succeeded in delivering the goal of the movement for Indian independence. How is India's economic journey germane to this assessment? It is so because attaining the goal of independence, as imagined by India's founders, was tethered to the economic prowess to be achieved by the newly formed country. The founders were acutely aware of this reality – unlike, it seems, the political class in whose hands the country is today.

To assess the extent to which the goal of Indian independence has been reached we would need to begin with an understanding of what it was to start with. It may seem something of a worn device to seek such origins in the writings of Jawaharlal Nehru, in particular the speech that he made to the Constituent Assembly on the eve of independence. There is, though, a compelling reason: from the liberal standpoint, there is no better statement of the goal of independence than that speech. This is confirmed when Nehru's vision for India, contained in his writing and speeches, is compared to the pronouncements made by many thoughtful Indians of the time. While all these others enable us to see through the thicket on some specific matter, Nehru's vision is not just overarching but came with a weighing up of the prospects for its attainment. On 15 August 1947 he pointed out that independence was "but a step" to "the ending of poverty and ignorance and disease and inequality of opportunity."[1]

Two things are striking about the speech, of which the passages I have quoted are a part. First, Nehru thought that the rationale of an independent India lay in the opportunity of the individual Indian to lead a fulfilling life, and not the pursuit of national power and glory brandished on a global stage. Second, even as he stated this goal, Nehru queried whether India's leadership, of which he was a part, had what it would take to succeed in achieving the envisioned goal.

Two innovations in social and political theory that were to come later help us place Nehru's thoughts in perspective. First, in the 1950s, in an essay that has received wide attention, the historian of ideas Isaiah Berlin made a distinction between two concepts of freedom.[2] The first of these, he said, is the absence of political interference in an individual's life – which he termed "negative" freedom. This is perhaps the understanding most easily

[1] Nehru (1958a [1947]).

[2] Berlin (1968 [1958]). Actually, he had used the term "liberty", but this is not consequential.

recalled when freedom is mentioned. However, as Berlin pointed out, it is possible to imagine another conception of freedom, which is a person's ability to do or to act in order to realise his or her goals. Quite intuitively, Berlin termed this "positive" freedom.

It is easy to see that the first of these two concepts of freedom does not imply the second. An individual may be unconstrained by law or convention, and thus be enjoying negative freedom, but it does not follow that he or she will have the capacity to act according to their wishes if deprived of positive freedom. How such situations can arise is taken up later in this book, but a knowledge of them is not needed to appreciate the distinction Berlin had made.

Before moving on, it should be noted that Berlin himself was sceptical of the practical significance of the distinction he had made almost as soon as he had made it. For, in the very same essay, he cautioned that the idea of positive freedom can be used by authoritarian regimes to mask their tyranny. In this, Berlin appears to have been influenced by his own experience of early communism in Soviet Russia, from where he was to emigrate to Britain, only to observe from afar what to him were unimaginable crimes committed by a state against its people. Not even the benign climate of 1950s Britain, which saw the installation of a globally unprecedented welfare state that promised its citizens freedom in both the above senses, seems to have reassured him.

Four decades later, Amartya Sen was to conceptualise development in a way strongly reminiscent of Berlin's second concept of liberty. He defined development as the "expansion of freedoms".[3] For Sen, freedom is to be understood as a person's

---

[3] Sen (1999).

capacity to pursue the "functionings", that is the "beings and doings", he or she values. This capacity Sen termed "capability". Surely this is a conception in the spirit of positive freedom, which idea we have just encountered.

From a practical point of view, however, Sen made an advance over Berlin. He identified "capability" as the functionings that the person can achieve, reflecting the person's freedom to lead one type of life or another.[4] Combining Berlin and Sen, we can see that an individual's capability set represents the constraint on his or her attainment of positive freedom. The immediate implication of Sen's intervention was in relation to the received idea of economic development, which now had to be recast. Sen seemed to imply that the idea of economic development prevailing at that time over the agendas of nation states and well-funded global institutions was focused excessively on goods and not people. It now followed that economic development should be seen as "human" development, with a view to expanding the individual's freedoms. Goods remain vital to our existence but capability is the source of our well-being, as it were.

It is significant that Berlin and Sen appear to be in sync in their unwillingness to specify the goals of the individual – in the case of the former the "doings" and in the case of the latter the "functionings" – that were to be thought of as relevant. Implicitly, for both of them, it was best left to the individual to decide. This is the quintessentially liberal position in politics. However, Sen did point to what might underlie capability, thus showing how public policy can be leveraged to advance human development. I shall return to this issue later.

[4] See Sen (1992).

Finally, neither Berlin nor Sen jettisoned the relevance of negative freedom. After all, generalised restraint by law or convention is incompatible with positive freedom. From the denial to widows of the freedom to remarry (decreed for long by the Hindu priesthood) to the suppression of women's agency under the Taliban in today's Afghanistan, we can appreciate the value of negative freedom to those who are denied it.

When individuals are free to pursue the functionings that they value, which Sen identified as development, they enjoy positive freedom in the sense of Berlin. Nehru had visualised the preconditions of such a life through the ending of poverty, ignorance, disease, and inequality of opportunity. He had at India's founding moment conveyed a clear idea of what such a project should aim for. But what is of equal significance is that he saw the goal could not be thought of as a guaranteed achievement. To study his speech in full would be to see he was not sanguine about the possibility of India's new rulers – not excluding himself – delivering a life free of deprivation to Indians, even if it could be safely assumed that the country would remain a democracy over the foreseeable future.

As I shall show in the course of my account, Nehru has proved prescient in his assessment. His importance, therefore, lies not solely in his identification of the goals for Indian democracy, but equally in drawing attention to the challenges in the journey that lay ahead of the country. As my account of India's economic journey progresses, it will become apparent that both the goals and the challenges have mostly gone unrecognised by India's leadership after Nehru.

Once we recognise the goal imagined at India's founding moment, the criterion by which we should evaluate its economic journey since 1947 follows directly. India can be said to have succeeded only to the extent to which all Indians enjoy positive freedom, so that they are able to pursue the life that they individually value. The outcome in this regard is largely related to the country's economic journey. For example, the consequence for human development of economic growth is closely related to how wide a section of the population participates in it. However, I believe that a recounting of India's economic journey is not just relevant for this evaluative exercise but valuable also as an educational one. The two academic institutions at which I have taught recently – one a private liberal arts and sciences university and the other a part of a set of public-sector management institutes – are as different as chalk and cheese. However, I am struck by a similarity among my students in their lack of appreciation of India's post-independence economic history. In the minds of many young Indians, we have made no progress at all during this time, with a dynamism finally coming to the economy only after the economic reforms of 1991. As if such a preconception were not bad enough, the all-pervading sense of hopelessness harboured about the future is quite astonishing, even for a wizened academic! I believe that this hopelessness is related to a lack of understanding of what has been achieved in India so far, and what stands in the way of our achieving a country where the people flourish – as was imagined in 1947.

A part of this misunderstanding is because of the absence of an accessible and evidence-based account of India's economic journey. So, in writing this book I see my task as, first, describing and then evaluating the journey in accessible terms, with the narrative based on evidence. In the course of my narration, I try to account for Indian economic history in terms of the politics –

both the ideologies and the social forces — that have triumphed at various stages in the past seventy-five years. In fact, I show that the extent to which India has made progress, measured in terms of the goal set out in 1947, can be understood only in terms of the country's politics. To run ahead a little, this can be seen in the significant variation in human development across the country. In light of this feature, it would be natural to ask why, if the laws — including economic ones — are the same for all of them, do some regions show greater development than others. The clue lies in the fact that in a large and diverse country the forces that make for progress are largely local and, therefore, mediated by the politics of a region. India's states are large both in terms of their populations and powerful enough in terms of their political reach to chart their own course. This can result in widely different economic outcomes across the country.

The book is arranged as follows: In the next four chapters I present my account of India's economic journey from 1947 to the present. The periodisation adopted is based either on political developments or a significant change in the economic policy regime, whichever happened to predominate at each turning point. Thus, the first period studied is 1947–64, which may justifiably be called "the Nehru era" — due both to the distinct economic model that was followed and the extraordinary influence on economic affairs of the country's first and longest-serving prime minister. In this section, having presented the facts, I weigh the criticism of the economic policy of the time, an exercise that has seen renewed interest in recent years. A conclusive evaluation is offered.

The second period studied is 1965–90. It has been titled "Watershed" to convey that this quarter-century, more often than not relegated to the back pages in accounts of the evolution of India's economy, marked an important break from the past. Political economy is deployed to account for the mercurial shifts in economic policy under Indira Gandhi and an assessment made of her role in shaping the country's economic future. There is also an account in this section of the brief stewardship of Rajiv Gandhi, and an evaluation of what his time in office meant for India.

The next phase studied is 1991–2013. The year 1991 witnessed an overhaul of the economic-policy regime, popularly known as "the economic reforms", which largely focused on a reintegration of India's economy with that of the rest of the world – which explains the title of the chapter. The political economy of this regime change is addressed first, followed by an analysis of the outcomes. The section concludes with an assessment of what the reforms actually accomplished, as against what some believe they did.

The last period studied is that from 2014 to the present. Politically, the period is marked by the return of a single-party majority in parliament and the emergence of a strong leader with a populist style. The lineage of the economic policy of the Narendra Modi government is explained and weighed in terms of what it has resulted in.

Through a narration of the journey of the Indian economy since 1947 I also answer some of the questions that I believe interest many Indians. Answers may be found in this book to the following: What difference did the economic policies of the Nehru era make? How should we view the impact of Indira Gandhi on the economy? Did Rajiv Gandhi's technical orientation help the country at all? How revolutionary, in terms of their impact, were the economic reforms of 1991? And, finally, to what extent has Narendra Modi delivered on the electoral promise *"Achche din aane wale hain"* (Good days are on the way), ostensibly to be brought about by his decisive political leadership?

In this book my aim is a popular account accessible to the lay person. It is undergirded by extensive research on the same topic contained in my book, *Economic Growth in India: History and Prospect* (2010), and subsequent writings in professional journals, where the details typically of interest to specialists may be found.[5]

In the final chapter of this book I assess the extent to which the goal set out by India's founders in 1947 has been achieved in the succeeding seventy-five years. As argued above, the goal is closely aligned with what has come to be understood as "human development" in the global discourse on the desirable social and economic arrangements in contemporary societies. So, I focus on the human development outcomes in India, resisting a fuller evaluation of the progress made in other dimensions – such as the growth and modernisation of the economy – despite these having been substantial. An evaluation focused on the latter aspects would be intrinsically of interest to any economist, and much of it does take place as part of my account of India's economic journey. However, the promise of Indian independence was that Indians would soon be free to lead a fulfilling life –

[5] In particular, the economic relationships presumed to exist have been empirically established by me in the works listed at *www.pulaprebalakrishnan.in*. The latter includes my commentary on contemporary economic developments in the media.

contained in the idea of positive freedom and inextricably linked to human development. Accordingly, the achievement of ends such as achieving a five-trillion-dollar economy, a complete integration of India's economy with the rest of the world and the freeing of all economic activity from regulation ring hollow so long as there remain Indians without the capability to pursue the life they value.[6] In assessing the extent to which the promise of Indian independence has been translated into human development, I shall show that this has varied across India.

I end the book by arguing that uneven progress is related to the varying extent of social transformation across the country, an argument that will immediately be understood by sociologists, even as its relevance is mostly underestimated by economists. Now, as I show in the final chapter of this book, it is also the case that the regions of the country that have witnessed greater social transformation have achieved a higher income. However, in this book the focus is on human development as an end in itself rather than as a means of promoting growth – because human development was the promise held out to Indians in 1947.

---

[6] For an example of the goals of economic policy as understood by diverse sections of the political leadership, see the following: "Though India embarked upon economic reforms in 1991, the [Indian Finance] Minister said, a lot was left to be done: "What was envisaged in 1991 itself hasn't happened, for very many reasons, the pace at which the opening up had to happen, the pace at which companies had to be liberated from the licence-quota raj, hasn't happened."" *The Hindu*, 5 October 2021. See also "Tamil Nadu can become $1-tn. economy in a decade: Thiaga Rajan", *The Hindu* 19 November 2021; P.T.R. Thiaga Rajan is the finance minister of Tamilnadu.

1

Breakout

To understand India's economic journey over the first seventy-five years of independent India – what drove it and why we are where we are – we need to start at its beginning. For, where an economy finds itself is influenced by the path that it has taken.[1] A second reason for the need to understand the path taken by India's economy is to be able to evaluate the extent to which an attempt was made to deliver on the goal set in 1947 – as outlined in the Introduction.

Where, in economic terms, was India placed in August 1947? The chaos of Partition was the culmination of almost two hundred years of conquest, plunder, and exploitation of the country as a colony. Accounts of this period, by Indian and British observers, are gruesome in their depiction of the disruption

---

[1] This property of a dynamical system, in this case an economy in motion, is known as "path dependence". Path dependence has been observed to be an important feature in the evolution of an economy, reflected in the history that economies starting out as similar in most ways often end up as very different. One needs only to think of the evolution of the states of India after independence to appreciate this, a matter to which I return in the final chapter.

and human suffering caused by an extractive state.[2] While the unsettling consequence for Indians of their country passing into colonial rule can be easily understood, its extractive nature requires some elucidation. When we use the term "extraction" in economics today we tend to think of the extractive industries, mining and oil being the examples that come to mind. However, extraction in the terminology of economics need not be confined to this form. The extraction in place in colonial India was the appropriation of the nation's economic product through taxes that flowed out of the country. Initially, under the East India Company (EIC), land revenue was the form that this extraction took. Later, it took the form of various levies charged to the Indian populace, the most notorious of which were the Home Charges, ostensibly for the service of good governance being provided to it by the British.

For the greater part of the two centuries over which much of India was under British rule, it was directly under the British state for only about ninety years. For the rest of the time it was under the EIC. So, since the latter was a company – one of the world's first multinationals – why do we speak of an extractive "state"? We do so because the EIC conforms fully to the Hobbesian view of the state as the entity with a monopoly on violence. The EIC gained its position as the ruler of much of India by military means. So it was a state all right, but a corporate one, in that it was run entirely on the profit motive, and for the benefit of its shareholders in England.

The EIC was impressively methodical in its approach to the exploitation of India. Having gained sovereignty in much of

---

[2] See Dutt (1902), and Dalrymple (2019), respectively.

eastern India after the Battle of "Plassey" (Palashi), it started its career as the state de facto by levying land revenue, thus extracting part of the economic product of India. This extraction was done indirectly, via Indian intermediaries – the zamindars. With a view to increasing the extraction, the Company soon devised other forms of land tenure in the north, south, and west of the country. The form of land tenure adopted was to have very long-lasting effects on the rural economy, with areas under zamindari showing lower levels of development than other areas even two centuries later.[3] Whatever the difference in the forms of land tenure instituted by the colonial government in the different parts of India, agriculture, the largest sector of the economy, did not prosper in colonial India. On the basis of the only systematic evidence we have of agricultural growth in British India, George Blyn has shown that in the last half-century of the Raj output growth was less than population growth for most crops other than wheat, and that the rate of growth itself was declining over time.[4]

A notable feature of colonial India was recurring famines. These were unprecedented in their impact on Indian lives. While the role of the colonial government in each of these famines has been debated – with some of the protagonists arguing that it was the Indian climate that was responsible – it is significant, as Amartya Sen has pointed out, that there has not been a single famine in India since 1947. Interestingly, Sen has put this down to political competition in a democracy, whereby a political party would have no chance of remaining in power if

---

[3] Banerjee and Iyer (2005) put this down to the greater degree of initial inequality induced by this form of land tenure.
[4] See Blyn (1967).

it were to preside over a famine. Governments in democracies strain every sinew even to ensure that the food supply chain is not too severely disrupted, leave alone allowing a famine to occur. In the context of the famines of colonial India, then, there is reason to believe that the government did little to prevent famines.

In the case of the famine in Bengal in 1770, it has been said that the EIC was not in administrative control of the entire region. But this cannot be said of the famines after 1857, when India was directly under the Crown, administered by bureaucrats and headed by a viceroy who represented the king of England. The historian Ambirajan has, using official documents, shown that, fostered by an adherence to the Malthusian ideology, there was a reluctance within the colonial government to intervene in famines.[5] For Malthus the poor were incapable of restraining reproduction and would end up multiplying at a rate faster than the food supply. Famines were an inevitable consequence of this, and deaths that occurred were nature's way of keeping population growth under check. Colonial administrators transferred this idea, originally conceived of in relation to the English poor, to India. Now famines in India were simply assumed to be the result of a population multiplying too fast. In this view, to prevent famine deaths would be pointless as the poor would eventually return to their irresistible pastime. Ambirajan does recognise a more compassionate approach among some colonial administrators, such as the Irishman Lord Mayo, but concludes that by and large colonial policy was resolutely Malthusian in its unwillingness to intervene to save lives.

[5] Ambirajan (1976).

That British policy in India cannot be absolved of responsibility for recurrent famines may actually be understood within the axes of the Malthusian framework itself. Food production increased and population growth declined significantly, though slowly, after 1947. The democratic order in India succeeded in reversing the seemingly immutable natural ordering Malthus had assigned to the growth of population and the food supply, respectively. It also, to an extent, has taken care of the vulnerable by strengthening and extending the public distribution system – actually, an arrangement put in place by the British colonial administration during the Bengal famine of 1943–4 to aid the war effort.

The corporate colonial state represented by the EIC gave way to the imperial colonial state, with direct rule by the British Crown instituted in 1858. It is worth mentioning that though Indians were in principle subjects of the English monarch, Britain was already a democracy – in the sense that it had a parliament, though with limited suffrage. It is important to recognise this as an instance of a democracy denying political rights to non-native peoples. The French Republic under Napoleon was not dissimilar in its treatment of its colonial subjects. It should not therefore be surprising that the colonial element in the relationship between India and Britain did not change after 1858. Extraction continued, even though land revenue grew to become a smaller share of the unrequited financial flows from India.[6] Prominent among their newer forms were the Home Charges, rationalised as a payment for the services Britain was rendering to India by governing it and extravagant guarantees to British

---

[6] See Mukherjee (2010).

investments in India. The use of Indian troops, paid for from the Indian exchequer, to protect Britain's imperial interests, and ad hoc "contributions" and loans commandeered by the colonial state during the two World Wars were other elements of the financial outflow that replaced the commodity flow which had taken place under the East India Company.

Though somewhat inchoate, the Drain Theory enunciated by Dadabhai Naoroji was to bring these invisible one-way financial flows to the attention of both the British and the Indian public.[7] It has been estimated that this drain could not have been more than 10 per cent of the national income of India. While this may not appear to be very large in itself, even a small outflow sustained for a long period of time can result in a very large amount of money. One estimate of the accumulated value of the drain starting from 1765 is that it amounted to thirty-eight times the GDP of the United Kingdom in 1947.[8]

Ultimately, there is a summary way of assessing the economic consequences of British rule in India, and this is no different from the approach still taken globally today when it comes to assessing economic performance among countries. This entails studying the growth of income. Two independent studies of growth in British India exist – one by the British economic historian A. Maddison and the other by the Indian economist S. Sivasubramonian.[9] The estimates of average annual per capita growth in these studies are close, though not identical. Over the period 1900 to 1947 Maddison's estimate shows a very slight

[7] Naoroji (1901). It must be noted, though, that British authors had written about the drain of wealth from India and attempted to quantify it much earlier.
[8] Patnaik and Patnaik (2021).
[9] See Maddison (2001) and Sivasubramonian (2005).

decline in per capita income, while Sivasubramonian's estimate shows a very slight increase. Going by these numbers, it would be safe to say that the final half-century of British rule in India was a period of stagnation in the living standards of Indians. That this was a period when financial flows out of India were positive suggests that the famed *Pax Britannica* really benefited only Britain.

This time capsule I have outlined of colonial rule in India was meant to convey an idea of the state of India's economy in 1947. It is aided by the graph in Chart 1.1, which plots the movement in India's gross domestic product from 1900 to the present.[10] In it we can see that, after a boom during the Second World War – which is believed to have yielded windfall profits to Indian industrialists – output collapsed, leaving India in 1947 with a national income that was lower than in 1930, the peak year of the Great Depression which had affected India by depressing the prices of commodities, India's principal exports. Compounding the impact of the collapsed wartime boom, the Partition of India which had accompanied independence was to prolong the depressing effect of colonial rule. Production suffered as the supply chain was severely disrupted. Some of the major industries of the country were based in the metropolitan ports of what became India, while the raw material was grown in what became Pakistan, cotton and jute being the best

---

[10] The vertical lines in the graph represent dates at which the rate of growth of the economy switches, i.e. increases or decreases. The figures in between are the growth rates for each phase. Note that the breakdates have been estimated by a statistical procedure and are not chosen by the researcher. For the procedure, see Bai and Perron (2003). The data are the national income estimates of Sivasubramonian (2005) and the CSO combined to give a continuous series at 2011–12 prices.

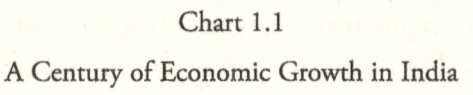

Chart 1.1
A Century of Economic Growth in India

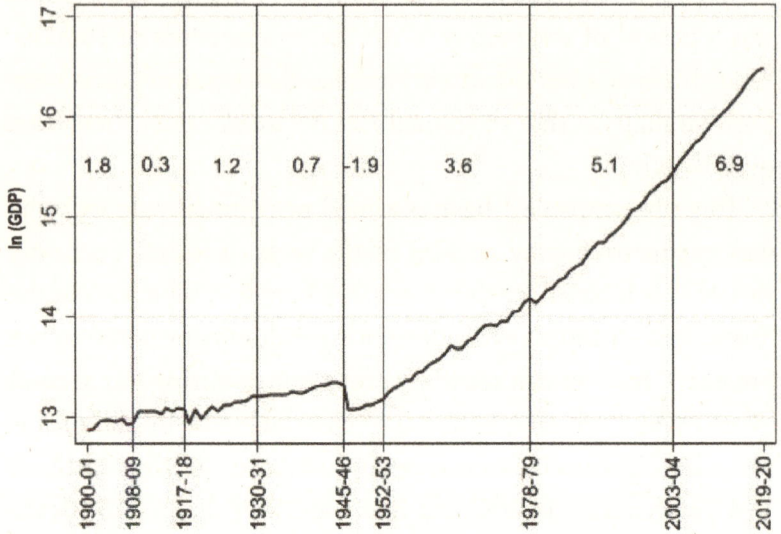

examples of this. Private investment is bound to have been affected as entrepreneurs would have shelved their plans in light of the uncertainty about the future of the new political entity that was India.

There was also the social dimension of Partition, which is likely to have cast a shadow on the economy. In August 1947, with mass migration across a poorly understood border and sporadic riots erupting, it must have seemed that nothing was moving well for the country, leave alone for its economy. Animal spirits, identified by Keynes as the urge among economic agents to act based on sentiment regarding the future, are likely to have been decidedly downbeat. To borrow an idiom from our times, surely nobody is likely to have imagined *"Achche din aane wale hain"* (Good times are on the way). How the political leadership of India dealt with this situation – of an impoverished economy facing political uncertainty – forms the next stage of our own journey through the economic history of early independent India.

Imagining the Post-colonial Economy

The Congress Party, which had led the national movement, had from the late 1930s been working on a vision of the economy for post-independence India. It also took the first steps to implement this vision. A significant milestone in this respect was the formation in 1938 of the National Planning Committee under the chairmanship of Jawaharlal Nehru, when Subhas Chandra Bose was the president of the Congress. The plan to industrialise India very likely germinated in the early deliberations of the Committee. It is interesting that economic policy in independent India had a distinguished lineage, with inputs from leading politicians and independent experts who had a global intellectual reach. Over the decades this great advantage was lost, the economic policy-making process having been swallowed up by narrowly partisan politics, which means that independent economists have been increasingly reluctant to be associated with it.

So, what was this vision that the National Planning Committee of the Congress had? For a start it envisioned an economy without the defining feature of India in the 1930s – the prevalence of extreme poverty. The elimination of poverty was to be achieved via industrialisation. The excessive preoccupation with the economy's architecture – i.e. whether it should be market-based, and whether state intervention should be allowed – that characterises much of the economic discourse today was relatively absent at that time, and the political leadership seems to have simply assumed that the state must play a leading role. What exactly this role should be had to wait till the 1950s, when P.C. Mahalanobis came to assume a central position in guiding economic policy. But it seems to have been taken for granted that there should be economic planning.

Much has been made of this approach of India's political leadership by critics of the economic policy of early independent India, the argument being that it represented a capitulation to the Soviet model of development. Two points may be noted here. Nehru himself is on record saying that India's economic future could not be secured by reference to either the American or the Soviet economic model since India's problems were unique. But the idea that India needed planning could not but have been influenced by a certain understanding of the wider implications of the Soviet experience. And this recognition was not confined to the politicians of the Congress party. In the 1930s M. Visvesvaraya, the visionary engineer from Mysore, spoke admiringly of the achievement of the Soviet Union in turning a backward economy into a veritable industrial powerhouse. Interestingly, the source of his information was an economic report of the League of Nations, an institution led by Western powers.[11] Very likely as a consequence of approaching the issue from the vantage point of his own discipline, he was particularly impressed by the engineering prowess Soviet Russia had achieved in so short a period. As a practitioner, it is unlikely that Visvesvaraya would have been swayed by ideological considerations

[11] See Visvesvaraya (1936).

and his assessment of the engineering achievements of the Soviet Union was prescient. The Soviets went on to play a major role in the defeat of Hitler, the Red Army being the first to reach Berlin in 1945. This would not have been possible without enormous industrial muscle, comparable to that of Germany, which was already a significant industrial power at the time of the birth of the Soviet Union.

Interestingly, a plan for the industrialisation of India that was not based on the experience of the Soviet Union but yet envisaged a leading role for the state was put forth by some leading industrialists of the country. Called the "Bombay Plan", it recommended an economic architecture with a significant presence for the state in what they considered the core sectors of the economy. Showing a precocious awareness of the discourse of "markets versus the state" that was to dominate global debates on the economy from the 1980s on, this document unapologetically made a case for government intervention as necessary, without in any way diminishing the private sector. Amidst the ideological cacophony in the country today, the Bombay Plan comes across as an extremely thoughtful proposal.

Altogether, far too much time has been spent on summarily dismissing the economic policy of independent India on the grounds that it was ideologically based on the Soviet model. This critique is an ideological approach in itself – on account of its insistence that economic arrangements are to be evaluated purely on the basis of their proximity to certain viewpoints rather than in relation to their anticipated outcome. A concerted drive towards industrialisation does not by itself imply an ideology-driven approach. Germany is an example of a country where industrialisation was a national policy in the nineteenth century. The first explicit case for protection from international trade as an aspect of industrialisation was proposed by the German thinker Friedrich List as early as the 1830s. Then, Germany's Chancellor Bismarck was to make industrialisation part of the state's economic policy. So too did South Korea in the mid-twentieth century, adopting industrialisation as a national goal. Interestingly, South Korea had a formal state planning authority, which, it has been pointed out, was inspired by India's own Planning Commission! Finally, what may surprise many is the claim that the first industrial nation, namely the UK, steered its industrialisation process by a protectionist trade policy.[12] First, to protect the British local wool industry the import of Indian cotton textiles was restricted in various ways. Then, in the twentieth century, Imperial Preference was clamped upon India, whereby imports into the country from Britain and its commonwealth had preferential access. This was meant to protect British manufacturing interests from competition by the Japanese cotton textile industry, which was merely to practise protectionism by another name. Britain also raised revenues for the imperial Government of India via customs duties, and such revenue ultimately made its way back to Britain as one of the many elements of the financial outflow from India already referred to.

Once the upheaval of Partition was behind the new country, Nehru turned with zeal to the task of economic reconstruction. Rafi Ahmed Kidwai, his close colleague over a long period, observed that Nehru was "obsessed with foreign affairs", leading him to spend less time on the economy than necessary.[13] This

[12] See Scott (1997).
[13] Quoted by Durga Das (1969), p. 379.

may well be true as Nehru did see India having a major role to play in the emergent world order. However, even a cursory glance at his speeches on the challenges facing the country would reveal that he gave its economy a great deal of his attention.[14] In any case, it is difficult to imagine a prime minister who held office for seventeen years failing to attend to his country's economy. Nehru's speeches in fact reveal considerable knowledge of the details of economic management, ranging from crop yields to the importance of raising industrial productivity. In 1950, when launching planning to achieve the goal of industrialisation, Nehru instituted the Planning Commission, with the prime minister as its chairman. This was very likely a unilateral move by him, not receiving the support of even all his cabinet colleagues. The finance minister, John Mathai, an economist and a director of Tata Sons, resigned soon after it was instituted on the grounds that it usurped the powers of the Ministry of Finance. Mathai's resignation also points to a certain ambiguity on the part of the authors of the Bombay Plan, of which he was a signatory, in that they viewed the state's role as an investor in essential areas as legitimate but were uneasy about its regulatory powers over the private sector.

With the constitution of the Planning Commission, economic planning was launched in 1951, giving rise to a series of successive five-year plans, until the institution was wound down in 2014 by Narendra Modi.

However, though begun in 1951, economic planning came into its own only five years later. This development can be traced

[14] Many of Nehru's speeches have been compiled in several volumes by the Publications Division of the Government of India. The speeches appearing in Volume 3 are from the period we are studying here.

back directly to the role of a single Indian, P.C. Mahalanobis. A physicist by training, Mahalanobis was to adopt statistics as his field of practice early in his career. By the 1950s he was a statistician of global repute. His writings on the Indian economy show him to be aware of the empirical aspect of growth as it had taken place across the world. Having been associated with the work of the National Planning Committee since its inception, he had a personal equation with Nehru.

Mahalanobis' contribution to planning and economic development in India is contained in the model that undergirded the Second Five-Year Plan launched in 1956.[15] It may be likened to an input–output model. A simple way to comprehend it is to see the economy as constituted by the production of two types of goods, namely, capital and consumer goods. Within the model, the capital good enters into the production of the consumer good and of itself, while, surprisingly, the consumer good is not an input into production at all. In an interesting departure from the received economic theory of the time, capital was not subject to diminishing returns. Now, as capital goods go into the production of both types of goods, a larger share of a given investment outlay allocated to the production of capital goods, if maintained indefinitely, would lead to greater final output, even of consumer goods, over time. This would be the case, as, with greater investment in capital-goods production today, the economy would be left with more capital goods and, therefore, with greater output in the future. Mahalanobis demonstrated this mathematically, and via a simulation exercise showed that a greater share of investment devoted to capital goods would lead

---

[15] Mahalanobis (1955).

to income rising sharply at some later date. The rise is postponed because there is a greater gestation lag between investment and the emergence of the output in capital-goods production than in the production of consumer goods. So, while a larger share of investment in consumer goods today may lead to a faster rate of growth of aggregate output initially, this outcome is trumped in the longer term by a greater allocation to capital goods production to start with.

Finally, Mahalanobis envisaged rising productivity of investment in the production of capital goods via a process akin to increasing returns. As the size of the economy increased, so would the utilisation of plants producing capital goods, resulting in a greater surplus – as fixed costs are spread over greater output. This would lead to a rising growth rate as the economy expands. It is useful to bear in mind this implication of the model when it comes to understanding the trajectory of subsequent growth in India.

The Mahalanobis model has been criticised on many grounds. First and foremost it has been pointed out that it ignored the issue of savings. Indeed it could not but have, as it was essentially an input–output model and not an economic model, as may be seen from the above description. While the model was based on investment it did not indicate where the necessary savings would come from. It should have been obvious that if production does not expand sufficiently to provide the savings counterpart of the investment, there would be inflation. Indeed this was to happen quite quickly in India. Within a couple of years of the launching of the Second Five-Year Plan, inflation rose. Yet, it is not clear whether this should be taken as an indictment of the Mahalanobis model. The inflation was triggered by rising demand for food in the face of a slow growth in supply. Any expansion of the economy, even if it were to be private-sector led, would have been inflationary had it not been accompanied by a commensurate growth in food supply. It may be said that the problem of increasing the food supply had been somewhat underestimated given the logic of the model, but not by the planners, including Nehru, as we shall soon see.

The second criticism of the Mahalanobis model has been that it ignored the question of the balance-of-payments.[16] This is perhaps motivated by the fact that, around the same time as the rise in inflation, which was soon after the Second Five-Year Plan was launched, India faced balance-of-payments stress. However, the criticism is misplaced. The balance-of-payments crisis has been related to the liberalisation of consumer goods imports in 1955–6 by the finance ministry and unexpected defence purchases from overseas. Neither of these are related to the investment outlays of the Second Five-Year Plan, which were intended to be focused on capital goods to be produced domestically. Secondly, it is odd to criticise Mahalanobis as being unaware of balance-of-payments considerations. He had envisaged an expansion of domestic production for the explicit reason of avoiding having to earn foreign exchange in an uncertain global environment. As an illustration, he had provided the example of a fertiliser plant, the role of which was to save the scarce foreign exchange required if the fertiliser were imported. And it is not as if it had not struck Mahalanobis that exports should be stepped up. He believed that through industrialisation India would be in a position to export some part

---

[16] Desai (2007) makes both these points.

of its increased production, and this was indeed set to happen by the late 1970s, though it was never on a scale sufficient to leave India comfortably off in terms of foreign exchange. It is, however, true that the possibility of stepping up the export of light manufactures, notably textiles among them, could have been pursued more vigorously.

It is not obvious that the rise in the inflation rate and the balance-of-payments crisis that followed the launching of the Second Five-Year Plan add up to a sufficient indictment of the Mahalanobis model that the plan was based on. The model was really only a vehicle for the larger plan for industrialisation, and the success of that project must be evaluated over a slightly longer time horizon than just a few years. It is to such an evaluation that I now turn.

Our first task, though, would be to establish the goal of economic policy at the time. Given that Nehru, based on his role in the national movement, was unchallenged in his party, his goal alone was what mattered, as well as how he believed it could be achieved. A succinct statement appears in the following intervention made by him in parliament in May 1956: "The whole philosophy is to take advantage of every possible way of growth and not to do something which suits some doctrinaire theory or imagine we have grown because we have satisfied some text-book maxim of a hundred years ago."[17] It is surprisingly clear-sighted and non-ideological given that Nehru had steered a motion pledging a "socialistic pattern of society" in the Avadi session of the Congress the year before, and had spoken admiringly of the "commanding heights of the economy"

---

[17] Nehru (1958b [1956]).

being in the hands of the state. He seems to have grasped that the project of removing poverty was going nowhere without growth, and that therefore maximising growth was paramount. It is not that he was not aware of the possibility of redistribution, but his speeches reveal that he viewed this as short-termist, resulting in lower output in the future.

While researching the history of the economy in the 1950s I met an Indian executive of a multinational bank who expressed admiration for Nehru's stance, remarking that it required considerable political conviction to initiate the Bhakra-Nangal dam project at a time when it would have been tempting to "distribute clothes instead". Critiques of economic policy seldom recognise the political challenges faced by the leadership of a democracy. Nehru's determination to place India on a higher growth path stands out in marked contrast to the distributivism that guides political parties of every hue in their choice of economic policy in 21st-century India. That the distributivist policies of the left-leaning United Progressive Alliance (UPA) in its second term (2009–14) and of the right-wing coalition the National Democratic Alliance (NDA) in its second term (2019–) have done little for economic growth serve as a marker when evaluating the turn taken by Nehru. But to dwell on this now would be to run ahead of the story. We are yet to see how Nehru and Mahalanobis intended to achieve their goal of maximising growth in a poverty-stricken economy.

By the mid-1950s the political leadership had defined their objective, which was the elimination of poverty through industrialisation, and visualised the economic policy that would take India there. This combination has been referred to as the "Nehru–Mahalanobis Strategy" by the economic theorist and planner

Sukhamoy Chakravarty.[18] It is crucial to understand what exactly it had entailed, as it has been the source of much criticism. Mahalanobis had seen his model, which we encountered above, as mere "scaffolding" to be dismantled once its purpose of demonstrating the possibilities had been served. He visualised economic planning as a means of channelling investment in the direction dictated by his model, simultaneously creating capacity and generating demand in the economy. The investment in the machine manufacturing sector was to be undertaken by the government. Today, the need for public investment in these sectors has been recognised in economic theory on grounds of the likely "impatience" of private capitalists to invest in long-gestation projects within an uncertain environment. What exactly the motivation of planners was in the 1950s we cannot be so sure of, though it may well have been a source of satisfaction to Nehru that this strategy conformed to his predilection for the commanding heights of the economy remaining with the state.

However, Nehru was clear that there was a role for the private sector: "May I say here while I am for the public sector growing, I do not understand or appreciate the condemnation of the private sector? . . . We talk about nationalisation as if it was some kind of a magic remedy to every ill. I believe that ultimately all the principal means of production will be owned by the nation, but I just do not see why I should do something today which will hamper my progress, my increasing production, simply to satisfy some theoretical urge."[19] However, under planning the private sector was to be controlled. This came in the form of

---

[18] See Chakravarty (1987).
[19] Nehru (1958b [1956]).

investment licencing. The rationale for this would have been that if planning was to channel resources in line with the goal of industrialisation, then resources should not be utilised for purposes that took away from the achievement of that goal. Thus the destiny of the investment plans of private entrepreneurs came to lie in the hands of bureaucrats. The consequence of this cannot simply be assumed, it needs to be evaluated – as done below.

In line with the Nehru–Mahalanobis Strategy, public investment flowed into what we term capital goods production such as machine tools, heavy electricals, transportation equipment, and the ultimate intermediate goods in the context of industrialisation, namely, iron and steel. Prior to the Second Five-Year Plan, undergirded by the Mahalanobis model, were the first of the post-independence infrastructure projects concentrated in the area of power and irrigation. Some of the prominent examples are Bhakra-Nangal and Nagarjunasagar, but there were many more. A state-led economic thrust, with a tilt towards industry, was to last with varying degrees of intensity for the duration of the first three five-year plans, i.e. over fifteen years. Regarding the choice of locations, there was some effort to distribute these investments across the country, which grew into a network of public sector steel plants, mines, power projects, dams and machine-building factories connected by transportation channels. The sociologist Satish Deshpande has suggested that this amounted to conceiving of "the nation as an imagined economy".[20] Undoubtedly, Nehru's goal of building a self-reliant India through industrialisation was based on a nationalist ideology. I now turn to an evaluation of its impact.

[20] See Deshpande (1993).

After Colonial Stagnation

The data in Table 1.1, taken from the work of the national income historian S. Sivasubramonian, are particularly well suited to an assessment of how India's economy performed during the Nehru era when this performance is set beside that in the first half of the twentieth century. The data are of the average annual growth in the three sectors of the economy, broadly corresponding to what we understand by the agricultural, industrial, and service sectors. They allow for one conclusion alone. The economy underwent a remarkable turnaround in the Nehru era.

First, compared to the last half-century of the Raj, the economy achieved a growth rate over four times as large. Having more or less stagnated during the Raj, per capita income now grew nineteen times as fast. Had population growth remained the same, per capita income would have grown much faster than it did. The faster rate of growth of population may actually be a reflection of the economic progress made. While a deeper analysis of the factors underlying the much faster growth of population in India

Table 1.1
Economic Performance in the Nehru Era

Sector/Period	1900–1 to 1946–7	1950–1 to 1964–5
Primary Sector	0.4	2.6
Secondary Sector	1.5	6.8
Tertiary Sector	1.7	4.5
GDP	0.9	4.0
GDP per capita	0.1	1.9
Population	0.8	2.0

Notes: Figures are of average annual growth.
Source: Sivasubramonian (2000).

after 1947 would have to take into account the change in the birth and death rates during this period, a general observation may be made about the factors underlying shifts in the rate of growth of a population based on global history. Thus, in the United States in the 1940s the birth rate had risen, perhaps reflecting the optimism of the American people emerging triumphant after the Second World War. Significantly, the US was the only major economy that saw a rise in GDP during the War. Equally, in Russia in the 1990s, following the collapse of the Soviet Union, the birth rate fell, presumably reflecting the pessimism of its population, reluctant to birth a future generation at a time of political uncertainty and economic deprivation. Thus, the dramatic increase in the rate of growth of the population in India in the Nehru era may be seen as a reflection of the optimism that Indians felt about their future, based on the changes they could see taking place in the economy; it is doubtful if Indians have felt as optimistic about their economic prospects since. They would not have been mistaken. They were actually living through a breakout by the economy, an escape from colonial stagnation. It is unlikely that they did not see this for themselves.

Perhaps no other phase of India's economic development has been criticised as much as the Nehru era. Criticism is the oil of intellectual engagement and should be met. So, what were the specific criticisms of how Nehru handled the economy in his time? I see four that merit engagement. First, there is the criticism that there was a neglect of agriculture in the economic policies adopted. The second is that the public sector was a white elephant. The third is that the private sector had been suppressed. And finally, it is asserted that the economic policy itself was flawed. I address each of these in turn.

Though the goal of economic policy in the 1950s was industrialisation, it would be wrong to claim that agriculture was ignored in any way. Nehru's observation, "Everything else can wait but agriculture", sums up how the leadership of the time viewed matters. In any case, industrialisation is not antithetical to agricultural progress. In the West, agricultural yields rose considerably with industrialisation, and some of the highest wheat yields in the world today are to be found in the first industrial nation, the United Kingdom. This should hardly be surprising, for industrial inputs matter for raising agricultural productivity. These come in the form of tractors, cement for irrigation channels, and chemical fertilisers. It is worth repeating that Mahalanobis' demonstration of the saving of scarce foreign exchange due to industrialisation was couched in terms of the domestic production of fertilisers. Even the most basic agricultural implements require iron for their production, and in 1947 India was severely short of it. So, we can see that there is no necessary contradiction between the goal of industrialisation and that of agricultural progress. In fact, agricultural productivity must rise if industrialisation is to proceed apace, for as labour leaves the farm to work in factories the remaining agricultural workers must produce more per person. It is difficult to imagine that this will take shape without industrial inputs, even if advances in knowledge derived from agronomy and superior seeds developed in the laboratory may contribute to raising the output of farms independently. This idea is embedded in the Mahalanobis Model itself as consumer goods, including food production, require produced capital goods, which are essentially industrial in origin. The planning process appears to have recognised this. The First Five-Year Plan was a collection of projects among which were dams and power projects.

Finally, the infrastructure that was built did not service industries alone. Agriculture would surely have benefited from the building of roads and bridges that were built through public investment. Two economists who had seen the planning process of the time at close quarters, namely, V.K.R.V. Rao and Raj Krishna, expressly stated that it is not correct to say that agriculture was neglected in the economic policy of the 1950s.[21] Actually, the data are unequivocal on this. From Table 1.1 we can see that the sector of the economy in which the most progress was made during the Nehru era was agriculture. With agriculture's share of the economy being by far the largest among the three sectors, the contribution of accelerated agricultural growth to the revival of the economy was by far the greatest.[22] The significance of this growth needs to be better understood. Again, from the same data we can see that agriculture barely grew during the final half-century of the Raj, unlike the other two sectors, which did record growth in this period. It is this that makes the performance of agriculture in the Nehru era an achievement of great importance, a triumph of economic policy.

I have already referred to the work of the American economist George Blyn showing that during the Raj the majority of crops grew at rates far below the rate of growth of the population, implying that per capita output was declining. The production of rice actually declined. Now, after 1947, for the first time agricultural production grew faster than the population. This could hardly have occurred in a regime of neglect of agriculture. Indeed, apart from the technical calculations of the

---

[21] See Rao (1971) and Krishna (1980).
[22] For the specific magnitudes, see Balakrishnan (2010).

economists of the Planning Commission, India's politicians personally led a campaign to "Grow more food" in the 1950s. Nehru himself displayed a knowledge of agriculture, such as of crop yields in India compared to elsewhere in the world that would be the envy of present-day politicians.

The second criticism of the Nehru–Mahalanobis Strategy is that the public sector created white elephants. To be sure, the public sector spread widely across the economy in the 1950s, and it would be valid to ask how it performed. Indeed the answer would form part of our evaluation of the strategy itself. The prime mover of the Nehru–Mahalanobis Strategy was an expanding public sector providing the inputs for industrialisation. Whatever may have been the history of the Indian public sector over the seven decades or so of its existence, the true test of its performance would be how it shaped up during the Nehru era, when there existed a will to govern it. A crude measure of the performance of the public sector would be the rate of growth achieved in the industrial sector, where it was concentrated. We find in Table 1.1 that the rate of growth of the secondary sector, which is mostly industry, increased fourfold during the Nehru era. However, this can only be indirect evidence of the role of the public sector, as industry did have a substantial private sector presence in 1947, and some of the growth would have been driven by private enterprise. Closely related to the argument that the public sector has turned out to be a white elephant is the belief that public sector enterprises gobble up the savings of the private. To ascertain the truth behind this I have undertaken a comparison of the savings performance of public and private sector enterprises. During the period 1950–65, the savings of public sector enterprises actually grew faster than those of the private corporate sector![23] So, whatever may have been India's experience with public sector enterprises in later years, in the Nehru era they actually generated savings and were not a burden on the Indian public – as is implied by the claim that they were white elephants. Of course, not all of the public investment made could be financed out of the savings of public enterprises. So the public sector did borrow from the public – but so did the private corporate sector. Both of them financed their investment by borrowing from the household sector.

Actually, the fact of the savings of public sector enterprises being positive and having grown even faster than those of the private corporate sector need not surprise anyone. The planners and the political leadership of the time had a clear idea of what the role of the public sector should be. Apart from its role in reviving the economy and setting it off on the path to higher income through industrialisation, the public sector was intended as an instrument of resource mobilisation. Thus we have Mahalanobis speculating on a possible role for a state trading entity, for markups were believed to be high in trade. Whatever may have been the rationale of a proposal of this kind, not only was there no ideological predilection against the public sector turning in a profit, but public enterprises were not loss-making.

A vivid illustration of this is evident in a speech made by Nehru at Bangalore in 1962. On the occasion of the inauguration of a second plant of Hindustan Machine Tools, he remarked that it was a special moment for India as this second plant had been funded by the surplus from the first plant. That this could have been achieved at all, and in so short a time,

[23] Ibid.

appears quite remarkable to us today when we have come to associate the public sector with inefficiency and sloth. Interestingly, on the occasion Nehru very likely chose to use the term "surplus" rather than "profit" due to the latter's association with capitalism, but it does not take away from the significance of my observation. In the minds of the political leadership of the time, public sector enterprises were meant not only to pay for themselves but to contribute resources to the nation's kitty. It just would not do if they had to be permanently subsidised by the public in a poor country.

A third criticism of the economic policies of the 1950s is that it suppressed the private sector. The following statement by the former corporate executive and writer Gurcharan Das nicely sums up this view: "Jawaharlal Nehru and his planners attempted an industrial revolution through the agency of the state. They did not trust the private entrepreneurs, so they made the state the entrepreneur. Not surprisingly, they failed, and India is still paying a high price for their follies."[24] It is worth remarking that in the Mahalanobis Model no distinction is made between public and private enterprise. The model only demonstrates the consequence for national income growth of the allocation made to the production of capital goods as opposed to consumer goods. A strategy based on it may be entirely driven by private enterprise. However, the industrial policy of the time was not neutral and reserved some areas exclusively for public investment. Moreover, the private sector had to apply for a licence to invest in the areas where it was allowed. So, unambiguously, the private sector had been controlled. It is possible to argue that this was excessive or even unnecessary, but the rationale for

---

[24] Das (2000).

licencing, set out by me earlier, had nothing to do with "trust", as Das puts it, and everything to do with the optimal allocation of scarce resources – "investment planning" to the economist.

Nevertheless, it is of interest to know how the private sector fared during this period. My own calculation shows that private corporate investment as a share of national income not only grew over two and a half times during the Nehru era, but actually grew faster than public investment.[25] This evidence hardly suggests a "suppression" of the private sector. Moreover, regulation notwithstanding, the overall effect of the policies pursued at the time could not but have been favourable to the private sector's expansion. What the Nehru–Mahalanobis Strategy did was to increase output via public investment. Growing aggregate output in the public sector is a growing market for the output of the private sector. We have already seen the extent of the expansion of output measured by the acceleration in GDP growth. It would be difficult to contest the argument that the private corporate sector as a whole was a beneficiary of the Nehru–Mahalanobis Strategy precisely because public investment on an unprecedented scale expanded its market. In the more formal language of macroeconomics, public investment very likely "crowded in" private investment in this phase of India's economic development. Note that this is being said about the private sector as a whole. The fact is that licencing would have ensured that some applicants for licences were denied them. So, not everyone could partake of the feast of an expanding economy, surely an "externality" for those from the private sector who found a place at the high table.

---

[25] See Balakrishnan (2010).

This episode serves to illuminate that there exist alternative uses of the term "market". In economic theory, the market is an arrangement in which outcomes are the result of private agents interacting with one another without regulation by the state. However, the term "market" is also used to represent demand for the goods produced by private agents. Perhaps the best example of this is the observation by Adam Smith that "the division of labour is limited by the extent of the market." Note that the market in this sense can expand, with beneficial effects for the private producer, as aggregate demand, stimulated by the state, grows. In the mixed economy that was India of the 1950s, the private sector's market grew via public investment. It is not at all obvious that India's private sector at that time would have expanded as much as it did had there not been public investment. That a private sector cannot lift itself by its bootstraps in all situations was apparent to Adam Smith, as seen in the passage quoted from *The Wealth of Nations*. Here he is using the term "market" to refer to demand, and implying that the growth of the market for its product is not always in the hands of a firm. Popular expositions of economic policy in India in the 1950s have emphasised the negative impact of the controls that were part of the policy regime. This tendency has missed the macroeconomic consequences of the same regime. Both of itself and by encouraging private investment it surely propelled the economy forward. Apart from creating capacity, what the Nehru–Mahalanobis Strategy did was create demand in the economy, and this was advantageous to the private sector, as seen in the rate of expansion that it achieved.

A fourth criticism of the economic strategy of the Nehru era is that India's leadership chose the wrong model for growth.

This model has been labelled "import-substituting industrialisation". The characterisation can itself be made sense of only in terms of the presence of high tariff rates, for in an open economy all domestic production is potentially at the cost of imports. Surely, we would not refer to the production of steel in today's United Kingdom as an instance of import substitution. So, "import-substituting industrialisation" is used explicitly for situations in which imports are kept out either through tariffs or/and quantitative controls. It is the case that till 1991 the policy regime in India included both these measures. Latin America was another part of the world in which a broadly similar policy regime prevailed.

In the 1970s, a critique was mounted internationally against such a strategy. Among the first of these was a study of the Indian experience by the economists Jagdish Bhagwati and Padma Desai. Titled *India: Planning for Industrialisation*, this may be seen as a critique of the Nehru–Mahalanobis Strategy. The main contention of Bhagwati and Desai is that closing the economy to foreign competition through protection had created a high-cost domestic industry that was incapable of competing in the world market. Critics of import-substituting industrialisation also argue that in such a regime the exchange rate tends to get overvalued due to the restriction of imports. It is thus seen as inherently anti-exports. Finally, it was pointed out that to be successful in world markets a country's products must use world-class intermediate inputs, a possibility that import restriction precluded. Above all, the Bhagwati–Desai critique was that the combination of investment licencing and bureaucratic allocation of foreign exchange was inferior to the use of the market mechanism to achieve the goal of industrialisation.

These are important criticisms, and it must be acknowledged that they did not receive sufficient attention in India at the time. The political climate was not conducive to a more market-friendly approach to economic policy. Two decades later, however, the climate changed drastically in its favour. We will have the opportunity to study the consequences of the policy shift incorporating the Bhagwati–Desai thesis later in this book. But it may be said right away that, in keeping with their contention that industrial protection led to an overvalued exchange rate, thus constraining export growth, a major devaluation of the exchange rate did take place in 1967, without any significant impact on the balance of payments.

Notwithstanding the plausible theoretical challenge to state intervention, including protection as a policy, most countries that attempted to industrialise after the Second World War relied heavily on state direction of their economies. These were so-called "late industrialisers" coming onto the scene at a time when significant industrial capacity had been built up in Western Europe, America, and Japan. It is not clear that they would have been able to grow an industrial base if they had left the task to the market mechanism. In fact, as has been argued, the successful late industrialisers of East Asia were bureaucratic in their economic methods and authoritarian politically, earning the acronym BAIR, i.e. Bureaucratic, Authoritarian Industrialising Regimes.[26]

It is often mistakenly assumed that these countries have been able to develop because they were dictatorships for a large part of their recent history. Reflexively, it is suggested that India is unable to develop because it is a democracy. This is a case of

---

[26] See Cumings (1984).

the most lazy reasoning. The countries of East Asia, including China, have made remarkable progress because they have chosen the right policies, that is, policies that contribute to growth. Almost to a country, they started with the modernisation of their agricultural sector while devoting resources to the education of their people. Subsequently all of them, including China, saw their exports growing. In all of these developments their states have had a role in directing investment and financing the private sector. Public investment in infrastructure has been very high too. This much is shared by all these economies, including China's. China is unique in having a very large share of production in public sector enterprises. The rest of East Asia was more private-sector driven, but, as Robert Wade (1990) has argued, by "governing the market" the state produced the results that we observe.

We shall come back to the question why India has made such little progress compared to East Asia in a subsequent chapter, but for now it may be pointed out that much of that part of the world had initially followed a path not very different from India's. This is particularly true of China. Till the second half of the 1970s, when Deng Xiaoping replaced Mao Zedong as the leader, it was far more state directed and closed to foreign trade than India ever was. This brief familiarity with the East Asian experience should be sufficient to convey that mere openness to the world economy and the absence of government intervention are not the only ingredients of the success of nations in creating wealth. So, what is it, particularly in relation to the history of economic development in East Asia, that India missed at the early stage of its economic journey? I shall move on to this question, but before I do that I present data on growth during the Nehru era in India in relation to that in some obvious comparators.

The data in Table 1.2 tell a definite story. India's growth in the Nehru era was much lower than that of South Korea, but substantially higher than that of China during the same period. We get even more perspective on India's performance in the early days of its economic journey when we compare it to the growth over a very long horizon in some of the world's most successful economies of all time, namely the United States, the United Kingdom, and Japan. With this information in Table 1.2 it becomes difficult to claim that India's performance in the early years of its existence was so disappointing after all. It also reveals that some of the criticism of the economic record of the Nehru era is either based on ignorance or is ideologically motivated. For instance, the description of the Mahalanobis model as a "model for going backwards" is so out of line with reality that it does no credit to its purveyor.[27] Given that the proof of

Table 1.2

Economic Growth in the Nehru Era in Comparative Perspective

	1950–64	1820–1992
India	4.1	–
China	2.9	–
Korea	6.1	–
United States	–	3.6
United Kingdom	–	1.9
Japan	–	2.8

Note: Figures are of average annual growth.
Source: Maddison (1995).

[27] See Bhagwati (1998).

the pudding is in the eating, as it were, one might concur that a growth strategy, which is what the Nehru–Mahalanobis Strategy was intended to be, should be evaluated by its outcome. Going by its growth record, it did not fare badly at all. Further, beyond the growth performance of the economy, by the mid-1960s India had built industrial capacity across a wide range of machines, consumer goods, and intermediate inputs. They were not of an international class, surely, but this was not unusual in the early stages of an industrialisation process. It may surprise many that in India in the 1940s "Japan" was a byword for exports considered to be of poor quality compared to European manufactures, particularly British. Within three decades, British manufactures had more or less vanished from the global market while the Japanese ones, from cars to electronic goods, became aspirational across the world.

Economic performance in the Nehru era cannot, however, be assessed in terms of growth alone. We have already spoken of Nehru's idea that an independent India was an opportunity to build a country without "poverty, ignorance and disease". One measure of how far India progressed in the direction of prosperity would be to study how far poverty was eliminated. This issue had come up early in the life of the republic, with Nehru's opponent Ram Manohar Lohia claiming in parliament in the late 1950s that very little progress was being made on poverty reduction. An assessment of this claim is indeed vital to an assessment of the economic policies of the time. Following the publication of an essay on Indian income inequality by Chancel and Piketty, in which the authors estimate the growth of inequality in India over half a century or so since the 1950s,[28]

---

[28] Chancel and Piketty (2019).

some have claimed that while inequality may have declined in the Nehru era, poverty actually *increased* in this period. And Twitter was on fire for two days! "Tweeple", however, are not known for the long attention spans necessary to settle so complex a matter.

Fortunately, we have access to a serious study of poverty in India during the 1950s done at the World Bank by Montek Singh Ahluwalia.[29] His conclusion is that "The evidence reviewed provides a fairly firm basis for documenting trends in rural poverty in India. We find that the Indian experience over the past two decades cannot be characterised as showing either a trend increase or decrease in the incidence of poverty. What we observe is a pattern of fluctuation, with the incidence of poverty falling in periods of good agricultural performance and rising in periods of poor performance." Ahluwalia's study is of rural poverty, but with the rural population being approximately 80 per cent of the whole at the time, the trend in rural poverty was very likely a good approximation to the trend in poverty across the country. It seems that not everything one reads on Twitter is true after all!

It is possible to argue that the failure of the economic policies of the Nehru era to make a dent on poverty is related to its success in providing an environment for accelerated population growth. From the data in Table 1.1 we can see that had the growth rate of population remained what it was during the final phase of the Raj, the rate of growth of per capita income would have been over 50 per cent higher. Actually, the claim that the surge in the rate of growth of India's population after 1947 reflects at least in part an improvement in living conditions

[29] Ahluwalia (1978).

cannot be dismissed out of hand. In India, the official measure of poverty has prioritised access to food, making estimates of poverty sensitive to the current price of food. In the 1950s, with irrigation poorly developed, food supply was dependent on rainfall, leaving it erratic. Food prices are likely to have fluctuated, and so would have measured poverty, accounting for the absence of a trend reported by Ahluwalia. Despite these caveats, the fact remains that during the Nehru era a downward movement in poverty was yet to set in despite the quite impressive, and permanent, step up in the rate of growth of the economy. Could there have been something in the economic policies of the time that, by neglecting the sources of productivity growth, may have held back the reduction in poverty that may otherwise have been possible? This is a question that must be asked.

A Momentous Neglect

In the debate about the policies of the Nehru era, what has generally been emphasised by critics is that the private sector was strangulated. The quotation from Gurcharan Das to which I drew attention is typical of this strand. At the other end of the political spectrum – from the left, that is – it is averred that Nehru was no more than the secretary to the Committee of the Indian Bourgeoisie, and it was only to be expected that he would not succeed in building a socialist state. Naturally, such criticism was bound to miss the essential failure, namely, the neglect of school education in the policies of the government. To some this may seem an outrageous claim, given that first the Indian Institutes of Technology (IITs) and later the Indian Institutes of Management (IIMs) had been started in the Nehru era, and went on to be highly prized by India's middle class. But that precisely is the point. The allocation of public expenditure on education at the time reveals a skewness towards higher education and a privileging of its technical segment. Not only was there insufficient emphasis on primary education, but there was also no evident assault on illiteracy among adults. Given the extent of literacy in India in 1947, this should have been the single most important short-term goal of public policy.[30]

The trend in the allocation of public expenditure across the three tiers of education during the Nehru era suggests too quick a shift away from schooling towards university education, designated "Higher" in Table 1.3. Of course, as the data in the table are shares, no conclusion can be drawn on the level, and therefore the adequacy, of spending. But we do have the word of economists of the time commenting on the allocation in the Second Plan to the effect that the sum intended for schooling

Table 1.3
The Allocation of Public Expenditure on Education, 1951–1966

Sector	First Plan (1951–6)	Second Plan (1956–61)	Third Plan (1961–6)
Elementary	58	35	34
Secondary	5	19	18
Higher	8	18	15
Technical	14	18	21
Others	15	10	12
Total	100	100	100

Note: Includes expenditure by the states and union territories.
Source: Government of India (2009).

[30] In 1951 the literacy rate was 18.3 per cent; women's literacy was far lower. See Government of India (2003).

was meagre given the scale of the problem. Thus, writing within months of the publication of the Planning Commission's "Recommendation for the Second Five-Year Plan", B.V. Krishnamurti of the Bombay School of Economics remarked on "how absurdly low are the sums allocated for education in the Mahalanobis Plan", characterising it as lopsided, with education given secondary importance compared to "heavy industries or river valley-projects". But it is Krishnamurti's prescience in identifying the role of education in India's economic development that is striking. He had stated: "A concerted effort to educate the mass of the population, specially in the rural areas, would undoubtedly have far-reaching benefits of a cumulative expansionist character. This would have greatly lightened the task of government in bringing about rapid economic development."[31] While this is rightly observed, it does overlook the fact that the objectives of the political class even in a democracy may not be entirely congruent with the aspirations of the population. In fact, as observed by the historian Romila Thapar, the political class does not particularly want an educated population as the educated tend to ask inconvenient questions of their rulers.[32]

I have already observed that during the Nehru era India grew slower than South Korea. It can hardly be that the level of expertise of India's planners was lower than that of those in Korea. The political conditions prevailing in the two countries were not the same. India had to recover from the severe dislocation caused by Partition and cope with the politics of the reorganisation of states along linguistic lines only a little later. And,

[31] See Balasubramanyan (2001).
[32] See Thapar (2009).

though India did receive considerable foreign aid, in per capita terms the aid received by South Korea, mostly from the United States, was far greater.[33]

But even this information cannot take away from the fact that there was a fundamental difference in the policies pursued by the two countries in the early stages of their development. It is instructive to read the Korean economist Linsu Kim on this question: "[W]hat distinguishes Korea from other developing countries is the way it has invested in human resources even before launching its drive to develop its economy. Had it not been for the formation of trained human resources in advance, Korea's economic development in the 1960s and 1970s would have been much retarded . . . What this implies is that investment in human resource development should precede industrialisation, as human resources cannot be trained overnight when needed."[34] With this insight, no deep search for the reason why India grew at a rate slower than that of Korea during the Nehru era, and for much longer afterwards, is needed.[35] India invested in machines but failed to do so sufficiently in the humans who would work them.

[33] See Bhagwati and Desai (1970).
[34] See Kim (1995), p. 286.
[35] There is also the factor that, though implemented at various dates, all over East Asia there had been land reforms that were believed to have the capacity to raise agricultural productivity and spur the growth of the economy. Land reforms are also expected to alter the rural social structure, with less immediate but nevertheless positive consequences for economic growth. Though there was some land reform in the Nehru era, it did not have a widespread impact on the rural economy as it mostly transferred land to the intermediaries rather than the peasantry. The states of Kashmir and Kerala were exceptions to this rule.

The failure to educate workers surely thwarted the industrialisation programme and held back growth more generally, but above all it was a major factor in the persistence of poverty on so large a scale. That education was essential for poverty reduction was known in the world of economists for at least half a century by the time India commenced planning for industrialisation. The following comment by Kahan on a debate in Russia in the late nineteenth century is instructive:

> Finance Minister Vishnegradskii's concern with the level of skill and education of the Russian industrial labor force in the 1880s both expressed and stimulated a concern for education as an economic investment of the society. His pronouncement was reflected in a large number of studies, both empirical and normative, or policy oriented. An early and probably representative example of the latter is an interesting collection of essays published in 1896 under the general title of Economic Evaluation of Popular Education. That by I.I. Yanzhul – which is still of considerable historical interest – is based upon the assumption that various external stimuli of economic growth (tariffs, subsidies, government regulations) are less effective than education and training. He invokes the authority of J.S. Mill, Thomas Brassey, and Alfred Marshall, and provides empirical data from American experience to argue that the level of productivity of labour in various countries is positively correlated with per capita expenditures on education and with rates of literacy.[36]

It is astonishing that a similar awareness of the crucial role of education for workers did not exist among India's elites who were in charge of the country at the time. Not even the fact that among the first acts of the Bolsheviks after the Russian Revolution was to set up good-quality schools moved Indian planning

[36] Kahan (1965).

to similar action, even though Nehru admired some of the early achievements of the Soviet Union.[37] India's economists, whether they supported or opposed the economic policy of the time, chose to give undue importance to "tariffs, subsidies and government regulations", the very interventions that Russian thinkers of the nineteenth century had considered of secondary importance to industrialisation when compared to education.

Why India did not launch an assault on illiteracy and expand education opportunities to the mass of the population immediately after independence remains an enigma. The British historian Percival Spear explains this as sabotage by India's lower bureaucracy, which was not sympathetic to the growth of mass awareness as it would threaten its position in the rural hierarchy. This, Spear suggests, meant that Nehru's intentions were not implemented effectively. The sociologist Barrington Moore is less generous in his evaluation of Nehru's role in shaping India:

> This is about as far as sociological analysis can penetrate. My own strong suspicion is that it already goes too far and that Nehru

[37] On the other hand, even the then conservative nationalist newspaper *The Hindu* had recognised the importance the Soviet leadership gave to the health and education of their young. In an editorial on 13 May 1921 it said: "Bolshevism may be a serious menace to the welfare of man, but we find that the Bolsheviks too are human beings, with an even greater regard for children than their vilifiers. From an account of the Bolshevik system of education, we learn that an elaborate scheme is at present worked out in Petrograd as regards the taking care and training of children. There are, we note, two important departments organised with special duties in the matter, the People's Commissariat for Public Health and the People's Commissariat of Public Instruction, both working in close co-operation." It is noteworthy that this was said over twenty-five years before Indian independence, but had very little impact on the political class that came with it.

personally ought to bear a very large share of the blame. Too great a concentration on circumstances and objective difficulties leads to the mistake of forgetting that great political leaders are the ones who accomplish important institutional changes despite such obstacles. Nehru was a very powerful political leader. To deny that he had a great deal of room to manoeuvre seems absurd.[38]

Considering that Nehru was for seventeen years the prime minister, it is somewhat difficult to accept that he was insurmountably handicapped in initiating a programme of human development, understood as the provision of reasonable health and education facilities to the mass of the population by the state. The conclusion cannot but be that it was less of a priority than it should have been. As the leader of the world's most successful national movement, for Nehru the movement's natural culmination was an India that would play an equal part in the governance of the world. The time he devoted to engaging with the global powers was inordinate, given the economic challenges at home. This could not but have resulted in some neglect of the latter.

As I said earlier in this chapter, Nehru's cabinet colleague Rafi Ahmed Kidwai captured this when he lamented the former's "obsession with foreign affairs [. . .] Does he not realise that the economic strength of a nation is the sole basis of its influence?" Kidwai had added that "Nehru does not understand economics, and is led by the nose by 'professors' and 'experts' who pander to his whims and fancies."[39] However, in

[38] Moore (1966), p. 407.
[39] Interview with Durga Das; see Das (1969), p. 379. The assertion that the prime minister understood no economics may not have been accurate; but, in the context, the implication is that the economists of the time did

governance it is not only a matter of what the leadership of a country knows but also as much of its aspiration. In the drive to achieve parity with the global elite, nationalist leaders end up jockeying for their country's position in the distribution of power between nations but underplay its unequal distribution within its boundaries.

Finally, revisiting the debate between Gandhi and Nehru on the desirable shape of India's economy after independence can be of use in evaluating the economic policies of the early years after 1947. Gandhi was for the acceptance of the idea of India as a network of village republics. These were meant to be self-governing and largely self-sufficient. Gandhi certainly was not for industrialisation, whereas Nehru saw industrialisation as the only means for the eradication of poverty in India. Gandhi seemed to severely underestimate the challenge of the highly unequal distribution of power and wealth in India's villages, for which Ambedkar's description "dens of localism" was surely more realistic. He had, however, acutely assessed the one factor that could influence the character of the soon-to-be-independent country, and this was education. Gandhi's view on its importance may be seen in the following excerpt from his *The Constructive Programme*: "Basic education links the children, whether of the cities or the villages, to all that is best

---

not alert him sufficiently to the consequence of not investing in education. This reflects a failure of the economics profession in India at the time. Excessive preoccupation with the mathematical properties of plan models, which were focused on growth anyway, seems to have blinded key economists to the reality that the models were intrinsically unsuited to addressing the distribution question, with its consequence for poverty reduction.

and lasting in India. It develops both the body and the mind, and keeps the child rooted to the soil with a glorious vision of the future in the realization of which he or she begins to take his or her share from the very commencement of his or her career in school."[40]

The "basic" here refers to Gandhi's idea of a holistic education, which included physical exercise, even beyond sports, so that students internalise the idea of the dignity of labour. But the message to be drawn from this passage is the idea that the future of a country is in a way determined by what children experience in school. It also contains the argument that an egalitarian school system based on equal opportunity generates a more equal society. This deep insight was totally ignored by India's elites after independence as the country continued with one of the most inegalitarian school systems in the world.

In fact, the inequality in the quality of education across India's school system has grown enormously since 1947. It is hardly surprising that India has a highly unequal distribution of income today. Equally, while Gandhi's idea of village republics may have been impractical, it should have nudged India's elites to design a more decentralised planning process and policy implementation architecture. This was to come, finally, with the Panchayati Raj Bill of 1987, but only after the realisation that much else had been tried and found unsuccessful. India's political class conveniently built memorials to Gandhi while ignoring his ideals. As the economist Bhabatosh Dutta has pointed out, while Gandhi may not have had a coherent plan for the economy, some of his ideas were not only highly relevant

[40] Gandhi (1941).

to the development of India, they could also quite easily have been incorporated into any plan for the industrialisation of the country.[41] Similarly, had the expansion of higher education been delayed a little, it might well have financed greater spending on primary schooling and the spread of literacy, reflecting Gandhian priorities. This leads to the conclusion that the relevant counterfactual in any evaluation of the policies of the Nehru era is how the future of India's economy would have been shaped had an educational foundation been built in the 1950s. To harp on the restriction of the market mechanism at the time is to engage in a mere ideological pastime.

Conclusion: A Visible Hand

The early years of independent India were a time when the economy decisively broke out of the shackles imposed on it by colonialism. This was achieved via the co-ordinated public-policy interventions that were part of the Nehru–Mahalanobis Strategy, which set off a growth process that has by now continued for over half a century.[42] It is yet to be demonstrated that the quickening of the economy in the 1950s, after close to two centuries of colonialism, could have been enabled by any other known strategy. However, we are also able to see that the failure in that moment to initiate a programme of investing widely in the health and education of the population has meant that

---

[41] Datta (1978).

[42] Indisputable evidence of this is seen in Chart 1.1. For a technical account, including a model and statistical verification, of the role of the Nehru–Mahalanobis Strategy in the long-term growth of the economy, see Balakrishnan, Das, and Parameswaran (2017).

growth here has been neither as fast nor as inclusive as it has been to our east in Asia. The spectacular reversal of economic stagnation and the disappointing neglect of human development represent the triumph and the tragedy, respectively, of the early days of the Indian republic.

2

Watershed

AFTER THE PASSING of Nehru, India experienced political turbulence periodically right up to the assassination of Prime Minister Rajiv Gandhi in 1991 – also remembered as the year of a significant shift in the policy regime.

Despite the political drift – likely to have been demoralising to those living through the times – from an economic point of view the period 1965–91 was a most interesting phase. In the mid-1960s growth slowed, remaining depressed for about a decade. Then, just when despondence may be expected to have been at its highest, it began to accelerate in the late 1970s. Moreover, whereas the slowdown was relatively short-lived, the subsequent acceleration of the rate of growth of India's economy has lasted for over three decades. It is in this sense that this period should be seen as a watershed.

The cyclical growth of this period, with the growth rate of the economy first falling and then reviving, may be seen in Chart 2.1. After attaining a peak in the year 1964–5, it remained depressed for the next decade, registering a lower figure in every year but one in this period. Actually, the growth rate declined twice, first in the mid-1960s and again in the early 1970s. Then, from the

Chart 2.1
A Growth Cycle

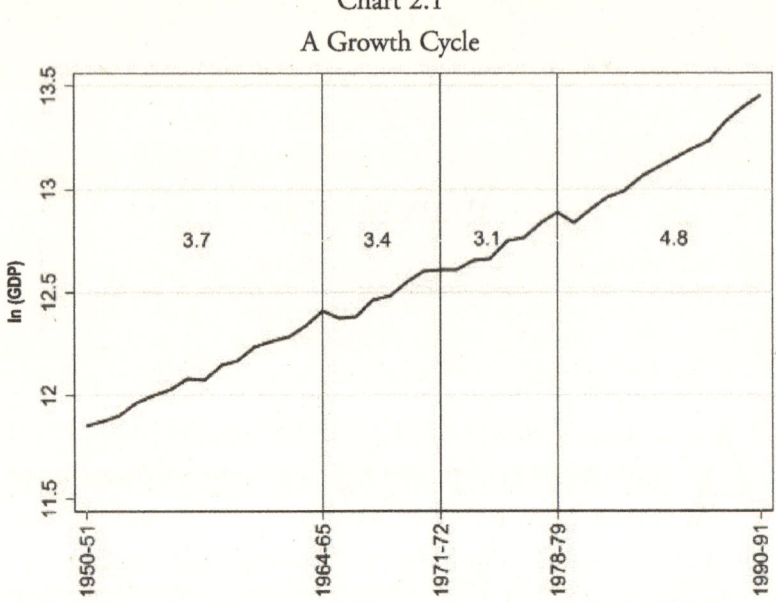

second half of the 1970s it revived but the tempo was not maintained. Only from 1979–80 was there a return to the kind of steady growth experienced in the Nehru era.[1] For the economist this growth cycle stands out as the feature of the quarter-century from 1965 that most needs explaining. The other one is the trend in poverty, which, as we shall soon see, was different from what may have been expected for the time.

Other than in the phases when history is governed by natural shocks, such as a pandemic, political economy is very relevant to

---

[1] The underlying methodology and the data used have been reported as part of the discussion of Chart 1.1 in ch. 1. For the reader who may wonder why the decline in growth from the mid-1960s is not captured in the latter, the answer lies in the fact that we are now studying growth within a shorter period of time. Breaks that are statistically significant within a certain time frame need not remain so as the frame is extended.

understanding major shifts in economic outcomes. This is particularly true of the fluctuating fortunes of the Indian economy after the Nehru era. As we will find, they are tied to the political moves of Indira Gandhi who succeeded Lal Bahadur Shastri – the prime minister who died in office in 1966 after a very brief stint. Neither her rise to the prime ministership nor the consolidation of her political position afterwards were smooth. India being a democracy, this had consequences for economic policy, for politicians are aware that they need electoral backing to stay in power. How Indira Gandhi's strategy for political survival influenced economic development and lives in a country of several hundred millions is a fascinating story in itself. However, I shall leave the account of her becoming prime minister and ensuring unlimited allegiance to herself by splitting the nearly century-old Congress Party to political scientists, focusing on the economic consequences of her economic policy alone.

Indira Gandhi faced an economic emergency even as she assumed the prime ministership of India in January 1966, the year previous having been the first of two consecutive years of crop failure due to drought. The crop failure of 1965 had coincided with a war against Pakistan. With hardly any food stocks – unlike today, when the Food Corporation of India (FCI) godowns are overflowing with grain – India had no choice but to import it. This, however, was an option that existed only in theory because the country's foreign exchange reserves were insufficient. In fact, the large current account deficit of the time itself required financing. So, the economy faced two deficits, a food deficit and a foreign exchange deficit.

In March of 1966 Mrs Gandhi made a visit to the US seeking a way out of both. Aid was promised via multilateral institutions controlled by the US, but conditional on changes to the economic policy regime. These took shape as a liberalisation of controls on trade and industry, and a devaluation of the rupee. The national movement having been propelled by the ideology of full political and economic independence, and Indira Gandhi being Nehru's daughter, this devaluation of the rupee by over a third – on a date easily remembered, 6.6.66 (6 June 1966) – was most likely done very reluctantly. Compounding Mrs Gandhi's unease was the fact that aid from the multilateral agencies did not follow to the extent promised, leaving the prime minister to devise economic policies entirely independently of what the US had wanted to see India adopt.

The Lurch to the Left

Political scientists define a populist leader as one who tries to establish a direct equation with the populace and then claims to speak and act on their behalf. History shows that populists can exist at both ends of the political spectrum, as seen in Latin America.

The political scientist's definition would make India Gandhi a populist.[2] Her early public stances were decidedly left wing, even

[2] On the other hand, Nehru, who had an unmatched "connect" with the Indian people, was not populist and was a stickler for parliamentary procedure. Except in the case of the first amendment of the Indian Constitution, which curtailed free speech, as shown by Tripurdaman Singh (2020), in general Nehru took pains to justify his party's, not his own, actions in parliament. This was particularly noticeable, as we have seen, at the launching of the Second Five-Year Plan in the mid-1950s. On the other hand, Indira Gandhi did not seem to care what political opponents thought of her policies or practices.

though in her "second coming" (1980–4) – after a spell in the political wilderness between 1977 and 1980 – she was to turn business-friendly. Prominent among the left-wing interventions she made were the nationalisation of fourteen major banks, the passing of the Monopolies and Restrictive Trade Practices Act (MRTP) in 1969, the abolition of the princely privy purse in 1971, the nationalisation of the coal industry in 1972, and the amendment of the Foreign Exchange Regulation Act (FERA) in 1973. In an outreach made over All India Radio she characterised the arrangement by which India's erstwhile rulers received payments from the public exchequer – termed a "privy purse" – as "unconstitutional", even though such payments had been promised to them by the Congress Party led by her father as recompense for ceding their power soon after 1947. Other interventions, less symbolically radical – but some of them potentially wider in their impact – were the nationalisation of the Indian Copper Corporation in 1972, and of general insurance and the wheat trade in 1973. Along the way there was recourse to vertiginous income tax rates, price control, and "no exit" clauses for industry. All of these were enacted with the slogan *Garibi Hatao* (Banish Poverty) audible, as it were, in the background.

The overwhelming consequence of the proliferation of controls witnessed in this period was to restrict economic liberty. This came to be spoken of, by both the government and its opponents, as "socialism". The advancement of positive freedom based on enhanced human capabilities (as outlined in the Introduction) – which are arguably more congruent with socialism, howsoever imagined – had little to do with it all.

This "leftward lurch", as it has been termed, by Indira Gandhi went mostly unchallenged in the political sphere except during the brief moment of success enjoyed by the Swatantra Party in the elections of 1967, after which it simply vanished. As her authoritarian personality did not brook dissent, there was little intellectual opposition either. The work of Bhagwati and Desai (1970) alone stands out as a critique of the policies of the time, though not all of these were initiated by Indira Gandhi herself. While it may be difficult to interpret the silence of the intelligentsia as approval, it is undoubtedly the case that some of her policies were received joyfully by the people. There was dancing in the streets of Delhi when nationalisation was announced. That over five years into her tenure Indira Gandhi was still immensely popular is demonstrated by her landslide victory in the general elections of 1971. With this she had a mandate to pursue the policies she desired. Surely a factor in her victory was also that her election slogan *Garibi Hatao* struck a chord with an electorate that had become tired of the grandiloquent speeches of politicians with little bearing on their everyday lives. Here at least, they seemed to be saying, is a politician who talks *to* us and not *at* us. We shall soon see if the promise was delivered.

The Capitalists Strike Back

There was an immediate drop in corporate investment in the very first financial year after Indira Gandhi assumed the prime ministership. This could of course have been due to the demand-contracting effect of the drought, but since investment as a share of the national income had remained depressed for the next fifteen years the fact is that it cannot be understood as a temporary response to an exogenous aggregate demand shock – it reflects the response of the private sector to the changed policy environment. Surely, it is a marker of how the private corporate sector, against whom the prime minister had directed her hostility, viewed her policies. Household investment, which includes what we would today term the "SME" (small and medium enterprises) sector, did no better, though, unlike corporate private investment, it at least showed a slight uptick during the more benign interlude of the Janata Party over 1977–9.

The history of corporate investment following the leftward lurch strongly suggests that Mrs Gandhi's policy shift is a suitable candidate among the factors responsible for keeping private investment in industry depressed for nearly one and a half decades. However, manufacturing is only a small part of the economy, and corporate investment only a part of total investment in manufacturing. So we would have to look for a wider segment over which a slowing of the economy took place. We know from econometric estimates that, apart from manufacturing, the largest segments of services, namely, "Trade, Hotels, and Restaurants" and "Transportation, Storage, and Communication", also slowed in the mid-1960s while the remaining segments barely grew.[3] So, at this point in time, growth over a wide range of sectors decelerated and overall economic growth slowed, as seen in Chart 2.1 above.

Though there is evidence of a slowing of the economy with the assumption of the prime ministership by Mrs Gandhi in 1966, a subsequent revival of growth in the late 1970s is coterminous with her return to power in January 1980, after two years of Janata Party rule. This may be seen in Chart 1.1 of the previous chapter. Indeed, the timing is exact! Also, while the slowing of

---

[3] See Balakrishnan (2010).

the mid-1960s was not very great, the acceleration of the late 1970s was substantial. Running ahead a little, it can also be seen in Chart 1.1 that it was greater than the acceleration that had followed the reforms of 1991. This phase in the history of the Indian economy has caught the imagination of India's economists like none other, and it is not surprising. The conundrum is well expressed by Kotwal, Ramaswami, and Wadhwa when they point out that the growth acceleration of the late 1970s "occurred at a time when India had acquired a reputation as one of the most protected and heavily regulated economies in the world."[4]

From the early 1970s the importance of openness and light regulation had begun to receive prominence in global fora concerned with economic development. While the pioneers in this approach were Bhagwati and Desai (1970), the view attained a certain power when it became the official position of two multilateral organisations, the World Bank and the IMF, which disbursed developmental assistance and hence could not be ignored. Anyway, the Indian experience at that time unambiguously bucked this view of what drives growth. Growth had accelerated at a time of increased control of the economy.

As evidence of the revival of growth in the Indian economy in the late 1970s came into view, a race began to account for it. The economists whose explanation has received the most attention are Dani Rodrik and Arvind Subramanian (2005). Theirs is an exercise in political economy. Such explanations are rare, partly because they are difficult to establish empirically. Rodrik and Subramanian first identify the source of the accelerated growth

---

[4] See Kotwal, *et al.* (2011).

of the economy in an accelerated growth of productivity. They then consider the possible explanations of the acceleration, namely, liberalisation both internal and external, public investment, and the Green Revolution. They conclude that these explanations are incompatible with the data and therefore deserve to be rejected. They then provide their chosen explanation. To make sure that I'm representing their case correctly, I shall quote them:

> We argue that the trigger for India's economic growth was an attitudinal shift on the part of the national government in 1980 in favor of private business. Until that time, the rhetoric of the reigning Congress Party had been all about socialism and pro-poor policies. When Indira Gandhi returned to power in 1980, she realigned herself politically with the organised private sector and dropped her previous rhetoric. The national government's attitude toward business went from being outright hostile to supportive. Indira Gandhi's switch was further reinforced, in a more explicit manner, by Rajiv Gandhi, following his rise to power in 1984. This, in our view, was the key change that unleashed the animal spirits of the Indian private sector in the early 1980s.[5]

Rodrik and Subramanian have recounted the twists and turns of Indira Gandhi's political manoeuvring quite accurately, but their argument cannot serve as the complete story. First, the links are not obvious. Because they identified productivity growth as the source of the growth acceleration, their account would have needed to identify the connection between a "supportive" policy and faster productivity growth without the intermediate step of capital formation. Otherwise, it is odd to suggest that capitalists,

[5] Rodrik and Subramanian (2005), p. 195.

reasonably assumed to be profit maximising, would wait for a friendly government to get the most out of their existing capital stock. Essentially, there is no theory of productivity growth in the Rodrik–Subramanian explanation. A second reason for scepticism is the dependence of their view on manufacturing being the fulcrum of the economy at that stage in its history. At less than 15 per cent of GDP, one would have to assume very high multipliers to suggest that faster productivity growth in manufacturing can by itself lift the growth of the entire economy. Finally, even if this can reasonably be assumed, there is the issue of timing. When we look at growth acceleration by sector, we find that manufacturing accelerates in the early 1980s but the economy itself accelerates in the late 1970s.[6] The economic transition during the quarter-century from 1965 would have to be accounted for in terms that are less reliant on any new-found dynamism in manufacturing.

The Growth Cycle Explained

Technically, it is quite easy to identify the sequence of events and the economic mechanisms at work in the slowdown and subsequent acceleration of growth in the economy during the quarter-century from the mid-1960s. An econometric investigation of inter-sectoral relations in the interval between the acceleration of the early 1950s and that of the late 1970s reveals a "recursive" structure, with agriculture driving services, which in turn drove manufacturing.[7] No feedback from manufacturing to agricultural growth is evident. This settles the issue of the role of manufacturing

[6] The evidence is presented in Balakrishnan and Parameswaran (2007).
[7] See Balakrishnan (2010) for the evidence.

in the revival of growth in this period, i.e. it is unlikely to have driven the growth of the economy. Finally, once again, economic growth accelerates in the late 1970s while manufacturing growth accelerates only in the early 1980s. This timing is not consistent with the idea of an economy-wide revival driven by manufacturing. Actually, it is consistent with the recursive structure of inter-sectoral growth referred to above, with an economy growing and reviving a slow-growing manufacturing sector.

Yet it could still be said that all of the observations of Rodrik and Subramanian regarding Mrs Gandhi's actions and the intention behind them remain valid. For instance, corporate investment, though not necessarily productivity — which is what they rely on in their account — revives within two years of her return to power in January 1980 and remains elevated for the next decade. This is entirely consistent with the argument that she turned business-friendly upon returning, with the corporate revival reflecting this turn. But it is still the case that manufacturing output growth accelerated *after* the economy-wide growth, and therefore could not have been the cause of the latter. Moreover, corporate investment in manufacturing is far too small a factor in relation to the rest of India's economy, both then and now, to make a big difference under growth rates that are to be expected. So what could this factor be that drove the acceleration of growth in the late 1970s?

Chanting "Socialism", Planting Capitalism

Everything points to the Green Revolution as having been the factor that contributed to the revival of growth in India in the late

1970s. But first, a brief historical recollection of its origins. As recounted already, after a year of very high growth of foodgrain production in 1964–5, India experienced a decline in production over the next two years. India's policy-makers had to find foodgrain to supply the population. At the time, as noted, the country was also short of the foreign exchange to pay for it. Food aid from the United States finally came, but grudgingly. This was not surprising. For close to two decades, India had been in the crosshairs of the Western power that really mattered, namely, the United States. The Cold War was on and India was not in the Western camp, though many developing countries, including Pakistan, were. This sometimes prompted the unasked question: Why was India not in the same tent when it was not hostile to the Western powers? The reason of course was that both Nehru and Indira Gandhi were always suspicious of capitalism, or at least of the dominance of private capital. Nehru, as a leader of the Non-Aligned Movement (NAM) – a grouping that remained independent of both camps during the Cold War – had initially worked non-alignment in India's favour, with all sides vying to extend aid to India. For instance, it is not known widely that the extent of foreign financing of the Second Five-Year Plan was as high as 25 per cent. The favourable consequences of remaining non-aligned had led the Polish economist Michal Kalecki to observe that India was like one of those clever calves that suckles milk from two cows! However, now came the food shortage, and the US was the only country capable of supplying a country as large as India the food it needed. India's representatives in the United States at the time described the process of convincing their American hosts to give food aid to India as "trying". It was put about that President Lyndon Johnson instructed his deputies to "send food to India by the shipload, so that she [Mrs Gandhi] is kept on a short leash." This construction is apocryphal, but it would surely have been humiliating to the Indian political leadership if the whispering did in fact reach its ears. The momentous transformation of Indian agriculture that ensued has been aptly termed the Green Revolution.

The Green Revolution should be considered one of the defining moments in India's post-independence history. In one stroke it altered the terms on which India faced the world politically. The politics is central to this. Particularly in the Nehru era, India has seen itself as a force for the good in the world, trying to nudge it, so to speak, in a more just and humane direction. This aspiration was worthy. However, as Nehru's cabinet colleague Rafi Ahmed Kidwai pointed out, the world tends to respect economic strength more than moral purpose. A fascination for Nehru's persona combined with the awareness that he had been incarcerated for almost a decade in British colonial jails bestowed on him a certain cachet in the democracies of the Western world. Ironically, Stalin was not as favourably disposed towards his government despite Nehru's receptivity to left-wing ideas. In any case, throughout the 1950s India found itself punching well above its economic weight in the global arena, particularly the United Nations, and actually influencing the global turn of events from Korea to the Suez.

All this came to a sudden stop with the food crisis of the mid-1960s, which developed into a perfect storm. There was not enough food, nor was there the foreign exchange needed to buy it on global markets, and the countries of the world that were in a position to supply the food were willing to oblige India only on their own terms. It was the moment of reckoning for Indira Gandhi's political leadership. While throughout her career she had demonstrated a willingness to dispense with democratic procedure, she was a resolute patriot. The begging to be done must surely have been difficult for her to bear. Moreover, the strategic relevance of "food sovereignty" could not have escaped someone as politically astute. Indira Gandhi moved everything she could to achieve it.

Actually, Indira Gandhi was hardly the first Indian politician to give attention to food production. As we have seen in the previous chapter, it was not as if the Indian leadership in the 1950s was ignorant of the importance of the food supply. After all, India's planning process had started with irrigation projects. Moreover, throughout the 1950s Congress politicians had hectored the population with their "Grow More Food" campaign. Indeed, so direct an involvement with India's economic problems no longer characterises the average politician of the twenty-first century, who is more concerned with remaining in power by dispensing favours than with finding solutions to lasting problems. We have seen in Chapter 1 that, as a result of the policies adopted in the 1950s, there was a remarkable surge in the growth rate of agriculture. But the population expanded as well, putting pressure on the limited food supply and tipping the balance into shortage at the first instance of drought. This sums up the situation India found herself in in 1965–6, the first of two consecutive years of drought. Indira Gandhi had inherited a whole institutional mechanism for the governance of agricultural production, namely, state agricultural departments, national agricultural research institutes, and a capable central bureaucracy. It also mattered that the Congress Party was in power in most parts of India. In the distribution of responsibilities laid down by the Indian Constitution agriculture is a State Subject, making states' acceptance of a centrally driven agricultural programme crucial. With the same party in power at the Centre and the states, a national plan is far easier to implement.

What actually happened on the ground to bring about the Green Revolution? The goal being to produce as much food as possible within a very short time, a fail-safe strategy had to be devised. It was decided to focus on some geographical areas of India. These were, initially, the wheat-growing regions of Punjab and western Uttar Pradesh, and later the rice-growing regions of Andhra and Madras – today's Tamilnadu. These were already agriculturally more progressive than the other regions of the country on account of their advantage of access to an assured water supply. Farms in these regions were supplied superior crop seed, termed "high-yielding varieties", and fertiliser. To mitigate the risk of a fall in prices, government intervention in the grain market was initiated, with a minimum support price being announced before each sowing season. As the minimum support price was based on costs, it was a form of guarantee to the farmers against losses on their output, over which they did not have full control due to variable weather conditions. Apart from a minimum support price, there was also a procurement price, which was higher. At this price, announced after the harvest, the government was to buy grain to supply the public distribution system. Finally, after the nationalisation of banks, focused lending meant that credit became more easily available to farmers than in the past.

This agricultural strategy of the government was to succeed like no other public policy initiative in India. To cut the story short, wheat production very quickly soared and rice production followed suit. India was no longer dependent on food imports. This was a game changer like none other, and self-reliance in food was now no longer just an aspiration. It was the last instance of the state in India coming so close to the production process – the first time having been when, in the mid-1950s with the launching of the Nehru–Mahalanobis Strategy, the state had set up public-sector production units. Today, a time when the idea of public–private partnerships (PPP) is bandied about as an innovation, it is useful to remember that the Green Revolution was one such initiative.

But one thing is clear: the Green Revolution was an agrarian revolution in the capitalistic mode, state-sponsored maybe but propelled by the profit motive. It seems Indira Gandhi was hardly squeamish about this and did not find it difficult to reconcile her role in encouraging the profit motive in agriculture with the so-called leftward lurch in the manufacturing sector, where her actions were decidedly anti-capitalist and intended to be seen as such. Her support to the Green Revolution never wavered, even as she inserted "socialist" before "republic" in the preamble to the Constitution during the Emergency, a time when the political rights of Indians were suspended. Her goal was self-sufficiency in food production and she remained focused, though flexible, in her efforts to attain it. Another example of this flexibility is how she quickly reversed, after just one season, the nationalisation of the wheat trade in 1973, when it turned out to be a complete failure. Food production it seems was more important than ideology, and Indira Gandhi carefully ensured that her predatory moves against capitalists would be confined to the much smaller manufacturing sector of India. In any case, they were producing goods essentially for the middle classes.

A granular account of the launching of the Green Revolution has been told by the civil servant B. Sivaraman, Secretary in the Ministry of Agriculture at the time.[8] He recounts the way in which India's government machinery moved to make it happen. He emphasises the co-ordinated effort made by the state's many organs, from the concerned central ministries to the Reserve Bank of India, the central agricultural research establishment, and state governments. It is difficult to imagine the government machinery today displaying such capacity and finesse in attaining a goal of public policy, even though we are far richer now. A major difference lies in the self-perception of politicians who, regardless of party affiliation or ideology, seem to be engaged in constant skirmishes on Twitter, apparently without the slightest awareness of their responsibility in providing solutions to the problems the country faces – understood as "governance".

The Green Revolution was the outcome of a political project to make India self-sufficient in food, and its real architect was the Minister for Food and Agriculture, C. Subramaniam. Encouraged by his prime minister, Lal Bahadur Shastri, this career politician changed the fortunes of his country through imagination, administrative capacity, and recognition of the relevance of scientific knowledge. The last was present in the role played by the agricultural scientist M.S. Swaminathan in choosing the right strains of wheat and, later, rice for India, which were the central elements in the Green Revolution. Speaking of "knowledge", Sivaraman states that several leading Indian economists were not just individually pessimistic about the government's efforts to increase food production at the time, but that they also joined hands to try and show why it was unlikely to succeed.

[8] See Sivaraman (1991).

Had this been just one historical instance of a significant section of India's economists backing the wrong horse, it would not matter much. An ideology-based predilection for how the economy works has been a constant among India's economists, lowering their efficacy in finding solutions.

One particular feature of the Green Revolution needs to be flagged. For a programme driven by the goal of making India self-reliant, it had strong international support, and not just in the form of goodwill. India had the benefit of the work done by the American plant scientist Norman Ernest Borlaug, and the seeds of the "Mexican short-stapled" wheat variety transferred to India's fields were developed in institutions funded by the Rockefeller Foundation based in the United States. The Green Revolution in India must be recognised as a great international collaboration, untouched by the politics of the Cold War then raging white hot. If there ever was a challenge to the hubris of overweening chauvinistic nationalism, it was posed by India's Green Revolution. India's self-reliance in food was achieved through international support.

Finally, it would be naïve to imagine that the Green Revolution came without costs. Francine Frankel, among the earliest and most perceptive observers of this transformation of Indian agriculture, has written of the "economic gains and political costs". We may credibly reverse this characterisation to speak of the political gains and economic costs. The political gains should be easy to see. If "food sovereignty", which may be construed as the freedom a country enjoys with respect to the production and consumption of food, is central to political independence, then the Green Revolution enhanced India's relative autonomy in the world. Quite simply, the country was no longer dependent on food imports. The second political gain is internal – in terms of what it implies. This is implicit in Norman Borlaug's assessment of the role of the Green Revolution. He had the following to say in his Nobel Lecture:

> The destiny of world civilization depends upon providing a decent standard of living for all mankind. The guiding principles of the recipient of the 1969 Nobel Peace Prize, the International Labor Organization, are expressed in its charter words, "Universal and lasting peace can be established only if it is based upon social justice. If you desire peace, cultivate justice." This is magnificent; no one can disagree with this lofty principle. Almost certainly, however, the first essential component of social justice is adequate food for all mankind. Food is the moral right of all who are born into this world. Yet today fifty per cent of the world's population goes hungry. Without food, man can live at most but a few weeks; without it, all other components of social justice are meaningless. Therefore, I feel that the aforementioned guiding principle must be modified to read: If you desire peace, cultivate justice, but at the same time cultivate the fields to produce more bread; otherwise there will be no peace.

One might only add that the gains of the Green Revolution in India went beyond just "keeping the peace" by avoiding the social strife that food shortages can cause. To not have to worry about food meant that India could now devote itself to the lofty task of ensuring social justice, promised in Nehru's proclamation at the dawn of independence, without being distracted by the spectre of mass hunger. It is unfortunate, though, that this moment was to come so late in its history.

Now, the economic costs. The agricultural transformation that was attempted was to turn India self-sufficient in food as quickly as possible. The costs were not even considered, it seems, leave alone fully understood. Today we can see the high environmental cost at which the transformation was achieved. The high-yielding variety of wheat and rice required greater inputs of fertiliser and an assured water supply. The over-use of fertiliser affecting soil quality and the over-use of water leading to the plummeting of the water table were the main costs. These were abetted by the subsidisation of fertiliser and the provision of free electricity to farmers, respectively, which was not necessarily part of the original plan. While it would be naïve to separate out the environmental and economic costs, we can now see the enormous cost of the economic policy regime that supported the Green Revolution. The original arrangement was that the minimum support price would act as a safety net and the procurement price would serve as an incentive. Very soon the distinction was erased and the government was compelled to buy whatever the farmers chose to sell to the FCI, often leaving the produce to decline in quality while in storage, if not actually to rot. Public stocks have as a result generally exceeded the official buffer norm by a large margin.

The mounting food subsidy reflects this aspect as much as the amount of grain distributed via the public distribution system. Over the past half-century, politics has intervened relentlessly to recast the whole panoply of intervention from the Agricultural Produce Marketing Committee to the subsidy regime as a sacred cow. Both the upfront economic costs and the less visible but deeper ecological consequences of this are heavy. The over-use of groundwater to grow rice, a crop unsuited to the region but a practice incentivised by procurement policy, is predicted to desertify Punjab by 2030. Even if this is an exaggeration, it does point to the direction of change that has come in the wake of the Green Revolution in India. These developments are clearly detrimental to the future of the country. They are not insurmountable, but politics alone can determine whether the threat will be eliminated.

The Revival

Whatever may have been the economic cost of the Green Revolution, it is evident that it had a positive impact on growth in the economy. I have already alluded to the evidence that establishes a prime-mover role for agriculture in this phase of India's economic growth. Conceptually, the recursive structure of intersectoral growth relations during this phase, which I have alluded to, implies that the acceleration of economy-wide growth is linked to a prior acceleration in the agricultural sector. And this is actually how it was during this period that I have referred to as a watershed in India's economic journey. The mechanism that undergirded the overall growth acceleration is that the faster *exogenous* agricultural growth would have had a multiplier effect. Here the rejection by Rodrik and Subramanian of any influence of the Green Revolution, based on the fact that there was no decline in agriculture's terms of trade, misses the mechanism by which an economy-wide acceleration can take place consequent upon faster agricultural growth. An acceleration takes place due to the rising demand from the agricultural sector. As farmers grow richer, rural prosperity itself could rise as wages are impacted, or when employment rises at given wages. For a start, one would expect farm employment to have risen, given the increase in production. Now the demand for non-agricultural goods, both services and manufactures, rises. In the actual course of events, over the decade and a half from the late 1960s when the Green Revolution was initiated, services growth accelerated soon after the accelerated growth of agriculture but manufacturing took much longer to grow faster.

It could be asked why, if the agricultural sector – the largest segment of the economy – was growing faster from the second half of the 1960s, the economy-wide acceleration had to wait till the second half of the 1970s.[9] There are two reasons for this. First, the increase in the rate of growth of agriculture was not of a high magnitude. Second, public investment began to grow slowly from the mid-1960s, reviving only a decade later. With this a significant exogenous driver of growth other than agriculture weakened for about a decade. As at that time much of the public investment was in the "heavy" industries, or capital goods production, its slowing would have produced a slowing of growth in the country's industrial sector as a whole. After public investment picked up in the mid-1970s, it remained high for the next decade.

Why public investment growth slowed for a while from the mid-1960s is an interesting question, of course. The following two explanations are offered. First, under the strain of having to deal with unexpected food shortages, a balance-of-payments crisis, and two wars with Pakistan within just over half a decade from 1965, the economic focus of the government is likely to have been distracted and public finances likely to have come under strain. Second, the recognition of the role of public enterprises in generating the funds for public investment seems to have faded

---

[9] See Chart 2.1 for the timing of the growth cycle in the economy. Evidence on the dates of the acceleration of each of its three main sectors may be seen in Balakrishnan (2010).

after the Nehru era, when, as we saw in the previous chapter, their savings had grown rapidly, indeed faster than the savings of the private corporate sector. Afterwards, political considerations began to enter into the making of economic decisions, particularly decisions regarding employment in public sector units.

A question that may strike the reader is how, when the growth of public investment declined, could the agricultural growth rate have accelerated. The answer lies in the fact that for fifteen years from the mid-1960s public investment tilted towards agriculture and away from industry. So the growth of public investment in agriculture did not decline.[10] This also confirms much of what we know about economic transformations. While knowledge or technology is crucial, major transformations require to be supported by resources. Apart from the very significant international transfer of technology to India, the Green Revolution was achieved by significant resource flow to agriculture represented by greater public investment. Capitalism it may have been, but it was not achieved by the private sector acting alone.

This completes my discussion of the journey of the economy for two decades from the mid-1960s. I now turn to the trend in poverty in this period.

Poverty

Indira Gandhi's chosen slogan *Garibi Hatao* tends to be viewed somewhat cynically, but this can be misleading. It is conceivable

[10] For the data on the growth of public investment across the economy during the 1960s and 1970s, see Balakrishnan (2010). For econometric evidence of the role of agricultural income and public investment in determining industrial growth, see Balakrishnan (1995).

that it reflected the politician's recognition of a major failing of Indian independence – that poverty on such a large scale remained in India even after two decades of active intervention in the economy. An assessment of Indira Gandhi's commitment to the eradication of poverty in India can only be based on a study of the trends in poverty in India. The challenges posed in this context range from the measure to be used to the availability of data. One commonly used measure is the headcount ratio or the percentage of the population that is poor according to some adopted poverty line. I shall refer to it as the "poverty rate". Gaurav Datt, Martin Ravallion, and Rinku Murgai have presented data on the poverty rate over six decades from 1950.[11] This reveals some very definite trends. First, the decline sets in in the late 1960s and continues all the way upto 1990. It is undeniable that poverty declined during the Indira Gandhi years, in fact the decline had commenced early in her tenure. All that remains is to identify the cause. In theory the causes of a decline in poverty could be many, being a combination of actions by the government to actions by individuals to increase their productivity by educating themselves. However, in the Indian case we can see a clear link between the Green Revolution and the onset of poverty reduction. With the estimates of Datt, Ravallion, and Murgai showing that the reduction commences in the late 1960s, when the agricultural growth rate rises, it is clear that growth rather than the anti-poverty interventions of Indira Gandhi may have mattered more – the latter were to crystallise only in the 1970s. Moreover, the foundation for the Green Revolution had begun to be laid in the early 1960s, even before she arrived on the scene as the prime minister. But energised by the food short-

---

[11] See Datt, Ravallion, and Murgai (2019).

ages of the mid-1960s, Indira Gandhi did give impetus to the existing efforts to increase food production in India. The link between the success of this project and the reduction of poverty is unmistakable. Indira Gandhi was unable to deliver fully on her stated objective of *Garibi Hatao* but the journey towards it started in her time and she presided over its undiminished progress during her lifetime.

A question of perennial interest to the economics profession is: What is the driver of poverty reduction – is it the result of growth, or of direct intervention by the state? While the relative contributions of anti-poverty schemes and the impact of faster growth following the Green Revolution remain to be ascertained, I would lean towards the latter as the crucial factor in poverty reduction in India so far. As in the case of the evaluation of the role of manufacturing in the transition to a higher growth path in the late 1970s, it is the timing of the onset of the decline in poverty that tilts the balance among possible explanations. Poverty begins to decline from the late 1960s. This is too soon for Indira Gandhi's poverty-reduction schemes to have influenced the trajectory of poverty.

It is striking that the decline in poverty starts when the growth of the economy begins to slow from the mid-1960s. There can be no better indication that the nature of growth matters for poverty reduction, in this case *where* in the economy growth is occurring. For about a decade and a half from the mid-1960s, while the growth of the economy slowed, agriculture grew faster as a result of the Green Revolution. The latter development was significant as the largest number of poor persons at that time were located in rural India. Ways in which faster agricultural growth can impact income generation and thus poverty levels have been identified above. Though the poverty rate in India today is far lower than it was in the mid-1960s, the likely role of agricultural growth in lowering it continues to remain relevant as at least half the working population is located in agriculture.

Apart from economy-wide growth and anti-poverty programmes, mass education – as already stated in the previous chapter – has been recognised as crucial to poverty reduction. It is interesting how little investment in it there was from a state that was veering leftward. Indira Gandhi's socialist rhetoric did not translate into a faster expansion of public schooling. Actually, the expenditure on elementary schooling in the 1970s grew slower than it did in the decades before and after.[12] It appears that when proclaiming *Garibi Hatao* she had meant a *maai baap sarkar* – i.e. providing succour to the poor and not necessarily equipping them for an independent life.

We have already encountered ideological blinkers among a section of India's economists in the form of the assertion that the policies to usher in a Green Revolution in India were unlikely to succeed. This came from the left of the political spectrum with its belief that profit incentives could not have worked in the semi-feudal agriculture of the time. Another instance of ideological blinkers has been the refusal to acknowledge that there was a dynamism to the economy even before the economic reforms of 1991. This characterised the thinking on the right of the political spectrum. The American economist Bradford Delong captures this perfectly when he says:

> The conventional narrative of India's post-World War II economic history begins with a disastrous wrong turn by India's first prime minister, Jawaharlal Nehru, towards Fabian Socialism, central planning and an unbelievable quantity of bureaucratic red tape . . .

---

[12] See the data presented in Sen (2010).

As a result, India stagnated until bold neoliberal economic reforms triggered by the currency crisis of 1991 unleashed its current wave of rapid economic growth.[13]

The evidence presented here shows how blinkered this view is and how ideological positions in general are a barrier to understanding the world.

An example of ideological expression on the period we have studied is contained in the statement by the economist T.N. Srinivasan that nothing much changed in India after the Nehru era as the government pressed on with an "interventionist framework of policy".[14] At the end of our examination of India's economic development over three decades we can see that this is not an accurate description of the evolution of economic policy. First, by comparison to what came afterwards, the economic policies of the Nehru era had been relatively liberal towards the private sector. Nationalisation on such a scale and the reneging on the privy purse came early in Indira Gandhi's career as prime minister, signalling a break with the past. Though Nehru had spoken of a "socialistic pattern of society" and expressed pride in a public sector poised on "the commanding heights of the economy", he was not enamoured of nationalisation, even though some of it happened on his watch. The shift to a more interventionist economic policy regime after Nehru has been rightly identified as ideological, even acquiring the taint "Nehruvian socialism" among its detractors, though measures such as nationalisation and discretionary use of the regulatory apparatus had played next to no role in the economic policy of the Nehru era.

A second reason why the observation by Srinivasan does not

[13] Delong (2003).
[14] See Srinivasan (2005), pp. 2–3.

work is that its scepticism of state intervention has proven to be ideological. The quarter-century that we have studied reveals both the successes and failures of such intervention. Indira Gandhi's predatory moves against India's capitalists led to an immediate plummeting of corporate investment and a slowing of industrial growth. On the other hand, her persistence with a state-guided agricultural transformation was one of the great successes of Indian economic policy. State intervention lies behind both the decline and the subsequent turnaround of the economy in the decade and a half commencing in the mid-1960s. We can see from this that it is the economic intelligence embedded in it that determines the outcome of a public intervention.

There is enormous interest in the role of Indira Gandhi in India's political and economic history. In general, the assessments have, naturally, brought up her authoritarian instincts, symbolised by the Emergency (1975–7), and the leftward lurch in economic policy in her early days. The theoretical literature in political science is able to explain some of this quite nicely. Thus, Hankla observes, "in democracies, interventions beyond those stemming from the coherent programme of political parties are driven by the imperative of ensuring survival, especially in the presence of unstable electoral linkages."[15] The timing of Indira Gandhi's interventions, closely following the Congress split of 1969, and their demonstrably discretionary nature lend credence to this argument. However, Mrs Gandhi's record in managing the economy must be judged by itself. To have taken the Green Revolution to its logical conclusion, to have reversed a growth downturn that had

[15] Hankla (2006).

set in before she assumed power, and to have been associated with the onset of a steady decline in the poverty rate that commenced during her prime ministership are achievements that should put her in the forefront of India's leaders. Her actions reveal her to have been highly pragmatic in her outlook. When she saw the food imperative she did not hesitate to encourage capitalism in agriculture. When she thought that it was politically advantageous to display hostility to the industrial capitalists she did so with gusto, but when she recognised the negative consequences of the latter she was quick to reverse her stance – as Rodrik and Subramanian correctly observe.

But there was a sting in the tail, so to speak. Ever watchful of the impact of other policies on the electorate, she hedged her bets no matter the possible negative long-term consequences of her actions for the country. For instance, she shrewdly checkmated, as it were, her own changed attitude towards the capitalists with a crumb tossed to labour. In this connection, Rodrik and Subramanian neglect a crucial piece of legislation that can under no circumstances be considered "pro-business", namely, the amendment of the Industrial Disputes Act of 1947. As it stands today, Chapter VB of the Industrial Disputes Act 1947 requires all establishments employing a "specified number" of workers to obtain prior permission of the appropriate government or designated authority before resorting to layoffs, retrenchment, or closure. "Establishments" include factories, mines, and plantations. Prior to 1976, at least there was no "prior permission clause" in the Industrial Disputes Act. When Chapter VB was first introduced, the specified number was pegged at 300 workers. Through a later amendment incorporated by Indira Gandhi in 1984, the specified number was reduced to 100 workers, thereby making the provision even more onerous.[16] The complication of exit written into the law is a deterrent to private investment. It is entirely Mrs Gandhi's contribution to the statute book, into which it first entered during the Emergency, to be fortified a few years down the road. This is another instance of her highly politicised approach to policy-making. While her record overall must be considered successful in the handling of the economy, everything suggests that her style of politics delayed the growth transition in India. Had private investment not stalled early in her tenure, the acceleration of the non-agricultural sector may have come a whole decade before it actually did, as the Green Revolution had set in by the late 1960s.

A Catalytic Disruption: The Brief Appearance of Rajiv Gandhi

Assassinated in 1984, Indira Gandhi was succeeded in office by her son Rajiv, who served a full term as prime minister. Though there were no signs then of a turnaround in any of the macroeconomic indicators, this was a highly significant phase of Indian economic development. There is a tendency to assume that it was under Rajiv Gandhi that the growth path of the Indian economy turned upward.[17] We now know that this is incorrect, and have seen that growth actually accelerated from the late 1970s. However, to assume from this that the tenure of Rajiv Gandhi was without significance would be naïve. It was catalytic in its impact on the economy.

---

[16] See Abhik Ghosh, "A Labour Litmus Test", *Indian Express*, 23 July 2015.

[17] An error implicit even in the perceptive study by Delong (2003).

A recurring expression in the late-twentieth-century management discourse was "disruption". It was meant to capture the positive impact of radical change to an existing industry or market due to technological innovation. Two modifications are needed when the term is used to describe the Rajiv Gandhi years. First, we are talking of a whole economy rather than the product of some specific industry. Second, in the context of the India of the time we are not talking of any major innovation – not just the introduction of technology or at times no more than technological consciousness – but of events which were significant in their impact. One of Rajiv Gandhi's early acts upon assuming the prime ministership was to announce six so-called "Technology Missions" pertaining to telecommunications, drinking water and water management, literacy, immunisation, dairy, and oilseeds. The question this gives rise to is that while this initiative may have identified the principal challenges from food to health in India, what did technology have to do with it? That precisely was the nature of the disruption: technology was to be leveraged to supply some of the most basic needs of Indians. In a country that had witnessed grandiose plans for the economy for three and a half decades without a significant change in the everyday life of Indians, here was a leader focussing on the absence from the economy of the most basic services needed for Indians. At least as far as the economy went, there were no major policy resolutions or even announcements, just an emphasis on bringing technology to how ordinary things are done. This was new.

The area in which this was most effective was telecommunications. As an adviser to the prime minister, the technocrat Sam Pitroda – who held international patents in the field – led the task of connecting India by means of a telephone network. An innovation that was not technologically noteworthy but was nevertheless highly impactful was the public telephone kiosk from which individuals could now make long-distance calls to their homes in other cities or villages of India. Nothing could have revolutionised everyday life in India more than this facility for ordinary Indians to stay connected with their families while they lived and worked elsewhere. Next, though not listed as part of one of the six technology missions announced by Rajiv Gandhi, the computer now emerged as a significant enabler. Perhaps the most significant disruption that it brought about was in the area of railway ticket reservation. As the railways were the biggest carriers of passengers in the country, the impact of computerisation of the booking of tickets could not have been anything but widespread. It brought in transparency, lowered transaction costs, and very likely reduced corruption. It would be appropriate to state that India experienced a telecommunications revolution during the Rajiv Gandhi years, and this young prime minister's intervention was central to it. It is this initial step that led to India's globally competitive software industry.

Though it took off only after the commercialisation of the internet in the mid-1990s, the business model itself had germinated a full decade earlier. In 1985, Texas Instruments installed the first satellite dish in the country, enabling a "tech company" to maintain a round-the-clock communication link with its US offices. Appropriately, it had arrived at its office in Bangalore on a bullock cart.[18] This heralded the concept of the outsourcing of

[18] "High-tech Bangalore Arrived on a Bullock Cart", by M.A. Arun, *Deccan Herald*, 22 September 2010, https://www.deccanherald.com/content/98795/high-tech-bangalore-arrived-bullock.html, accessed 19 July 2021.

production by multinationals. India's software services industry has never looked back. For the economy it was reflected in the foreign exchange earnings that it brought in. Rajiv Gandhi may have had a fascination with technology for its own sake, but through the telecom revolution he was able to bring its fruits to bear on the lives of millions of his countrymen. Today, when the Indian software engineer is a common sight in the world's capitals, it is too seldom remembered that a young prime minister of India made this possible. Seldom have a politician's dreams for a whole country materialised so concretely so quickly. Alas, the outcomes from the other technology missions turned out to be far less impressive.

An indicator of the reception of Rajiv Gandhi's policies is to be found in the investment response of the private sector. While it had slowed immediately upon Indira Gandhi's assumption of the prime ministership, it accelerated in the second half of the 1980s. Lest it be imagined that Rajiv Gandhi's policies were purely pro-corporate, it should be noted that the acceleration of corporate investment was marginal. It was investment by the "household sector", which we now think of as the SMEs in the economy, that showed an unprecedented surge.[19] The term "animal spirits" is heard quite often in India today, though mostly in the form of a lamentation over their absence. On the other hand, Rajiv Gandhi seems to have contributed to a bullishness among Indian entrepreneurs merely on grounds of what he seemed to represent by his presence at the top, a kind of "Pygmalion effect". There had been in this period no major policy shift – Finance Minister V.P. Singh's tax reforms notwithstanding – or greater public investment to serve as an engine of growth

---

[19] For the magnitudes, see Balakrishnan (2010).

by creating demand. Most politicians can only dream of such a response to their leadership. India under Rajiv Gandhi serves as an example of the intangible factors that go into the making of a favourable investment climate. If ever there was an instance of the private sector responding to an attitudinal change, this was it. Private investment, and not just corporate, responded with alacrity to the promise of this youthful prime minister.

It is true that Rajiv Gandhi had inherited an economy that was accelerating across all sectors, one which also did not experience any external shocks whether of war or of the balance of payments during his tenure.[20] However, he had used this favourable situation imaginatively to improve the lives of ordinary Indians by leveraging technology. He also prepared India for entry into the digital age that was to come. It is due to his efforts and quite early in his term that India began inching towards the creation of an internationally competitive IT industry. Qualitative changes are hard to measure, and their impact is not amenable to quantitative assessment, but most people who lived through the time recognise that something changed in India in the second half of the 1980s – a decline in the sense of general hopelessness. It is perhaps this very confidence in their future, which Rajiv Gandhi had catalysed, that led the people to vote out his government over suspicions of corruption in the state's purchase of Bofors guns from overseas, even though no directly incriminating evidence has been found against Rajiv Gandhi so far. The confidence is evident in the fact that the opposition that was voted in was not distinguished by any capacity for governance. Indians seemed to be saying that, come what

[20] Ibid.

may, they did not wish to be ruled by a tainted government, however efficient.

Finally, though he was of a technical bent of mind, Rajiv Gandhi was able to grasp one aspect of governance in India that few other politicians seem to have been able to – or, if they had, have chosen to remain silent about. This is expressed in his observation that "only about 15 paise of a rupee of public expenditure actually reaches the intended beneficiary."[21] This was an open acknowledgement of the leakages in the delivery of welfare schemes in the country. Over three decades later, it was to be quoted by the judges of the Supreme Court of India when adjudicating the validity of the Aadhaar card. It is interesting that the judges chose to speak on matters pertaining to the delivery of welfare schemes, which most Indian economists are reluctant to discuss critically for fear of being seen as being unsympathetic to the poor. Rajiv Gandhi was clear-headed about how India's government machinery worked, as we can see in this excerpt from his speech to his party's workers assembled to celebrate the centenary of the Congress Party in Bombay in 1985:

> And what of the iron frame of the system, the administrative and the technical services, the police and the myriad functionaries of the State? They have done so much and can do so much more, but as the proverb says there can be no protection if the fence starts eating the crop. We have Government servants who do not serve but oppress the poor and the helpless, police who do not uphold

[21] https:// www.hindustantimes.com/india-news/only-15-paise-reaches-the-needy-sc-quotes-rajiv-gandhi-in-its-aadhaar-verdict/story-I8dniDGXF6ksulggTDgb9L.html, accessed 20 July 2021.

the law but shield the guilty, tax collectors who do not collect taxes but connive with those who cheat the State and whole legions whose only concern is their private welfare at the cost of society. They have no work ethic, no feeling for the public cause, no involvement in the future of the nation, no comprehension of national goals, no commitment to the values of modern India. They have only a grasping, mercenary outlook, devoid of competence, integrity and commitment.

Rajiv Gandhi did not remain alive long enough to be able to address the issue of how the governance of India may have been holding back its progress. Nor did his party follow up on his thoughts on the issue. With this, an opportunity to radically reform the machinery of government to improve the lives of millions of Indians was missed.

Conclusion: The Watershed Years

The reader should by now have been able to see how the quarter-century from the mid-1960s was a watershed moment for India's economy. This was a period when the economy had been buffeted by natural, economic, and political shocks. In 1965 there was both a drought, which led to food shortages, and a war with Pakistan. A balance-of-payments crisis arose the next year while the drought struck once again. Five years later, in 1971, there was a second war with Pakistan, which brought with it an influx of refugees from East Pakistan who needed to be fed and housed. On the political front, there was the succession struggle of the mid-1960s after the long tenure of Jawaharlal Nehru, followed, though much later, by the assassination of a serving prime minister and that of a former one (Rajiv Gandhi in 1991) during elections. Political uncertainty discourages investment, and capital formation, both private and public, slowed for a time.

It is conceivable that the economy could have been left mired in stagnation. However, ultimately, it pulled through with some determined and intelligent political leadership. Since then, India's economy has modernised continuously and mostly grown faster for four decades.

3
Return to the World

IN 1991, the Government of India undertook a major overhaul of the economic policy regime that has come to be known as "economic reforms". I shall henceforth use this expression to describe the changes that were effected. While, as we have seen, various governments in India had experimented with changes in economic policy throughout the preceding four decades, this time was different. The changes were comprehensive within the areas of focus, and in themselves constituted a radical change from the past. The specific features of what came into effect and their consequences is the concern of this chapter, but before that I shall devote some time to the political economy of the regime change as this is an aspect that has evoked interest. In short, what were the politics and the economics that drove it?

The Politics and Economics of the Reforms

Going by the policy statements of the Government of India at the time and the contents of Finance Minister Manmohan Singh's celebrated budget speech in July 1991, the guiding principle of policy at that juncture was the integration of India's economy with that of the rest of the world. At the same time, the world over, the inevitability of embracing globalisation was assumed by reference to the implosion of the former Soviet Union (FSU). The event itself was interpreted as evidence of the unsustainability of the autarkic Soviet economic model upon which India had allegedly based its own. Everything, according to those who held this view, pointed to the imperative of granting freer play to market forces.

It is important to flag the rather casual reasoning involved in arriving at this conclusion. First, even as the unsustainability of the Soviet economic model was presented as a predictable outcome after the event, the FSU's collapse had come entirely unexpectedly to economists.[1] Its roots had perhaps lain more in Gorbachev's policy of *glasnost* ("openness") – a radical regime shift in the sphere of politics – than in *perestroika* (the "restructuring" of the economy). This had cut at the foundations of single-party rule by the communists, as well as at the vice-like grip of the bureaucracy and the secret police, and spread out to

[1] Consider the following observation: "Every revolution is a surprise. Still, the latest Russian Revolution must be counted among the greatest of surprises. In the years leading up to 1991, virtually no Western expert, scholar, official, or politician foresaw the impending collapse of the Soviet Union, and with it one-party dictatorship, the state owned economy, and the Kremlin's control over its domestic and Eastern European empires . . . Although there were disagreements over the size and depth of the Soviet system's problems, no one thought them to be life-threatening, at least not anytime soon." Aron (2011). The author goes on to provide economic data ranging from the growth rate of the economy to the size of the fiscal deficit to argue that there was nothing inevitable about the collapse of the Soviet Union from an economic point of view.

dislodge the more than half-century of ethnic Russian hegemony over the so-called "union of nationalities". The FSU's unravelling as a political entity had followed, and with it the collapse of the entire socialist bloc of Eastern Europe. With hindsight, a potential application of the "domino theory", albeit in a part of the world far from that for which it was originally proposed, had remained unimagined for over three decades!

A recognition of politics as the most proximate cause of the collapse of the FSU does not reinstate confidence in its economy at the time, but it does help us see that the forces making for the disintegration of the European socialist bloc were largely political, and its timing almost entirely determined by them. It is not irrelevant to note that China had, for at least three decades by then, adhered to a highly *dirigiste* model of import-substituting industrialisation, which for a decade and a half from 1950 had yielded a growth rate lower than India's – as we saw in Chapter 1 – without a threat to its political order. The argument advanced here – that political liberalisation may have been the more important factor in the disintegration of the FSU – is strengthened by reference to the experience of China, where the move to a largely capitalist economic model has been underpinned by a severely repressive political regime, which alone could have contained the political disaffection that tends to accompany growing income inequality and regional imbalance.

The second reason why the case for a regime change in India based on the Soviet experience would have been inappropriate is that in 1991 India was quite far from ever having been a Soviet-style economy. Apart from the total absence of the coercive allocation of labour, which was perhaps the most significant marker of the erstwhile communist economies, even in 1991 over 80 per cent of GDP in India was generated in a barely regulated private sector, which was far from the case in the FSU. In India, organised manufacturing had been tightly regulated indeed, but it comprised a highly developed private sector and constituted less than a fifth of the economy. By 1991 the Indian corporate sector was also highly organised politically and boasted of a lobby with increasing access to the political class. Where India's economy had a strong resemblance to the Soviet economy, however, was with respect to the foreign-trade regime. Here, import quotas were widespread, and, when they were absent, there were tariffs which were among the highest in the world. So it can be said that India, like the FSU, had attempted to industrialise under the umbrella of protection, no matter that some trade liberalisation measures had been initiated from the mid-1970s on.

However, the broad economic strategy would by itself hardly qualify India as a Soviet clone, for much of East Asia too had pursued what has been termed import-substituting industrialisation. But something a little more than mere economic strategy had been in the balance when the policy regime had been chosen by India's political leadership in the 1950s. Foreign capital had not just been discouraged, it had over time been more or less expunged from the economy. It was this closure to foreign capital, at times in forms not envisaged in the early 1950s, that was to change in 1991. This was the truly radical shift accomplished by the reforms of that year. There is every indication that it was deliberate and intended to be irreversible. In any case, it is a move that has held for three decades now and shows no sign of waning. Interestingly, one of the first things done by the hypernationalist government of Narendra Modi when it came to power in 2014 was to court foreign investors through its "Make in India" campaign.

Within the overarching objective of integrating India with the rest of the world, specific changes to the policy regime were undertaken. For the sake of convenience, these may be grouped under the rubrics "internal" and "external", even as we realise that some of their elements may overlap and, moreover, need not always be autonomous. The principal changes in the former group were the scrapping of investment licensing and amendments made to the Monopolies and Restrictive Trade Practices Act of 1969, originally promulgated to regulate the "large industrial houses". Among the most visible features of the "policyscape" for at least a quarter of a century, their disappearance was of considerable symbolic value.

As for the changes with respect to India's interface with the rest of the world, three may be noted. First, the tariff rate was reduced across the board, clearly intended to lower the protection hitherto enjoyed by Indian industry. Second, after a devaluation of the rupee early in the reforms, it was left to float for current account transactions. This amounted to allowing a greater role for market forces in determining trade flows. In the context, this could also have been rationalised as necessary to curb a likely influx of imports when quantitative restrictions on imports were being rescinded. Finally, a simplification of procedures for inward foreign direct and portfolio investments was announced. As a signal of the intention to integrate the country with the global economy, this remained unsurpassed.

These changes to the external-policy regime of the economy were unilateral. Other changes were to come into effect in the mid-1990s, following India's accession to World Trade Organisation (WTO) rules. These were part of a simultaneous move by member countries to a set of rules jointly agreed upon. Prominent elements of this new set were a commitment to phasing out quotas, legislating a new patent regime granting recognition to product patents (hitherto non-existent in India), and recognising trade in services. Though these were not ceded unilaterally and came with reciprocal rights for India, the move was viewed with deep suspicion by vocal sections of the polity within the country. Arguably, however, it was the trade and industrial policy reforms of 1991 that constituted a greater shock to the economy and were in this sense the more potent of the changes.

The expression "liberalisation, privatisation, globalisation" (LPG for short) has been used to describe the shift in the policy regime initiated in 1991. But this is misleading, and it is pertinent to demonstrate why.[2] Liberalisation, in the form of the trade and industrial policy changes recounted here, was in the forefront of the economic reforms alright but of privatisation there has been relatively little, with the high-visibility privatisation of Air India coming after over three decades. Evidently, the politics of the public sector run far deeper than the superficially differentiated agendas of India's political parties. This we can infer from the fact that alliances of nominally both the right and the left have governed India since, but have moved little in the direction of privatisation. The Indian political class' relationship with the public sector appears to be independent of ideology, the reluctance to privatise perhaps reflecting more an unwillingness to let go of a significant lever of power.

That privatisation had featured at all in the policy announcements of governments in the early 1990s, only to be dropped as soon as the crisis of 1991 had passed and the economy had stabilised, has encouraged speculation on the role of some external

[2] Admittedly, the usage is found more often in the media than among professional economists, but then in India the media has emerged as an important influence on public opinion.

agencies in its inclusion in the agenda for reforms. Finally, we come to the globalisation component of LPG. User-specificity is a hazard often encountered in the parleying of this term, and not just in India. One might ask if globalisation is the adoption of international standards in economic arrangements within a country, or whether it refers to the unrestrained cross-border movement of goods, services, and labour. We can see that, either way, far too much by way of globalisation is attributed to the reforms of 1991. For a surplus labour economy such as India, true globalisation should encompass the possibility of labour emigration. This is restricted by immigration controls in the rest of the world, paradoxically among the labour-scarce economies of the Organisation for Economic Co-operation and Development (OECD), which would count at present as the obvious destination, and not just for Indians.

On the other hand, the barriers to adopting certain kinds of global standards are largely internal. Take, for instance, the adoption of global standards in evaluating the education and health status of the population. For a large country such as India, which has been growing for a long time and has considerable administrative reach, the public provision of health and education upto a certain level is no longer unattainable. However, no move in this direction was made as part of the reforms of 1991. The reforms themselves were almost entirely in the nature of liberalisation and did not initially address the issues of either human development or social protection.[3] As we shall see in a later chapter, India lags behind much of the world on almost every indicator of human

[3] These were to come over a decade after 1991 in the form of the Sarva Shiksha Abhiyan and the National Rural Employment Guarantee Scheme (NREGA), respectively. The budget for 2018–19 introduced Ayushman Bharat, which

capital and welfare provision. Therefore, while the share of trade in India's GDP has risen, the extent of globalisation, as described above, that has taken place is limited. The one notable move in the globalising direction was that after a gap of four and a half decades India once again became exposed to foreign capital flows.

Another feature of the reforms of 1991 may now be noted. The liberalisation that occurred was mostly in what is constitutionally recognised as the central government's policy space. In the case of foreign trade, central legislation defines policy-making, but this cannot be said of policies that govern industry. In India, foreign trade is on the "Union List" and trade policy the preserve of the central government. This is not the case with industrial policy broadly understood. Here, state governments retain substantial powers and a central legislation is not the last word as far as policy governing industrial investment is concerned. So, while the Industrial Policy Statement of 1991 may have scrapped industrial licensing, fresh proposals for industrial investment continue to be dependent on state governments for other clearances, especially environmental ones. In practice, some states have turned out to be more attentive to such proposals than others. That this is so is partly revealed by the growing divergence of industrial performance among the states. Yet the scrapping of industrial licensing, once a potential barrier to even a demonstrably profitable capacity expansion, was a significant event, marking the end of an era as far as the policy regime is concerned. Returning to the question of how the reforms of 1991 and after

---

the finance minister in his speech asserted was "the world's largest government-funded health care programme".

are to be characterised, we might say that while there have been liberalising trade and industrial policy reforms, LPG is not a particularly helpful account of the evolution of the economic policy regime in India.

As may be imagined, the politics of regime change leaves the economist on less sure ground than does its economics. Judging from their writings, however, it does not appear fully mapped territory for political scientists either.[4] The main "axis of contestation", an expression favoured by one of them,[5] is whether the economic reforms package of 1991 was only an egregious event in a sequence of market reforms that had been experimented with earlier by the domestic leadership, or was an imposition by global multilateral agencies, notably the IMF. Political scientists may be expected to bring along the element needed for a fuller understanding of regime change, rendering their perspective invaluable. However, even while they may be united by their interest in the origins of the reforms, the question of the factors underlying the regime change in India has not been answered by them similarly. Among the most recent accounts is that of Sengupta (2008), who rejects the portrayal of reforms "as the outcome of a linear, cumulative process of 'learning' by the country's policy elites", preferring instead an account of 1991 as a "political event".[6] What makes it political for her is the defeat of the old paradigm by the Washington Consensus, a manifesto on the ideal economic-policy architecture that was ascendant in

---

[4] See especially Kohli (2006a, 2006b); Pedersen (2000); and Sengupta (2008).

[5] Sengupta (2008).

[6] Ibid., p. 36. Though a reference is made to the career of the idea in political theory, no evidence is advanced by the author for any argument in the Indian context that answers to such a description.

the 1990s. In this defeat, a significant role is said to have been played by professional economists of the Indian government who subscribed strongly to the worldview that was emerging as dominant globally.

Despite a self-conscious effort to provide a political explanation for the reforms, Sengupta's approach lacks a base in political economy, showing nothing like a sufficient role for domestic political parties, global institutions, and historical events.[7] En route to an account that encompasses these, it would be instructive to note the views of two other political scientists. One of them sees southern Indian engineering firms with an interest in the global market constituting an interest group. The managers of these industries had links with the global managerial elite and viewed themselves as positioned differently vis-à-vis the West by comparison with the first generation of Indian industrialists after independence. Pedersen (2000) sees this group, which coalesced into the Confederation of Indian Industry (CII), as having been a strong lobby for the kind of reforms which were undertaken in 1991.

Among political analysts, as he describes himself, Kohli's work on the politics of reform is the most grounded, scouring first the policyscape of the 1980s in order to provide a longer view of the regime change of 1991.[8] While he is astute in recognising the role of the newly emerged industry associations, Kohli is at his most

---

[7] However, her characterisation of the essence of the regime change is worth noting: "This was far more than a transition from 'state' to 'market', since much 'market reform' had occurred prior to 1991. The most significant aspect of the 1991 reforms is that they signalled a transition to the political ideology of neoliberalism, and to its attendant assumption of a benign (liberal-capitalist) global order." Sengupta (2008), p. 39.

[8] Kohli (2006a, 2006b).

insightful when he links the change to the implication for India of the collapse of the Soviet Union.[9] The interpretation that regime change in India was inevitable as the collapse of the Soviet Union signalled the bankruptcy of communism, and that free markets were the only solution to India's problem, we have already discussed. However, Kohli is referring to something more palpable. This is the ending of the strong economic links that the Indian economy had enjoyed with the FSU for almost four decades. A pivotal feature of this was rupee trade, which had enabled India to buy oil and defence equipment without having to pay in foreign exchange, a trade facilitated by the export of tea, textiles, and raw materials. The ending of this possibility, not to mention the drying up of the market constituted by the Eastern European economic bloc, COMECON, as it faced temporary political turmoil had grave implications for the Indian economy. Kohli points to the recognition among India's elites that defence equipment would now have to be sourced from the United States. And, more importantly, that a move in such a direction would require the opening up of the Indian economy to American capital and goods, a demand other developing countries of the world had experienced all along but which India had not experienced thus far.

To this important insight we might add the following: with the collapse of the FSU, India would have had to export more to an open global market to earn the necessary foreign exchange. And rather like the historically observed relationship between markets and prosperity, it could not but have been apparent to any unbiased observer of the time that it was virtually impossible to be a successful exporter while remaining ensconced behind

[9] Ibid. (2006b).

protective trade barriers. The latter has less to do with any ethical element of reciprocity expected in trade relations, having instead everything to do with an exporter needing access to globally competitive technology and capital goods which can only be imported. Of course, for India there had been present, all along, an imperative to export to make up the foreign exchange needed to finance its voracious consumption of oil and gold. We may add that adjustment in the form of reducing oil dependence was politically inconceivable, given a state far too populist to restrict consumption.

Having surveyed the views of political analysts of the reforms of 1991, we may now sift them through the history of the Indian economy since 1947, which we are by now familiar with. Some form of incipient reforms of the trade and industrial policy regime had begun in the mid-1970s. This continued in dribs and drabs right through till the middle of Rajiv Gandhi's tenure as prime minister, which lasted till 1989. The intervening two years before 1991 had seen two governments, led by V.P. Singh and Chandrashekhar, respectively, which could devote little attention to economic matters as they were more concerned with political survival. However, except for the ones undertaken by Rajiv Gandhi, liberalising reforms in one area were mostly accompanied by enhanced restrictions in others, a pattern akin to "two steps forward, one step back". For instance, as we have seen, Indira Gandhi's mildly liberalising initiatives in the mid-1970s and the early 1980s were accompanied by a tightening of labour law, introducing a legal barrier to exit in industry. Earlier, the Janata Party, led by the politically conservative Morarji Desai, had signalled its intention to liberalise licensing and external commercial policy by appointing the Alexander Committee on Import–Export Policies and Procedures in 1977. However, it granted further concessions to small industry and actively discouraged foreign direct investment, as may be seen in the highly publicised expulsions of Coca-Cola and IBM.

As for the Rajiv Gandhi phase, Rodrik and Subramanian (2005) have shown that the effective tariff actually rose during this period, thus neutralising the removal of import quotas for some products. However, Rajiv Gandhi's role cannot be sufficiently captured by indicators of the restrictiveness of the trade regime. The young prime minister had positioned himself as one who was unafraid of initiating change without rejecting everything in past Indian economic development. The radical rhetoric talked by Indira Gandhi, and walked by George Fernandes in his brief tenure as the minister for industries in the Janata government, was by now a thing of the past. There was a strong sense of using state-of-the-art technology to transform India. Also, without in any way dismantling the public sector, Rajiv Gandhi provided room for the private. This was most noticeable with respect to information technology and telecommunications. The now extinct "STD booth" was at the moment of its first appearance in the mid-1980s symbolic of some intrepid private entrepreneurs having been allowed to scale the ramparts of a public sector monopoly in telecommunications. Given that, after the Nehru era, the privileging of the public sector had become a marker of left-wing political virtue signalling, this was a truly radical shift. Further, it could not have been missed by the political class that the move had a widely distributed welfare impact which was not without a significant political payoff.

Evidence of a liberalisation of the policy regime having been initiated in the decade before 1991 is not to deny that the reforms package of 1991 may have been influenced by the IMF. Indeed, the influence is there for all to see. However, it is likely to have been more with the macroeconomic than the structural reforms. Lowering of import tariffs, reducing the budget deficit, and restricting credit and devaluation all bear the hallmark of the Fund's standard stabilisation package for a balance-of-payments-constrained economy. That the reduction in the fiscal deficit must clearly have been influenced by the IMF is also suggested by the feature that the sharp reduction in the early years of the programme was to be followed by a slippage from targets as soon as it was wound up. Promptly, public savings turned negligible in the second half of the 1990s. On the other hand, it is unlikely that the Industrial Policy Statement of 1991, which abolished licensing, would have been solely at the behest of the Fund, and, even if it was, the reforms for licensing had been contemplated in Indian government circles for close to two decades by then.

In conclusion, it is not particularly difficult to separate, on the one hand, the elements of regime change imposed by external agencies as the price of balance-of-payments support, from, on the other hand, those adopted quite willingly by the Indian political leadership, even if India had been hectored by the agencies to make these changes. The balance-of-payments crisis had left India with little alternative but to travel, cap in hand, to Washington. This gave the IMF–World Bank combine the perfect opportunity to impose its views of an ideal economic architecture on the last major country that had for long resisted its writ. In fact, an opportunity had been missed by the combine in 1981, when, having granted the largest-ever loan made by the IMF to a member, India had declined to take the final tranche of the $5 billion assistance, for the economy had recovered quickly from the impact of the second oil shock. The recovery itself had been made possible by Finance Minister Pranab Mukherjee ingeniously tapping non-resident Indians for foreign exchange support. The end of communism in the FSU and China's knocking at the doors of West-dominated international fora had left India isolated as a practitioner of extensive restrictions on international trade and capital flows. It should not come as a surprise at all that the IMF had weighed in with its trademark conditionalities, intending that the country's resistance should end forever. However, at least as far as the internal liberalisation was concerned, it was the culmination of what had been toyed with, though hesitantly for fear of political repercussions, by India's major political parties for some time by then.

The progress of the reforms, both macroeconomic and structural, provides an insight into the role of external agencies relative to that of domestic liberalising forces. It would be a fair summary to say that next to none of the structural reforms – whether of the "external" or "internal" type according to our classification – has been reversed. On the other hand, the principal macroeconomic reforms of permanently reducing the budget deficit, an important element of the IMF package, were more or less abandoned since the end of the IMF programme in the mid-1990s, only to be revived under pressure from foreign outflows in 2011. The Fiscal Responsibility and Budgetary Management Act of 2003 had a shaky start, largely because India's politicians were aware of the restrictions that it placed on their established practices, particularly the buying of political allegiance through subsidies while at the same time keeping taxes low. Clearly, budgetary rectitude had been imposed from without in 1991. On the other hand, structural reforms, in evidence at least since the 1980s, were very likely perceived by the political class as potentially contributing to growth, and therefore beneficial to their prospects, even if some sectional interests were likely to be hurt in the process. It is plausible to imagine the presence of such a calculation in sustaining structural reforms. However, it is more difficult to locate the proposed privatisation of public sector enterprises within the perspective offered here. The IMF actually refuses to acknowledge the accrual of revenues from privatisation as a legitimate form of fiscal correction.

The liberalisation of 1991 stands out in marked contrast to the liberalisation episode of 1966 when, faced with a balance-of-payments crisis, India had first gone to the IMF. At that time, a sharp devaluation and some liberalising reforms were implemented in return for promised balance-of-payments support. When this did not materialise, Indira Gandhi, smarting from the ignominy of having been outplayed by the international powers that be, and goaded by domestic public opinion, had simply reversed the reforms. On the other hand, since 1991 we have thus far only had strongly liberalising governments of all hues at the centre, and even in the states for that matter, each advancing India's continuing integration with the rest of the world.

Outcomes

India has now seen over three decades of what is termed "market reforms", indicating a greater role for market forces in the economy. In 1991, the government had embarked upon an economic reform programme that was largely propelled by an external payments crisis. The focus of the reforms then was mainly the economy's trade and industrial policy regime. The reforms may be distinguished by whether their focus was on the internal or external sectors of the economy. As far as the domestic economy was concerned, the most important change made in 1991 was that industrial licensing was rescinded and private entry permitted in almost all areas of the economy other than the railways, ports, defence, and atomic energy. In subsequent reforms, private investment was permitted in all areas other than the last among the above-named sectors. Though clearly intended to increase competition and productivity – defined widely enough to include the quality and variety of goods, and therefore believed to potentially benefit the consumer – the ending of licensing may be viewed as contributing to inclusion among private entrepreneurs. After all, investment licensing, irrespective of its motivation, implies a winner-takes-all outcome. Though delicensing is among the rare instances when market liberalisation is inclusive *per se*, this feature must nevertheless be acknowledged. In terms of economic theory, it is a move towards a more competitive market structure.

As far as the external sector was concerned, the main changes of 1991 amounted to lowering substantially, if not entirely eliminating, the protection of domestic industry. A significant across-the-board reduction of the import tariff was implemented. This was staggered over time, with the reduction itself continuing well into the decade, when, finally, the average tariff rate stabilised at a level far below what it had been, though in some cases yet higher than that in the other non-OECD economies.[10] Within two decades after the onset of the reforms, India was a far more open economy than it was in 1990, even though the rupee

---

[10] Some of this was reversed to an extent by the Modi government some three decades later as part of its Atmanirbhar policy.

was not yet fully convertible on the capital account. However, the extent of capital account liberalisation must not be understated either. Foreign direct investment is highly encouraged. Portfolio capital flow is controlled, though asymmetrically, with restrictions placed on domestic investors while international financial institutions are permitted to move their capital freely across the border. In particular, quantitative restrictions on trade have disappeared, though this has come about via an international move towards a more open global trade regime under the WTO, rather than having been unilaterally implemented by India as part of its policy of economic liberalisation. Nevertheless, in terms of the character of its policy regime, India's economy became far more integrated with the rest of the world due to the liberalisation initiated in 1991. Economists remain divided on the question of whether openness is to be judged in terms of the degree of restrictiveness of the trade regime or in terms of outcome indicators such as exports and imports, combined, as a share of GDP. Keeping this in mind, we may point out that trade, i.e. exports plus imports, as a share of output has increased very significantly in India since 1991. So, whatever the metric, India has become a far more open economy. Overall, combining the implication of industrial delicensing and the opening up of the economy to global trade flows, market liberalisation has proceeded quite far in India over the past three decades. As India is increasingly transforming into a major economic entity of the world, at least in terms of its size, it would be interesting to know the consequences of this development. I shall focus on two issues. First, it is sought to be known whether the reforms have yielded results in line with the stated objectives of the government when undertaking the reforms. Next, it is asked whether the market liberalisation has brought opportunity evenly across society.

Two goals had motivated the economic reforms launched in 1991. The first was faster growth, and the other was greater efficiency.[11] The precise relationship between the reforms and these two desired outcomes that may have been imagined by its architects was not adequately revealed at the time. However, there was the claim that greater competition following market liberalisation would lead to faster productivity growth. It has been shown that this has not materialised.[12] So, I shall focus on the growth of output, the economic indicator more centrally placed in the public consciousness than perhaps any other.

Within the two decades after 1991 the growth rate of the economy has definitely accelerated, but it took well over a decade for the trend in the growth rate to shift upwards.[13] For five years starting from 2003–4 India registered unprecedentedly high growth rates, though falling a little short of the 10 percent figure aspired to by its policy-makers. This phase ended abruptly with the onset of the global financial crisis of 2008. However, despite the slowing of growth in India from 2008, and until the pandemic struck in 2020, the country had been among the fastest growing economies of the world.

But it is the nature of growth in India that is interesting, especially from the point of view of its capacity for spreading opportunity and thus advancing inclusion. While it is the manufacturing

---

[11] The government's view on the rationale of the reforms may be gathered from the Economic Survey releases of July 1991 and February 1992.

[12] See Balakrishnan, Parameswaran, Pushpangadan, and Suresh Babu (2006).

[13] See Chart 1.1 in ch. 1.

sector that the reforms had focused on – directly in terms of the restructuring of the trade and industrial policy – it is mostly services that have grown the fastest among sectors. After 2008, manufacturing growth has been tardy. As for the agricultural sector, growth here has not only fluctuated, but in the case of foodgrains the growth of production has not even kept pace with the rate of growth of the population. For the first time in about five decades, the per capita availability of foodgrains in the country has been declining.[14] While this is a cause for grave concern, there is reason to doubt that the slowing of agricultural growth is related solely to market liberalisation *per se*. According to an influential line of reasoning, in a two-sector economy the protection of industry is tantamount to a bias against agriculture. Now liberalising trade and industrial policy reforms are expected to shift the terms of trade, and thereby income, towards agriculture. This is believed to create the incentives for producers to expand output in this sector.[15] Going by this view, agriculture ought to have gained fresh dynamism as a result of the reforms. However, it did not.[16]

Most assessments of the growth that has taken place in India since the market reforms tend to be quantitative, which though

---

[14] Evidence, based on reports of the Government of India, on the decline of the growth rate in the agricultural sector may be found in Dev (2008). For evidence on foodgrain availability since 1991, see Deaton and Dreze (2002).

[15] The view has been expounded in a public lecture by Manmohan Singh while he was the finance minister. See Singh (1995).

[16] For an empirical assessment of relative roles of structural factors and the changed policy regime in determining agricultural growth since 1991, concluding that the former are likely to have been more important, see Balakrishnan, Golait, and Kumar (2008).

important is a limited form. We now move on to a qualitative assessment. First, though industrial growth had not till well after 1991 shown the marked acceleration that was expected of it, segments within manufacturing have experienced remarkable growth and transformation. Automobiles are a case in point. Here, not only is fast growth evident but a growing sophistication suggests a potential for India to become a global manufacturing hub for this good. A further development, though not confined to manufacturing, is of India becoming a preferred international location for R&D, some of it for global manufacturing giants, but more prominently for information technology firms from IBM to Microsoft. In manufacturing, India is also being seen as a site for both high-end design and re-engineering of manufacturing processes. Some of this is related to the development of cheap international communication networks, including the internet, which has made it possible to leverage the globally competitive skill base, built up over the long haul in India, rather than market liberalisation *per se*. But it is also true that some of the import liberalisation and easing of foreign exchange restrictions have helped, and that there has been a shift in the understanding of the role of government.[17] This role has since 1991 been reinterpreted to mean the enabling of business. That this may have taken the form of a relatively greater attention to the needs of foreign over domestic investment, and, among domestic investors to the needs of large corporate houses over smaller enterprises, cannot be ignored, however. Finally, the increased presence of prominent global firms in India is, of course, related to the liberalisation of foreign direct investment.

[17] See Narayana Murthy (2004), though this author's argument is perhaps more pertinent for the software industry.

To conclude this section, it may be said that the map of material production gives the impression of dynamic enclaves within manufacturing and a stagnant hinterland represented by slow-growing agriculture. This is significant from the point of view of attaining inclusive growth, an objective articulated by both the political formations that have formed the Government of India in the past decade, as the largest number of India's workers are located in agriculture even as the sector is shrinking relative to the rest of the economy. I shall return to this issue.

Liberalisation and the Quality of Life in India

But what of the "quality of life", and how may market liberalisation have contributed to its advance in India? This important issue was not explicitly on the agenda of the government when the reforms were launched in 1991. It would, however, be improper to assume that the government was indifferent to the question, only that it appears to have assumed that growth was all that needed to be focused on. However, the question asked is of the essence, as economic growth is mainly to be valued from the point of view of its contribution to human well-being. Nevertheless, in fairness to the policy-maker, silence may be related to the understanding that "the quality of life" must come into our reckoning only after the issue of employment is sorted out – a direct relationship between faster growth and a widespread growth of employment, it would seem, having been assumed. Despite the difficulty inherent in defining it and the challenging paucity of the statistics needed to establish the progress made in achieving it, it is absolutely essential to make the effort here to assess the contribution of market liberalisation to the quality of life in India.

Even the most casual observation suggests that in certain spaces the quality of life in India has improved. In particular, there has been a very substantial improvement in the range, quality, and availability of manufactured goods produced in the country. This is undoubtedly related to the liberalisation of entry into the sector. Interestingly, it appears to have been achieved without much foreign entry, either in the form of foreign direct investment or imports. We also see an improvement in the quality of certain services, notably of air travel and telephony. The mobile phone revolution has swept the country and transformed the opportunity for both business and interpersonal communication. Here the wherewithal – the technology and the hardware – had initially come from overseas and the liberalisation of foreign direct investment had a major role to play. A similar transformation is also to be seen in air travel, with direct benefits in the form of reduced cost and greater choice. This owes to the liberalisation of entry into the aviation sector. Interestingly here, while all the private capital is domestic, some part of the manpower, both of pilots and managers, has often been international. The entry of private players in airlines, telecommunications, and banking has had a tangible impact on the quality of services offered to the Indian public. To a lesser extent, this has extended to an improvement in the quality of services rendered by rival public sector counterparts which had hitherto been monopolies but now faced competition.

It appears, then, that to an extent the assumed strategic role of privatisation, defined broadly enough to include entry, has been borne out. It may safely be assumed, though, that except for telecommunications this improvement in the quality of services is largely confined to services consumed by the social strata extending from the middle classes upward. This can be inferred from the cohort that uses internet banking or relies on the airlines for transportation. Thus, the reforms have certainly ensured that the aspiration of the Indian middle class to world-class manufactured goods and access to better services has to a large extent been satisfied. When flagging this, though, it is important to recognise that even as the numbers constituting India's middle class are sizeable, the middle class itself is only a small proportion of the population.

While on the topic of the quality of life, it would readily be agreed that constitutive of a good life are goods and services beyond banking and the airlines. Examples of these range from the courts of law to urban governance, and physical infrastructure from roads to sewerage. Economists refer to these as "public goods". They are public in the sense that they are accessible to all. It has the implication that, given their characteristic of non-rivalrousness and non-excludability in consumption, they are likely to be under-provided by the market and therefore have to be publicly provided. There is little evidence of either the quality or quantity of public goods having increased substantially in India since 1991. On the other hand, we have reason to believe that faster growth may have stretched the limits of the meagre infrastructure in existence. Even the most basic awareness of economic theory would remind us that the fixity of public goods in India despite a more liberal economic regime, and indeed faster economic growth, need not be a matter of surprise. After all, the goods are referred to as "public" for a reason, harbouring the presumption that the market on its own is unlikely to deliver them optimally. We may safely assume, therefore, that their emergence in India in sufficient quantities would require specific interventions beyond market liberalisation.

Actually, public goods assume an importance that goes beyond their contribution to the quality of life of those presumably already in employment. If the problem of ensuring inclusive growth is to draw much larger numbers into employment, then public goods are central to achieving the goal of inclusive growth. Instances could be when agricultural produce rots due to the absence of a roads network, or the absence of irrigation lowers the productive capacity of land.

The role of public goods in the sphere of production, as opposed to consumption, has tended to be underestimated in the discourse on growth and development in India. The first round of reforms in India had, to some extent rightly, focused on incentives for investment or expansion of output, but the time may have come for economic policy to focus aggressively on the factors that enable the production process itself. Where such enabling factors are absent, a putatively favourable incentive structure represented by freely formed prices, or even a predictable legal framework, would make little difference to the producer. Examples in India range from the water-starved peasantry of Marathwada to the electricity-short small entrepreneur in Karnataka.[18] By comparison with statistics on income, and therefore on poverty, we have no summary statistics on the availability and distribution of public goods and services in India. We must perforce rely on piecemeal reports in the media, and these are not

---

[18] Though water and electricity are not, strictly speaking, public goods, relieving the environmental constraint and enhancing infrastructure invariably requires an element of what economists refer to as "collective action".

reassuring. The flooding of Chennai in November 2015, allegedly due to poor water management by the public authorities, is a case in point. Some years prior to this event the entire electricity grid of northern India melted down temporarily. I shall take up the matter of the availability of public goods in determining the impact of the COVID-19 pandemic in the next chapter.

While the faster growth of the economy has been in accord with the predictions of the managers of the reform process in India, there have also been some surprises. First, the greater integration of India's economy with that of the rest of the world has been far smoother than anticipated. Though the balance of payments in 2009–10 recorded the largest trade deficit in six decades, private capital inflows were abundant, and the country was able to finance its payments far more smoothly than was claimed to be ever possible by critics of the external liberalisation when it was announced in 1991. Capital inflow poses its own problems for macroeconomic management, but it also reflects the confidence of the rest of the world in the recipient's economy. The fact that India has withstood the exposure to both the goods and capital markets of the world economy speaks of both the inherent resilience of its economy and the quality of the macroeconomic management.

In particular, the three decades since 1991 are the longest period India has witnessed without experiencing a foreign exchange shortage. Earlier, despite the heavy controls of capital flows, there was a balance-of-payments crisis almost once in every decade. Now, in a remarkable reversal of roles, in 2010 India lent to the IMF!

It is important, though, to appreciate how the balance-of-payments situation turned around favourably. Though export growth did rise after 1991, especially of services, so did imports, especially after quantitative controls on consumer goods were eliminated. The increase likely reflects a rise in the income elasticity of imports. In any case, the current account has remained in deficit, except for a single year, even after 1991. So, how has India avoided a balance-of-payments crisis since? It has been possible because the persisting current account deficits have been financed by capital inflows, which possibility did not exist before the economic reforms that liberalised transactions on the capital account of the balance of payments.

This may be seen from the data in Table 3.1. We can see that over time the importance of portfolio capital inflow has increased. In this sense, India's experience from integration with the rest of the world has been altogether different from that of China. Following its integration, the latter has been able to generate huge trade surpluses. Though it has been alleged that this reflects a deliberate undervaluation of the renminbi, the export performance underlying these surpluses has served as an engine of growth for the country. India's economic reforms have not had a similar success. The quite impressive increase in foreign exchange reserves, yet paltry when compared to China's, has come

Table 3.1

Financing External Payments

	1990–1	2000–1	2010–11	2019–20
Trade balance	–3.0	–2.7	–7.8	–0.05
CAD	–3.1	–0.6	–2.7	–0.01
FDI (net)	0.0	0.8	0.6	0.01
Portfolio capital	0.0	0.6	1.8	negligible

Note: Figures are as a share of GDP.
Source: Economic Survey, GoI, various issues.

about as a result of financial inflows rather than export surpluses, which is what had been expected. It is now apparent that competitiveness cannot be established by simply reducing government control over the private sector or liberalising external-sector transactions. The history of globally successful economies shows that publicly provided infrastructure, private R&D, and a facilitating government machinery are crucial for a country's export competitiveness. Most of these ingredients have been present in the case of India's software-services exporters, but are not equally available for exporters of goods. The occasions since 1991 when there has been a trade surplus have been rare, except of course in software services. The balance of payments has been shored up by foreign capital inflows, including portfolio capital. Again, as seen in Table 3.1, portfolio capital is volatile, and flows out just as easily as it comes in, leaving reserves to deplete rapidly. That is why some countries control them, but India has chosen not to, perhaps out of an anxiety to appear a globally integrated economy. The only guarantee against balance-of-payments stress is a consistently strong export performance. The reforms are yet to take India there. In the table above we can see that, on occasion, the trade deficit has swollen to two and a half times what it was in 1991.

The improvement in India's balance of payments following the economic reforms has pleasantly surprised some observers. It suggests the resilience of its economy when thrown open to global competition. But there have been unpleasant surprises too. Most unexpected has been the performance of the agricultural sector. There, when growth has not been lacklustre, it has been volatile, particularly since 2008. Altogether, since 1991 agricultural growth has on average barely kept up with the rate of growth of population. For an economy with low levels of food consumption per capita by global standards, this is disappointing at a time of the high growth of the economy. In fact, a high overall growth rate has masked a failure on the agricultural front. Evaluations of India's economic performance since market liberalisation have tended to overlook the fact that over the historian's *longue durée* the richest countries of the world are those that have succeeded in making food plentiful and cheap for their populations.[19] An indicator of this is the low share of food in average household expenditure in rich economies. In a cross-country comparison, we would find a strong inverse correlation between the level of GDP per capita and the share of food in household expenditure.[20] At least since the time of the classical economist David Ricardo we have had an understanding of what underlies this relationship. It represents the mechanism whereby cheaper food releases household demand for other goods and services, implying that, for poor economies, continuous improvement in agricultural productivity can be an engine of growth, at least in its early stages. In fact, in the absence of international competitiveness in manufacturing, it is the one potential force that holds most promise. Contrary to the historical experience of the wealthy economies of the world, in India the real price of food has not only not declined since 1991, it has actually increased by over 50 per cent.[21] Food price inflation has been

---

[19] See Johnson (2001) for a global history extending over half a millennium.

[20] Evident from the cross-country data released by the United Nations. See http://www.data.un.org.

[21] By "real price" is meant the price of a particular good, in this case food products, in relation to the general price level in the economy. For movement of the real price of food in India referred to in the text, see Balakrishnan and Goyal (2019).

very high during phases in the past decade and a half, and though it has abated recently it continues to lead other factors in contributing to inflation, even during the pandemic when economic activity contracted substantially. Persistent food-price inflation is not expected in a country hailed by some as a rising economic power.

Of course, higher food prices could well have been more than compensated by rising incomes. Whether this has actually been the case is best answered by looking at the trend in poverty. For this I draw upon the investigation by Deaton and Dreze (2002). It helps that these authors take a slightly wider view of what constitutes poverty by focusing on development indicators such as health and education, in addition to the standard consumption expenditure of households. Based on their estimates, the authors conclude, "poverty decline in the 1990s proceeded more or less in line with earlier trends." On development, they conclude that "Most indicators have continued to improve in the nineties, but social progress has followed very diverse patterns, ranging from accelerated progress in some fields to slowdown and even regression in others. We find no support for sweeping claims that the nineties have been a period of 'unprecedented improvement' or 'widespread impoverishment'."[22] The Deaton and Dreze study is of the early post-reform phase, though, and there are by now official poverty estimates for at least upto a decade more. Now the question would be whether the trend of a reduction in poverty has continued. We shall soon see, but the following observation may be made right away. It is possible that while the condition of the poor is improving, the better-off may be doing even better out of the growth taking place, implying greater

---

[22] See Deaton and Dreze (2002), p. 3729.

inequality. Could it be that it is this that characterises India since 1991 – declining poverty but rising inequality?

As pointed out by Thomas Piketty, inequality is shaped by national economic policies. For India, the government's budgetary policy reveals, to an extent, the section of the population that is gaining from overall economic policy in the era of market reforms. While in the absence of specific empirical investigation such commentary can only be tentative, it may be observed that much of the central government's budgetary allocations since 1991 may have disproportionately favoured the middle classes. Note the reduction in the tax rate, both corporate and personal, the expansion of higher education – especially the new IITs and IIMs – and even the farm-loan waivers. As if to compensate for a policy bias towards the better-off, as it were, the government has targeted the poor via the National Rural Employment Guarantee Scheme.

Poverty

Some economists have pointed to an accelerated reduction in poverty in India since 1991, suggesting by implication a role for the reforms in this.[23] The fact of an acceleration is incontestable, but the role in this development of the reforms as we understand them, as opposed to other contemporaneous public policy interventions, needs sorting. To get there, we need to first acknowledge that poverty measured by the number of poor begins to decline in the 1980s itself. Official estimates of poverty exist for two time points in the 1980s, namely, 1983 and 1987–8. Poverty declined at both these points, 1983 being the first time ever

[23] See Rangarajan and Dev (2017).

that a decline in the number of poor was registered. The rate of decline in poverty accelerated between 1983 and 1988. But this was not to last, and the next estimate, for the year 1993–4, actually showed a mild increase in the poverty rate.[24] It is important, though, to see the recorded fluctuations in poverty in perspective. Poverty estimates appear at intervals that are not always uniform, and are influenced by the prevailing prices as consumption expenditure is adjusted for price movements. Despite this, we have reason to believe that the recorded rise in poverty in 1993–4 need not be an artefact, for the estimated number of poor rises further, though marginally, in 2004–5. It is only the estimate for 2009–10 that shows a decline in the number of poor in India once again. This is followed by a quite spectacular decline over the next two years. To get an idea of the magnitude of the decline, the numbers for 2004–5, 2009–10, and 2011–12 are 407 million, 355 million, and 270 million, respectively. So, while it is correct to say that poverty declined rapidly since the reforms, it actually declined only after about one and a half decades from 1991. Moreover, a decline in poverty had started earlier.

The extent of poverty reduction over the period 2009–10 to 2011–12 is very high by historical standards, and needs explaining. When we understand the process that may have undergirded the decline in poverty, we are also able to assess the role of liberalising reforms in the outcome. The decline in poverty is observed soon after a period when growth in India was the fastest ever – the five-year period from 2003–4 onwards. In three of these

---

[24] These observations are based on poverty estimates using the "Lakdawala Method". The analysis that follows is based on poverty estimates using the "Tendulkar Method". Data in both cases is from Planning Commission (2014).

years, growth came close to breaching the double-digit barrier. More crucially, however, the reduction took place when agricultural growth was at its fastest ever too. Deokar and Shetty (2014) have estimated average annual agricultural growth at 4 per cent during 2005–6 to 2013–14 compared to 2.5 per cent for the decade prior to this. A 60 per cent increase in the rate of growth of agriculture sustained for close to a decade is sure to have impacted poverty significantly. Similarly, the 1980s, when poverty reduction first accelerated, too had been a period of accelerated agricultural growth. The relative roles of the reforms and agricultural growth in driving poverty reduction after 1991 are clear from the differential trends of rural and urban poverty.[25] It is only after 2004–5 that we see, for the first time ever, a reduction in the number of the urban poor. Till that date this figure had steadily risen while rural poverty had resumed its downward trend after 1993–4 itself.

This places the role of the reforms in perspective. The economic reforms had focused on trade, industry, and the financial sector. Activity in these sectors is mostly based in urban areas. For well over a decade after 1991, it had not succeeded in reducing the number of the urban poor. Only after the agricultural sector began to grow faster from that time did the number of the urban poor begin to decline. Two processes are likely to have been at play in this. Growing rural incomes may have fuelled a demand for urban products and, following the significant decline in rural poverty, migration from the villages – swelling the numbers of the urban poor – may have slowed. The role of agricultural growth in reducing poverty is apparent in

[25] The poverty numbers referred to in the discussion that follows are from Planning Commission (2014).

the fact that between 2004–5 and 2009–10 the number of the rural poor declined by 15 per cent while the number of the urban poor declined by only 5 per cent. This points to the possibility that economic reforms without robust agricultural growth may not have made a difference to urban poverty. The faster growth of agriculture itself very likely came from sector-specific public policy that was not a subset of what has come to be understood as reforms, defined by the liberalisation of the policy regime. The relevant policies have been identified by Deokar and Shetty as increased public investment, a faster rate of growth of credit for private investment, and the launching of the National Horticultural Mission.[26] There is a lesson in this. Future strategies for the elimination of poverty are advisedly based on the historical record, i.e. what we have learned has worked in the past, rather than the promise of "more reforms". One thing, though, is clear from the episode we have studied. Elimination of the significant level of poverty in the Indian economy would require not just growth but sustained high growth in the agricultural sector. So far, all phases of significant poverty reduction – the late 1960s, the 1980s, and even the early decades of the twenty-first century – were phases of high agricultural growth.

Why Agriculture Still Matters

Since 1991, measured in terms of the rate of growth of output, the agricultural sector has performed far less well than the other two sectors, namely industry and services. However, the greater part of the workforce, i.e. over 50 per cent, is concentrated in

---

[26] See Deokar and Shetty (2014).

the agricultural sector. So, agricultural income per worker has grown more slowly than per-worker income in the other two sectors. Under present trends, a significant section of agricultural workers would have to move out if they are to have an equal opportunity to earn the incomes rising faster in the other two sectors. This, however, is not a matter of will, i.e. it is not as simple as us asking "Why don't they just move, then?"

Two conditions are entailed in a successful move. First, except for manual labour deployed in construction, participating in the non-agricultural sector requires a higher level of education and a certain degree of skilling for the worker contemplating such a move. This is especially true of manufacturing activity where, in a globalised world, firms compete on the basis of the productivity of labour as the other variable inputs are all tradable, implying that firms have equal access to them. On the other hand, immigration controls ensure that labour is largely domestic. Now, firms ultimately compete on labour cost, which is determined by productivity. The skilling needed for agricultural labourers to move out of their normal work area is not acquired costlessly. Either the firms receiving them would have to pay for their reskilling or the workers would need to retrain themselves. Historically, by European standards, firms in India have been quite reluctant to train potential workers. On the other hand, much of the landless rural labour is almost destitute and thus incapable of training itself. It is obvious that under these circumstances the state needs to step in.

The second factor to reckon with is that the increased non-agricultural production of the migrating labour would have to find a market. I shall digress momentarily in order to place this proposition in perspective. The central insight of the Keynesian

Revolution in economic theory is that the demand of labour is a derived demand, i.e. there is demand for labour only if there is a demand for goods. This implication of the market economy is overlooked both by enthusiasts for the free market economy and their opponents. So, the transfer of workers to the non-agricultural sector cannot merely be wished for. It would have to be dovetailed with developments elsewhere in the economy, to enable which a co-ordinating role by the state may well be necessary. The central issue is that for the expansion of the non-agricultural sector, where the agricultural population would move in pursuit of employment and higher incomes, the demand for its goods must expand too. In the first instance, the market for expanded non-agricultural production would have to be provided by the growth of agriculture. For, while in principle the demand could come from the rest of the world, a slow-growing world economy today implies that external demand cannot be relied upon to enable the desired transition.

Does this make me an "export pessimist", among economists a taint perhaps more damning than the "anti-national" of the vocabulary of the dispensation governing India at present? I believe that it does not. My observation has been made in light of the fact that Indian exports were struggling even before the pandemic slowed the world economy from early 2020. For instance, in mid-2016 exports from India were still recovering from seventeen consecutive months of decline. Now, as the pandemic may be waning, the world economy has been plunged into uncertainty following the war in Europe. India may have found a window of opportunity for its agricultural exports as supplies of food from Ukraine are temporarily affected but demand for its other exports may be affected due to the global slowing that is likely. Nevertheless, it is important to not be bound by the present as a guide to action, and everything ought to be done to develop the international competitiveness of Indian enterprises. But this brings us back to what I have already highlighted as a constraint to achieving it, namely the skill level of our workforce.

To sum up, I have said that while there are two sources of demand for an economy's goods, namely the domestic and the external, in the immediate present we would have to rely on the former, and sustained steady agricultural growth is a necessary part of such a strategy. But if agriculture is to serve as an engine of growth at least for a while, it would have to expand without an increase in the price, for a rise in agricultural prices will stymie the growth of demand for manufactures envisaged in such a strategy. An agricultural expansion without a rise in prices can yet be profitable if there is a concomitant growth of yield. Before I come to the question of what can be done to raise agricultural productivity I should mention an important reason – one that goes beyond the pursuit of expanding opportunities for our youth – why we must encourage worker movement out of agriculture. Indian agriculture is witnessing a progressive decline in average farm size due to fragmentation. If this continues, per household income from farming will shrink even if the yield is constant. We would be well advised to treat this as an important instance of how India's prospects are constrained by natural resource availability, a possibility scarcely imagined at both ends of the political spectrum.

Increasing agricultural productivity would require at least three interventions by government. First, an effective physical infrastructure will have to be provided. This can come only from government. Here I wish to briefly clarify what I mean by "effective". It refers to the actual availability of the input. It has been pointed out that official statistics in India may not reflect the true position with respect to availability in different areas. Scepticism has ranged from the data on irrigation statistics to the food stocks of the Government of India. Second, a far greater knowledge input is required from India's extensive archipelago of agricultural research institutions. Recall that these had been in the forefront of the Green Revolution in the 1960s. Nothing but a governance deficit explains their current dormancy. The reference to the Green Revolution should also remind us that the last major agricultural thrust in India was made fifty years ago. Today, a whole new challenge to agriculture, represented by ecological factors and climate change, has raised its head. A second agricultural transformation, taking into account these factors, is now needed. Finally, education matters not only to manufacturing. Increasing agricultural productivity requires a more educated farmer as farming will have to be increasingly undertaken under conditions of natural resource adversity due to climate change, as well as growing competition due to the integration of markets globally.

The Great Disappointment

The success of the reforms in ending balance-of-payments stress and raising the rate of growth has blinded attention to the fact that in one area reforms have had very little success. This is manufacturing. By the 1980s it was apparent to all concerned that India's economic performance was deficient when compared to that of East Asia, and not just Japan – which was already industrialised when India won freedom. Korea and Taiwan were not just exporting to the rest of the world, they were exporting high-quality manufactures based on electronics. The Chinese example of exporting low-quality and low-cost household utensils was to come much later. Reading the annual Economic Survey of the Government of India at the time the reforms were launched suggests that the East Asian experience of growth through manufacturing success was positioned centrally on the radar of its architects. The fact that reforms mostly contained measures that directly or indirectly affected the industry and trade sectors of the economy attest that. Of these, the dramatic reduction in tariffs and the complete elimination of quantitative controls were the most egregious changes in policy.

There are of course purely theoretical arguments for emphasising manufacturing. Many years ago, Nicholas Kaldor observed that faster growth of manufacturing was associated with faster growth of labour productivity, suggesting a route to the prosperity which results when at least part of the growing productivity is passed on to labour in the form of higher wages. Moreover, for an economy such as India's with a low land–man ratio, there is the added attraction that manufacturing is "land saving". Despite all this theoretical rationalisation, however, what must have tipped the balance towards manufacturing in the reforms of 1991 was most likely the spectacular manufacturing success of countries in the East. Now, three decades after the reforms, a similar manufacturing success has eluded India. I have already referred to the far greater range of consumer goods, and of far higher quality, produced in India since 1991; but on one important count the reforms have failed to produce the expected result. As seen in Table 3.2, the size of the manufacturing sector relative to the

Table 3.2
Manufacturing's Share of the Economy

1990–1	2000–1	2010–11	2019–20
16.2	15.3	14.8	14.7

Source: Author's calculation from national income data released by the Ministry of Statistics and Programme Implementation, Government of India; https://www.mospi.gov.in.

economy has not grown; in fact, it has declined. The economies of East Asia, including China, have a substantially higher share of manufacturing than India does. This suggests that for India the inability to grow its manufacturing, potentially the most dynamic sector of an economy, may have had a role in keeping its per capita income low, and thus poverty high.

The question to be asked is: Why is it that, despite the focused reform of the policy regime in relation to manufacturing, it has had no success in raising the share of manufacturing in the economy? I can think of four factors underlying this outcome. They are based on what we can infer from the experience of East Asia, which is a meaningful thing to do as these are Asian economies which were not much richer than India in the 1950s. Of these, two factors are economic and two are rooted in political economy.

Perhaps the most important point is the superior level of schooling in societies to the east of India. Let us for a moment ignore the much-cited examples of Korea and Taiwan and look at economies closer to India, both culturally and in terms of per capita income, when they started out. In this connection, this observation is pertinent: "The proportion of the population that was illiterate in India in 2004 was similar to that observed around 1970 in China or 1960 in Malaysia. The fraction of the population that had completed secondary education in India in 2004 (16 per cent) is half of the figure that had prevailed in China in 1975."[27] These numbers show the staggering gap between India and her eastern neighbours in terms of education levels. In the twenty-first century, literacy can hardly be a sufficient qualification for a member of a globally exposed manufacturing sector. So, even if India may have made strides in making its population literate, it would have remained backward in terms of the skill level of its population well after the liberalising reforms of 1991, for little has been done on this front until very recently. It does not take much to infer that India's manufacturers would have difficulty competing globally while employing a labour force that has had less schooling and possesses less skills than the workers of the rest of the world.

The second economic factor in the East Asian success in manufacturing is the availability of infrastructure. Infrastructure is not easy to measure, as implied in Pierro Sraffa's quip "How many tonnes is a tunnel?" But we are able to gather from the time taken to travel from Beijing to Shanghai, and the quick turnaround possible for container ships in Singapore, to assess the infrastructural prowess in the East compared to India. An aspect of this is that, at least in China, the infrastructure has been built by the state.[28] Interestingly, unlike in the Nehru–Mahalanobis Strategy, as implied by the allocation of public investment, in the economic reforms of 1991 there seems to have been no real appreciation of where the infrastructure needed for the faster

---

[27] Riboud and Tan (2009), p. 209.
[28] See Sahoo, *et al.* (2010).

growth imagined would come from. As has been conveyed already, these reforms were largely in the nature of the liberalisation. That infrastructure is important, and that much of it would have to be provided by government, is apparent from the phase when India's economy grew at its fastest ever – the five years from 2003. This was a period of very high public investment in infrastructure. Of course, private investment grew too, but public investment grew faster. This brief phase was one of the few when a growth transition was dominated by manufacturing, i.e. it was the increase in the rate of growth of manufacturing that contributed most to the rise in the growth rate of the economy. It points strongly to the importance of public provision of infrastructure for the growth of manufacturing.

Finally, the third and the fourth factors both relate to political economy. These refer to the role of the bureaucracy and the capacity of vested interests to undermine the growth orientation of the state. As may be seen, they actually go together. Political economy explanations of the East Asian miracle see it as having been engineered by a bureaucratic, authoritarian industrialising regime (BAIR). The economist Robert Wade has attributed to the East Asian state the achievement of "governing the market",[29] but it is important to appreciate that the state also succeeded in governing the bureaucracy to the extent that the latter had to play a supportive role in the industrialisation process. This may have been altogether different from the Indian experience as identified by Prime Minister Rajiv Gandhi very early in his tenure (as discussed in the previous chapter). In India the bureaucracy has remained relatively ungoverned, thanks to colonial-

---

[29] See Wade (1990).

era rules that have enshrined their independence. Apart from the bureaucracy, India has experienced the role of vested interests in the form of rich farmers, industrial capitalists, and a small but militant labour force in the organised sector of the economy. At various times India's governments have bent to these interests, thus sacrificing growth opportunities. At least in the early days of industrialisation in East Asia, the fact that they were dictatorships meant that economic vested interests such as the ones described above were virtually non-existent.

But even the taming of vested interests and the disciplining of the bureaucracy would not have sufficed to produce the East Asian miracle, which was underpinned by intelligent policy design and the public provision of infrastructure and education on a significant scale. The latter was largely absent in India. To see the East Asian experience of growth and development entirely in terms of free markets and openness to trade would be to completely misread it. As a metanarrative it may be said the it is human development that underlies the rise of these countries. They created a healthy and educated population, which constitutes the sinews of the economy. India can learn from this history.

By comparison with East Asia, India's bureaucracy has been left relatively ungoverned. The consequences of this were clearly understood by Rajiv Gandhi, as I showed in the previous chapter, but he did not live to possibly make a difference to this arrangement. An independent bureaucracy that can slide into unaccountability reflects the governance model during colonial rule in India, starting with the East India Company. In an insightful commentary on his compatriots, Adam Smith observed that their only concern was to build a fortune by any means and to get out of the country as fast as possible, no matter what the consequences for its inhabitants. However, even this understanding of the rationale of colonialism is not enough to appreciate its debilitating consequences for India. To hold India, the British invented an intermediary class standing between themselves and the "natives" – as they saw Indians. That class was the bureaucracy and for Indians there was no redress against its depredations. The colonial regime, on the other hand, tolerated its excesses as a small price to pay for retaining a remunerative colony.

The colonial administrative apparatus has been retained intact in independent India. Of course, this was not inevitable. The Supreme Court recently asked the Government of India to state why it retains a sedition law long used to immobilise Indians during colonial times. While many understand the absurdity of a sedition law today, the crippling effect of colonial practices that govern economic activity has gone unscrutinised. Random inspection of a company's premises by state functionaries sits at the pinnacle of these practices, preventing India's industry from achieving its potential.

Economists are hard put to resolve the puzzle that the manufacturing sector has not expanded relative to the economy following the reforms. We can now see that while the elegantly crafted trade and industry reforms have addressed the policy regime, they have not addressed the conditions under which production takes place in this country, notably the need for the producer to continuously interact with an unaccountable government machinery. This may have held back the expansion of the manufacturing sector as intended. India's regulatory regime needs radical overhauling.

A second reason for why manufacturing did not grow relative to the economy, despite it being the focus of the reforms, is very likely the slow growth of demand. The reforms themselves had focused on the supply side. Above, it was argued that demand would have to grow for some part of the Indian population to move out of agriculture into the non-agricultural sectors of the economy. But the reforms did not include a mechanism by which demand would expand. Interestingly enough, at a time when the economics of growth was far less well understood by the profession, the Nehru–Mahalanobis Strategy had already accounted for demand growth. The external source of demand identified by Mahalanobis was public investment.[30] It is worth noting that the share of manufacturing in the economy did grow during the Nehru era. In trying to understand from the demand side the factors underlying the stagnant share of manufacturing after 1991, the following development may hold a clue. The very improvement in the quality and diversity of goods produced along with the manufacturing sector not registering significantly higher rates of growth on a sustained basis may be a reflection of growing inequality. The demand for superior goods could be coming from the section of the population that is doing better out of growth. If growth is unequalising, the demand for goods of mass consumption is unlikely to grow fast. Chancel and Piketty have provided evidence of sharply rising inequality in India after 1991. In fact, after having declined for about a quarter of a century, inequality began to grow again in the 1980s.[31] Both the absolute level of inequality and its trend are quite staggering. The share of the top 1 per cent of the population was only 6 per cent in the early 1980s but rose to 22 per cent in 2015. It is plausible that worsening distribution smothered the growth of

---

[30] See Balakrishnan (2010) for Mahalanobis's observation on this issue.
[31] See Chancel and Piketty (2019).

demand. The rich are perhaps more likely to spend on high-end real estate than manufactures. Moreover, some part of their demand may be diverted to imports, even when they are manufactured goods. The Chancel–Piketty estimates have been contested, however, and the relationship between growing inequality and the growth of manufacturing remains to be fully worked out.

Conclusion: Returning to the World Unprepared

An economic assessment of the development of India's economy since 1991 would read as follows. There has been an acceleration of economic growth accompanied by a widening of the range of consumer goods produced and improvement in the quality of services available. Furthermore, the economy has passed the longest period since 1947 without facing balance-of-payments stress. However, not all sectors of the economy have shown the same dynamism, with the performance of agriculture actually becoming a cause for concern. One aspect of this uneven growth has been an unequal distribution of opportunity within the economy. This unevenness has left a significant section of the population with a low income, even though the extreme poverty that is captured by India's official poverty line has continued to decline.

Studies of the economic history of the country since 1991 tend to drown in the minutiae of economic policy changes considered, obscuring the essence of the reforms which was to re-integrate India with the rest of the world. Long before discussions of the possibility of India becoming a Great Power had begun – in fact even before the Common Era – India was a great trading nation. Its goods – one could even say "services" if Buddhist missionaries who had travelled eastward are included – were prized in the countries to which they found their way. This character of India's economy altered significantly after 1947. The shift may be considered a failing of the economic policy of that time, even if on balance that policy was far more successful than acknowledged, as I have shown in Chapter 1. It is not possible to be a significant player on the global economic stage and remain protectionist. India has since recognised this and undertaken the steps necessary to make a return to where it belonged in the distant past. Though the economic reforms of 1991 have had some successes, as recounted here, they are yet to establish the country as a successful world trader. Indeed, after thirty years we can see that liberalisation is a necessary but not sufficient condition for this to be achieved. An educated workforce with globally comparable skills, world-class infrastructure, and an enabling government machinery are necessary for a country to hold its own in the world market.

4

Momentum Lost

BY 2014 THE United Progressive Alliance (UPA), having been been elected for a second term, had been in power for a decade. The coalition led by Manmohan Singh had had a spectacularly successful first term, though the enviable growth run had actually commenced in 2003–4, the last year of the Vajpayee prime ministership. The success did not carry over into the UPA's second term in office, however. First, the global financial crisis (GFC) of 2008 punctured prospects for continued export growth as the world economy slowed. Second, in the five years after 2009 there occurred several negative agricultural shocks, most likely weather-related.

Apart from these exogenous events that adversely affected India's economy, there was also a change in the orientation of the UPA. A more populist approach is evident in its second term, with an emphasis on legislating rights and aiming at inclusion, with attention to the economy seemingly diminished. Public investment, which had grown very impressively in the first term of the UPA and served as an engine of growth, slowed in its second term. Procurement prices were raised considerably, leading, predictably, to high food inflation. And, most importantly, the governance process foot-faulted by attracting negative publicity on the allocation of spectrum and coal-mining rights. A perception of corruption on a grand scale was created.

Interestingly, as seen in the discussion in the previous chapter, the pace of poverty reduction did not slow during this period. But it could not have helped the UPA government that, soon after the macroeconomic stimulus following the GFC was withdrawn by 2011, the economy began to slow. The extremely poor are no longer the majority in the country, and the aspirations of the better-off are likely to have begun to diverge from those of the former. This was the background against which the elections of 2014 were fought.

The Promise

For the 2014 elections Modi positioned himself adroitly as the right man for the moment. It is likely to have aided him that anti-incumbency was rife as the economy had lost steam by then. Modi had been installed as the chief minister of Gujarat for four terms and was feted in this role by India's big business, even though Gujarat's development indicators were not impressive by comparison with some of India's states. In an unusually energetic campaign, he painted a picture of "policy paralysis" having overtaken the incumbent government, and made a hefty pitch for a more decisive and capable governance. But the most important offering was the promise of employment creation. In a country with very high unemployment, this may be expected to have had high value in an election campaign. Of equal value in striking a chord with the electorate must have been his promise to end corruption at a time when a perception of corruption in the highest echelons benefiting the very rich had taken hold. Modi's promise was expressed as *Na Khaunga, Na Khaane Doonga*, to be understood in the context as "I shall not steal, nor let others do so". At a time of high inequality, and judging by the electoral result, this is likely to have resonated with the majority.

In a campaign that emphasised development (*vikas*), there was emphasis on infrastructure and jobs.[1] And it was not to be just *vikas*, it was to be *sabka saath, sabka vikas*, signalling that the development to come would be inclusive. The promise of an improvement in the lives of the people was contained in the slogan *Achche din aane wale hain* (Better days are to come). Altogether, a superior economic performance was high on the campaign promise of Prime Minister Modi. Given the centrality of an improved economy to the campaign, it bears mentioning that no plan had been outlined, i.e. there was no clear road map to the transformation being announced. Since then we have seen repeated emphasis on "the ease of doing business", giving an impression that the government saw its advancement as a crucial ingredient of its economic policy.

Faster growth may not have been explicitly mentioned, but jobs were. However, it is difficult to deliver jobs without growth, while the reverse is not necessarily true. So perhaps it was just left unsaid that there would also be a superior growth performance. In any case, this was implied in the promise of better days ahead, which had rung out through much of Modi's campaign.

Finally, there was the maxim "Minimum government, maximum governance". What exactly this meant was not spelt out but it very likely promised a turn away from government intervention towards a greater role for markets in determining economic

---

[1] See https://economictimes.indiatimes.com/news/politics-and-nation/bjps-election-manifesto-15-salient-points-of-its-5-year-road-map-for india/articleshow/33376625.cms?from=mdr.

outcomes. The scale of the ambition is revealed by the name chosen for the replacement to the Planning Commission, the dismantling of which was one of Modi's first actions. The newly minted body was named NITI Aayog. While Aayog still meant a "commission", in Sanskrit *niti* could refer to ethics or policy, depending upon the context. But the NITI in the name of this new agency is the acronym for National Institution for Transforming India. This matched the newly elected prime minister's public statements that his vision for India is rapid transformation and not some gradual evolution. In this intended transformation, though, NITI Aayog was to play only the role of a public policy think tank generously funded by the Government of India – unlike the Planning Commission, which had a role in the allocation of the nation's finances across the states of India, apart from a forum for consensus-building.

For a political leader who had projected himself as a transformer of the economy, Modi did not lay out his vision for the economy, leave alone articulate a strategy to achieve it. In this respect he was different from former prime ministers who were successful in leaving their footprint on the economy, among whom were Nehru, Indira Gandhi, and Rajiv Gandhi. Narasimha Rao, whom many would consider the most successful prime minister in ushering in change, may not have stated a vision, but in Manmohan Singh he had a trained and highly experienced economist as his finance minister who, along with his team of accomplished economists, did articulate one – which was that of a market economy integrated with the rest of the world. What precisely this entailed and how much success it had we have already examined in the previous chapter.

By not declaring any new vision or approach to the economy and its management, Modi's stance implied that he was just carrying on with the policies of the UPA without the corruption. It appears not to have struck him that this left unanswered the question of how the promised growth in employment could come about without a substantial change in policies. An escape route to this challenge does of course exist via the unleashing of the animal spirits that govern private-sector behaviour. Arguably, some such unleashing had taken place when Rajiv Gandhi assumed office. Private investment had strongly revived then. Perhaps Modi had imagined that the very installation of him as prime minister would drive a similar recovery.

While there was no specific strategy announced to achieve the transformation, the economic policies of the finance minister, Arun Jaitley, during Modi's first term in office bore a strong resemblance to the main tenets of the policy package termed the "Washington Consensus", which had first appeared in the 1990s. This refers to a set of principles on how the ideal economy should be managed. The background to it was the collapse of the Soviet Union and its basis was a particular understanding of the event. This policy package eschewed all form of intervention in the economy. Industrial policy which appeared to involve any targeted focus on the development of an industrial sector was particularly frowned upon. The policies recommended had mainly to do with macroeconomics and did not directly address development.

It would be useful to set out the areas on which management of an economy policy should, according to the Washington Consensus, focus. John Williamson, the economist who coined the expression, listed the following ten "reforms": Fiscal Discipline, Reordering Public Expenditure Priorities, Tax Reform, Liberalising Interest Rates, A Competitive Exchange Rate, Trade Liberalisation, Liberalisation of Inward Foreign Direct Investment,

Privatisation, Deregulation, and Property Rights.[2] Actually, a move in the direction of almost all of the above had been made by the Government of India well before Modi arrived on the scene. The three areas where this movement had been weak were the restructuring of public expenditure, privatisation, and the strengthening of property rights.

Though Modi would have been very comfortable with each one of these reforms, the policies of his government did not effect them all. Instead, from the very beginning it focused on the issue of fiscal discipline, understood as cutting the fiscal deficit. The guideline was given by the Fiscal Responsibility and Budgetary Management (FRBM) Act of 2003, enacted by the coalition named the National Democratic Alliance, led by Prime Minister Vajpayee. For Finance Minister Arun Jaitley, in particular, pursuing a path laid down by a venerable mentor in the party may have had a significance far greater than the impact to be expected from pursuing "fiscal consolidation", the term used for paring the deficit. The FRBM Act had envisaged a fiscal deficit of 3 per cent of GDP as the target. It is a sad commentary on economic policy-making in India after 1991 that so much of it has been derivative. In this instance, the 3 per cent cap seems to have been borrowed from the figure adopted by the European Union as part of its "Growth and Stability Pact" by which certain fiscal rules came into effect in 1999. Be that as it may, a fiscal deficit figure of 3 per cent of GDP appears to have played the role of the North Star in the economic policy calculations of the Modi government.

The size of the fiscal deficit has a direct implication for the size of the government's borrowing requirement, and public debt is

---

[2] See Williamson (2004).

expected to have negative consequences for the economy – that is, when it is not impotent. The impotence of fiscal policy implicit in Ricardian equivalence has been shown to be dependent upon restrictive conditions, and it would be meaningful to ask why the national debt should be a burden as the population owes it to itself, as it were, unlike debt owed to the nationals of other countries. Now, the supposedly negative consequences would have to be significant indeed to oppose public debt. However, an argument has survived in the armoury of those opposing debt, and it is based on the notion of inter-generational equity. Here the poser is whether it is ethical to borrow and leave it to future generations to repay our loans. This issue cannot be brushed aside, of course. However, its negative implication for raising public debt must be set against the assets that may be financed out of government borrowing. The impressive public goods of Europe's welfare states that the current generation enjoys were not built by it and were financed by public funds, some of which would have been borrowed. It would therefore be fair to expect the current generation to contribute to the servicing of the debt incurred to fund the public goods they enjoy. Only an extreme libertarian, arguing that the consent of future generations was not sought when the debt was contracted, would overlook this.

The Modi government's placing of fiscal consolidation on a pedestal may however have had little to do with arguments from public finance. If we are to look for the economic reasoning underlying it, it could be that a stable macroeconomic environment is necessary for economic growth. This idea was implicit in the Washington Consensus, and the case for it was most explicitly made in a highly cited article by the one-time chief economist of the IMF, Stanley Fischer: "It is now widely accepted that a stable macroeconomic framework is necessary though not sufficient for sustainable economic growth."[3] What Fischer meant by "stable macroeconomic framework" may be seen in the following excerpt:

> The concept of a stable macroeconomic framework is used to mean a macroeconomic policy environment that is conducive to growth. The macroeconomic framework can be described as stable when inflation is low and predictable, real interest rates are appropriate, fiscal policy is stable and sustainable, the real exchange rate is competitive and predictable, and the balance-of-payments situation is perceived as viable.[4]

Recognising the "practical difficulty" of defining and measuring the stability of the macroeconomic framework, Fischer had identified the indicators that would matter most for macroeconomic policy when he stated: "I shall use the inflation rate as the best single indicator of the conduciveness of macroeconomic policies to growth, and the budget surplus as the second basic indicator."[5]

Though he was a lawyer by profession – and not an academic like several previous finance ministers of India had been – Jaitley's public statements and specific actions suggest that his actions as finance minister were mostly directed by an approach that saw macro-economic stability as a sort of guarantee for achieving growth. However, while adherence to pre-set deficit targets was fully under his control, inflation was not. For inflation control, Jaitley put in place a specific mechanism. By an amendment of the Reserve Bank of India (RBI) Act of 1934 in 2015, the Modi

---

[3] Fischer (1993), p. 485.
[4] Ibid., p. 487.
[5] Ibid.

government made inflation control the main objective of monetary policy in India. Though under the colonial Government of India the RBI did not exactly have the interests of India in mind, it was after independence governed by a "multiple indicators" approach that allowed for a concern with variables other than inflation, such as the exchange rate and output growth. With the amendment mentioned above, the RBI was given a target inflation rate to pursue, with some leeway for missing it in practice. With this move the institution transited to an inflation targeting central bank, as were many of the world's central banks at the time. However, it must be noted that even today not all the central banks of the world pursue this goal exclusively. The Federal Reserve – the US central bank – for instance, has a mandate to "promote maximum employment".[6]

If we are to divine the approach to the economy of the Modi government, it would be that of pursuing macroeconomic stability via fiscal consolidation and inflation targeting. Fiscal consolidation, when achieved by contracting public expenditure, would have been in line with the maxim of "minimum government" announced by Modi at the time of the election campaign in 2014. The control of inflation as the central goal of a government is not without a trade-off. When inflation is actually generated along with growth, prioritising inflation control implies a lowered concern with growth.

Interestingly, the two pillars of the macroeconomic policy of the Modi government, inflation targeting and fiscal consolidation, are at odds with developments in the world of economic ideas. Ever since the GFC of 2008, a considerable rethinking of

[6] https:// www. federalreserve.gov/aboutthefed/the-fed-explained.htm, accessed on 27 October 2021.

the tenets of macroeconomic policy has taken place. The question asked within the fold of the global economic establishment's most prominent wings was, "Are all the sacred cows dead?"[7] After all, in the Western hemisphere at least, the period immediately preceding the GFC was one of such low inflation that it had been dubbed "the Great Moderation". Nor did the US economy, the epicentre of the crisis, have a particularly large fiscal deficit by historical standards. Yet the crisis had erupted in the United States. After the GFC, it was plain that to define macroeconomic stability in terms of the magnitude of the fiscal deficit and rate of inflation, as Fischer had recommended in the 1990s, would be simplistic. An unanticipated financial crisis had brewed under the very nose of the high priests of macroeconomic stability.

Globally, what followed was to open up to intense scrutiny the macroeconomic truisms of the past two decades. In the United States fiscal deficits, generally ignored as ineffective, or, worse still, harmful, were resorted to on a scale not seen in half a century. It is widely agreed that this stemmed the tide and a depression was avoided. Further, monetary policy was used aggressively in the US to try and keep the long-term rate of interest low. The money supply with the public grew from the billions to the trillions, but inflation did not accelerate in keeping with the monetarist prediction. The New Classical Macroeconomics that had earlier captured the minds of policy-makers in the US and Europe was eclipsed, at least in the world of policy.

It was well after this change in mindsets globally that the Modi government in India was adopting the main proposals of

---

[7] See Demirguc-Kunt and Serven (2010).

a rejected school of macroeconomics. This reflects an ideological rather than an evidence-based approach to economic management. Some confirmation that this understanding of what the government saw as the centrepiece of its economic management of the economy is correct may be found in the following. Towards the end of the Modi government's first term, its most articulate spokesman had taken credit for restoring macroeconomic stability.[8] The official Economic Survey had dutifully harped on the theme earlier. Reflecting upon the government's performance in its second year in office, it was stated that India "stands out as a haven of macroeconomic stability".[9] In the Survey of the next year the "robust macroeconomic stability" attained through the government's economic management is extolled.[10] Interestingly, this was written within less than a quarter after the demonetisation of November 2016, following which scenes of chaos at the banks and stalled economic activity – which I discuss later in the chapter – has been imprinted in the public's mind. The term "stability" has many different uses, it seems!

The Record

In an evaluation of the Modi government's record it would be appropriate to start by looking at the indicators of macroeconomic stability, as this was its avowed aim. Following Fischer, I study movements in the budget deficit and inflation, given in

[8] See https://www.thehindu.com/business/Economy/macro-economic-stability-has-improved-says-Jaitley/article6785651.eco, accessed on 27 March 2019.
[9] Economic Survey (2016), vol. 2, p. 21.
[10] Economic Survey (2017), p. 17.

Table 4.1. It is without doubt that the fiscal deficit has mostly been lower since 2014 than before. What about inflation? The Modi years turned in unambiguously lower inflation. So, going by these two indicators, it can be said that macroeconomic stability improved, as claimed by the government. However, it is not an achievement unique to it. For, we can see from the data in the same table that the reduction in the fiscal deficit and inflation commenced well before 2014, as decreed by the requirement of the FRBM Act. In fact, by the time Modi assumed office for the first time, the fiscal deficit had been brought down by almost a third from its peak in 2009–10, and a much smaller reduction would have taken it to the targeted figure of 3 per cent of GDP. Furthermore, after having pledged to attend to the task of fiscal consolidation, quite quickly the government's resolve appears to have wavered. In 2017–18 the fiscal consolidation was halted. In 2018–19 the fiscal deficit target was breached to provide direct income transfers made to farmers, a move coinciding with an upcoming general election.

We now turn to the declining inflation rate recorded since 2014–15. Again, it is indeed true that while inflation has declined since 2014, having peaked in 2009–10, it too had commenced its decline earlier. Unlike in the case of the fiscal deficit,

Table 4.1
Inflation and the Fiscal Deficit Since 2014

	09–10	13–14	14–15	15–16	16–17	17–18	18–19	19–20
Fiscal Deficit	6.6	4.4	4.1	3.9	3.5	3.5	3.4	4.6
Inflation	13.5	9.5	5.8	4.9	4.5	3.6	3.4	4.8

Source: Fiscal deficit data are from "Budget at a Glance", various issues, Ministry of Finance; Inflation (CPI) figures are from the *Handbook of Statistics on the Indian Economy*, Reserve Bank of India, various issues.

for which, given that a considerable adjustment towards the cap of 3 per cent of GDP had taken place prior to 2014, a greater rate of decline was not necessary, the decline in inflation has indeed been faster after the Modi government took over. Of the government's role in this outcome, the question is whether the decline in inflation was due to monetary policy, which since 2016 has become synonymous with "inflation targeting".

Superficially it may appear so, for even though inflation targeting was adopted as the centrepiece of monetary policy in India only from 2016, the RBI has virtually been an inflation targeting central bank since 2013, when it came under a leadership committed to low inflation. However, disaggregated data on inflation gives us reason to believe that extraneous factors may have mattered more than monetary policy for the decline in inflation. From 2014–15 there has been a sharp fall in food-price inflation. Further, oil prices actually declined.[11] Close to 80 per cent of India's oil consumption is imported, implying an externally determined price for the commodity. Changes in its price feed into the inflation rate, of course, but are beyond the reach of monetary policy. As for the price of food, monetary policy can affect it but only indirectly, by depressing output growth. So, if during this phase monetary policy has affected food-price inflation at all, it could have done so only by reducing the rate of growth of output and thereby squeezing consumer demand.

The issue of the model of inflation that best describes inflation in India has been investigated through econometrics in a study conclusively establishing that the inflationary process in India is fully explained by the behaviour of agricultural prices

---

[11] See Balakrishnan and Parameswaran (2021) for the evidence.

and the price of oil, both outside the purview of the central bank.[12] The study further establishes that the model used by the RBI to justify inflation targeting cannot explain recent inflation in India. Thus, there is reason to believe that, as far as inflation control is concerned, monetary policy is unlikely to have played a role and that the Modi government benefited from exogenous factors beyond its reach. However, it may not have stoked inflation by raising the procurement prices of agricultural goods to the same extent as its predecessor.

So, the Modi government has maintained a stable macroeconomic environment but the question is what has this achieved in terms of its stated goals. It would be natural to start with economic growth. Though Modi's promise had been of jobs, as I have already mentioned, it is difficult to imagine employment growth without growth of output. The trajectory of growth in India since 2014 may be seen in Chart 4.1.

We see that growth was accelerating, quite strongly at that, before 2014. It continued to accelerate till 2016–17, though at a decreasing rate. Since then growth has slowed, at times at an increasing rate. No favourable impact on the growth rate by the pursuit of macroeconomic stability by the Modi government is evident. The growth rates achieved are not an improvement over what was achieved during the phase of high growth 2003–8 that we spoke of in the previous chapter. This is also confirmed by the econometric estimation of the phases of growth, graphically represented in Chart 1.1.

We can see in this that the attainment of macroeconomic stability is no assurance of resurgent growth. From 2017–18 the

[12] Ibid.

Chart 4.1
Economic Growth since 2014

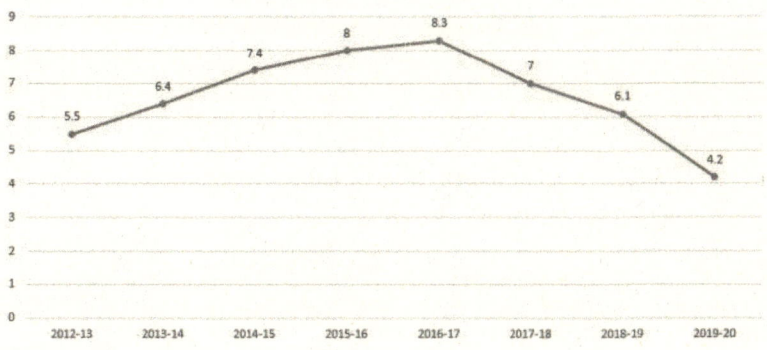

Note: Figures are of the annual rate of growth.
Source: Author's calculation from GDP data released periodically by the Ministry of Statistics and Programme Implementation; see https://mospi.gov.in.

growth of the economy slowed continuously, and by 2019–20 it had fallen to a level far lower than that inherited by the government. This deceleration itself cannot be put down to a worsening of the macroeconomic environment. It can be seen in Table 4.1 that the budget deficit and inflation indicators actually improved as the slowing set in.

So, what could have caused the downturn? Everything points to the direct impact of the demonetisation implemented in the middle of 2016–17. The rate of growth slowed from the very next year. I shall return to a discussion of the consequences of the demonetisation, turning now to the question of employment. It is difficult to be fully certain when pronouncing on this question as we must rely on patchy and discontinuous data. However, we must proceed and I have done so with what is available. Chart 4.2 shows the unemployment rate over the past decade starting with the first year before 2014 for which data are available.

Chart 4.2
Unemployment

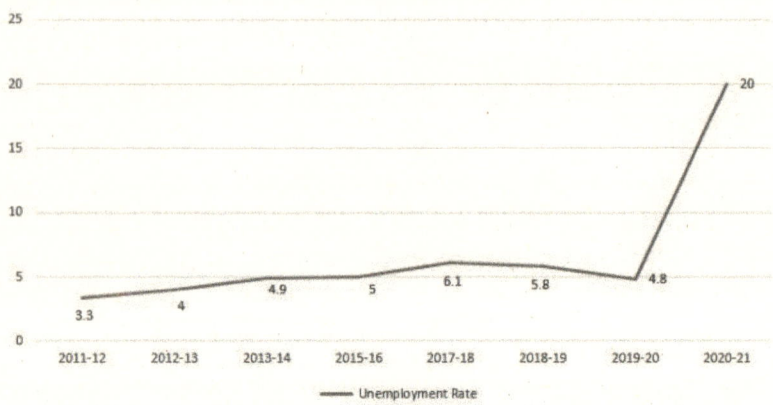

Notes: The figure for 2020–1 alone is the urban unemployment rate for the period April–June. Others are the economy-wide rate.
Sources: Data for 2011–12 are from NSS (2014), the rest are from the PLFS (various issues).

It shows that, for the greater part of the tenure of the Modi government, the unemployment rate has been higher than in the first half of the decade. The Modi government has had very little success in making a dent in the unemployment situation in India, contrary to the promises it had held out during the elections in 2014. The sharp increase in the unemployment rate in 2020–1, due to the lockdown following the onset of COVID-19, has been kept out of this assessment.

The mild decline in the unemployment rate from 2017–18, seen in Chart 4.2, comes as a surprise when considered along with the growth data, as we know that growth had begun to decline from 2017–18 following the demonetisation. It would be difficult to square a declining unemployment rate with a declining growth rate. But there is a plausible explanation of what we have here, and it is this. We know from recent history that the labour force participation rate in India fluctuates. A declining unemployment rate can result from falling labour force participation as discouraged workers no longer seek work, dropping out of the labour force altogether. That this occurred after the demonetisation, when growth slowed and new entrants to the labour market found it difficult to find employment, is not inconceivable.

The Unconvinced Investor

The Modi government's first pronouncements all suggested that it desired a decisive shift away from a state-driven model of economic development. This much was apparent in its slogan "minimum government". If this was to be achieved, the private sector would henceforth have to take the lead. Modi had a reputation as a business-friendly chief minister of Gujarat, even though one may ask if this meant exclusively "big business" represented by the corporate leaders who had flocked to the Vibrant Gujarat business summits of the time. Once Modi reached Delhi, he emphasised that his government would improve the ease of doing business in India. The last by itself is a worthy objective, as anyone familiar with the working of the regulatory apparatus in the country would agree.

Given the self-avowedly business-friendly attitude of the Modi government, it would be of interest to see how the private sector responded. I focus on capital formation in the private sector. If attitudinal shifts on the part of governments matter for private sector activity, as Rodrik and Subramanian (2005) have suggested, then a strong response of private investment to the accession of Modi to the prime ministership may be expected to have taken place.

The data on capital formation starting from 2013–14 presented in Table 4.2 are not flattering to the Modi government. Note that capital formation, measured in relation to GDP, has been lower than it was in 2013–14, the year before it took over the reins. In a disaggregated view, we find that while capital formation in the public sector has held, it is the decline in private capital formation that has pulled the aggregate down. Further, its disaggregation by capital formation in the corporate and household sectors, respectively, shows that it is the former that has decisively declined after 2014.

It is important here to state that capital formation last peaked in 2011–12.[13] So, declining capital formation is something that the Modi government inherited. However, it has had no success in stemming the decline. In fact, since 2014 it is public capital formation that has held up the investment rate, a feature acknowledged by multilateral agencies such as the World Bank that have a stake in India by virtue of their lending activity.

Table 4.2

Gross Fixed Capital Formation (GFCF)

	2013–14	2014–15	2015–16	2016–17	2017–18	2018–19	2019–20
Public/GDP	7.3	7.3	8.0	7.6	7.3	7.6	7.7
Private/GDP	25.3	23.9	22.7	23.2	23.7	24.3	24.8
Corporate/GDP	12.6	11.5	12.7	12.0	11.3	11.4	11.9
Household/GDP	12.6	12.3	10.0	11.2	12.4	12.9	12.9
GFCF/GDP	32.6	31.1	30.7	30.8	31.0	31.9	32.5

Source: Author's calculation from *Estimates of National Income, Consumption Expenditure, Saving and Capital Formation*, published online periodically by the National Statistical Office; see https://mospi.gov.in.

[13] See Balakrishnan (2019).

Having observed that capital formation has not picked up since 2014, it is not difficult to understand why growth has not either. In the workhorse Solow model of growth, growth is a function of the investment rate and the exogenously given rate of technical progress. With the investment rate more or less stable in India after 2014, a rise in the growth rate could not have been expected. Now, the question would be why the investment rate did not pick up.

Once again, it is private investment that did not rise. This has the implication that macroeconomic stability, so assiduously pursued by the Modi government, has not been able to revive it. This is not surprising. As has been pointed out already, the claim of the importance of macroeconomic stability for growth is not based on economic theory but on some economic relationships dredged from cross-country data. There is the question of causality in the adoption of this method, and then there are the outliers to contend with. Outliers would suggest that individual country characteristics matter for growth. After all, we would not expect the economies of India and Vietnam to function identically. Informed by a scepticism on the causal role of the macroeconomic environment in driving private investment, I look at the supply and demand conditions prevailing at the time.

Finance is a factor on the supply side of investment and credit from commercial banks an important source of it. The non-performing assets (NPAs) of commercial banks had been building up even before the Modi government took charge of the economy, but the situation took a considerable turn for the worse after 2015.[14] Having resulted from lending to infrastructure

---

[14] See the trajectory of the non-performing assets (NPAs) of Indian banks as reported in https://dbie.rbi.org.in, accessed 27 October 2021.

projects, this left commercial banks reluctant to lend. The public sector banks were the ones most saddled with NPAs, leaving their executives, caged-in by external vigilance, reluctant to lend. The other side of the banks' NPAs are the balance sheets of the corporates that had taken the loans. The objective of the latter now becomes to deleverage rather than invest. So, the emerging incentive structure was not conducive to either lending by the banks or investment by the firms. This "twin balance-sheet" problem directly impacts capital formation in the economy. It may well have contributed to the decline in investment that started in 2011–12, which has not been reversed.

But even if supply constraints, such as credit availability, were a factor, the question remains whether Modi has created a climate for private investment. Answering this would require some recourse to economic theory. In a highly nuanced treatment of what drives investment, Keynes in the *General Theory* identifies the role of "long-term expectations".[15] For Keynes these expectations, formed behind a veil of ignorance about the future, were driven by animal spirits and not economic calculus. This makes it difficult for the economist to be fully sure of what drives investment. However, after Keynes, economists have come to recognise the presence of "hysteresis" whereby present states of economic activity can persist. This can result in the economy not returning to its prior state after a shock. With respect to investment, the implication of hysteresis is that if agents recognise it as a possibility, they are likely to factor in the present state of capital formation when forming expectations of the future state of the economy. Indeed they would be rational in doing so.

[15] Keynes (1936).

Once we appreciate the factors that go into the formation of expectations, it is possible to see that both the state of the economy Modi inherited and his ideological predilections, as they influenced the government's economic policy, may have left private investors unmoved by the stability, both political and macroeconomic, that they were being asked to admire.

First, what was the state of the economy then current. The boom had ended by 2008 and the economy had been held up only by the Mukherjee stimulus, which could not have been expected to last. The upsurge in public investment had long since ended and agricultural growth had become erratic. In fact, in the first two years of the Modi prime ministership, agricultural growth was near zero. Finally, with the global financial crisis and the consequent slowing of the world economy, the future of exports was uncertain. All this added up to a slowing of the exogenous drivers of demand, and investors could not but have seen that if hysteresis was to be expected, the situation was not likely to revive soon. Also, investors would not necessarily have been enthused by the possibility that the ideology of "minimum government" could put public investment on hold, as public investment has the potential of crowding in private investment. So, based on the situation in 2014, India's investors would have been fully rational had they anticipated a not-so-rosy future for the economy unless some exogenous factors were to turn favourable or the government were to act decisively to energise it.

The one lever that the government could have pulled as it watched private investment decline was to step up public investment. As can be seen in Table 4.2, it resolutely refused to do this for its first six years in office. Only ideological blinkers combined with the hubris that there is nothing to be learned from history can explain this inaction. Historically, every turning point of growth in India, including the downswings, have been associated with a significant shift of the public investment rate. This includes the growth accelerations of the 1950s, the late 1970s, and the early 2000s – all seen in Chart 1.1 – and the downturns of the mid-1960s as well as the GFC of 2008.[16] The ideological aspect is to believe public investment crowds out the private sector. Indeed, all the three instances of growth acceleration that I have mentioned above were phases when high private investment accompanied the public investment thrust. This suggests that crowding in rather than crowding out characterises the relationship between public and private capital formation in India. An aversion to the government playing a role in capital formation is peculiar to economists and politicians of a certain persuasion. As we shall see, it does not afflict capitalists as much.

Two Initiatives

In its first term, the Modi government had projected three of its reforms as particularly transformational in terms of their potential. These are, in the chronological order of their implementation, "Make in India", the demonetisation, and the introduction of the goods and services tax (GST). Of these, the last mentioned, which was implemented in 2017, is the culmination of a project initiated by the UPA that did not see the light during its tenure due to the partisanship of the BJP-led opposition. The BJP was quick to seize upon the

---

[16] Interestingly, even the very strong Mukherjee stimulus in response to the GFC, that lasted for two years, boosted consumption rather that capital investment by government, explaining its short-lived nature.

opportunity of launching it, with considerable fanfare, as soon as it returned to power. As it is still a work in progress, with continuing changes in the rules, I shall not proceed to a discussion of it, mentioning only that the claims made – that it would bring in substantial revenues to the government and spur economic growth, for reasons not fully specified – have not been particularly evident, so far at least. The evidence on growth I have presented already. The evidence on tax revenues is as follows. Indirect tax revenue as a share of the gross domestic product has been lower in every year since 2017, having increased in every year of that decade prior to it, which amounted to an increase of approximately 25 per cent over the period.[17] Finally, independent economists have claimed that, by increasing the compliance effort needed and unleashing a variant of the "inspector Raj" in the name of GST enforcement, the launch of the GST in 2017 has suffocated the smaller production units.[18] This cannot be ascertained from macro data but cannot be ruled out prima facie either, for we find that manufacturing output slowed considerably from the very next year on.[19]

Make in India

"Make in India" targeted manufacturing production with the aim of raising its share of output to 25 per cent of GDP. In this respect it was almost identical to the objective underlying the constitution of the National Manufacturing Council by the UPA. The council had been set up in 2004 by the UPA in its first term

[17] See MinFin (2021).
[18] See Singh (2022).
[19] See Table 4.4.

to provide a forum consisting of representatives from government, industry, and academia for a policy dialogue to energise and sustain the growth of the manufacturing industry. There were two differences, though, in the "Make in India" programme. The latter did not envisage a forum for the exchange of views, an arrangement that has potential as a source of inputs into policymaking. External evaluation of policy is essential to bring about course correction when needed, and the need for the latter could be missed if the evaluation is confined to committees comprising politicians of the ruling party and bureaucrats.

The second difference was that through "Make in India" Modi seemed to be addressing his call to the foreign multinationals, implied in the outreach "You may sell wherever you want but make in India". Again, as set out in the previous chapter, the objective of turning India into a global hub for manufacturing is desirable given the potential of manufacturing to create employment. To an extent, the emphasis on "making" was a progress over the presumption underlying the reforms of 1991 which appeared to have overlooked the need to encourage production, having assumed that an overhaul of the policy regime would be sufficient to spur it. That the PM took a personal interest in the "Make in India" pitch is reflected in his publicised meeting, soon after assuming office in 2014, with the CEOs of some of the world's leading multinationals when he was in New York for the annual meeting of the United Nations General Assembly. That meeting, in particular, gives the impression that Make in India was a pitch made to foreign companies rather than a programme focused on creating an ecosystem for production in India, for producers both Indian and foreign. In my earlier discussion of why manufacturing growth has disappointed in terms of its response to the reforms of 1991, I had flagged the issue of bureaucratic hurdles and infrastructural shortage as constraining manufacturing growth in India. These were not the main focus of "Make in India", however, though the Modi government should have had ample time to observe that history.

The call to multinationals to invest in India did not go altogether unheeded. There was a surge in foreign direct investment (FDI) of over 50 per cent in the very first year of the Modi government, and it has remained elevated ever since. The data on FDI inflows are presented in Table 4.3.

By 2019–20 FDI was close to two and a half times its level in 2013–14. This is quite impressive, and may well have been a reflection of the confidence in the leadership of Modi and the pursuit of macroeconomic stability as the centrepiece of his economic policy. However, a far greater net FDI inflow had been registered during the boom years of 2003–8.[20] It is not sufficiently

Table 4.3

Foreign Direct Investment

Year	Net FDI inflows (Rs crores)
2013–14	129969
2014–15	191219
2015–16	235782
2016–17	238913
2017–18	195052
2018–19	214036
2019–20	304820

Source: Reserve Bank of India, *Handbook of Statistics*, various issues.

[20] See RBI (2016) for the data. In recent years a debate in India reveals some

well known that FDI has also begun to flow out of India in significant volumes.

We have seen that the "Make in India" initiative has had considerable success in attracting FDI to India. Now let us look at the record of manufacturing production after 2014. Data on the growth of this sector are presented in Table 4.4.

Data show that manufacturing growth revived after 2014–15 and has remained elevated for the entire first term of the Modi

Table 4.4

Making in India

Year	Manufacturing	Agriculture
2012–13	5.5	0.2
2013–14	5	5.4
2014–15	7.9	–3.7
2015–16	13.1	–2.9
2016–17	7.9	5.3
2017–18	7.5	5.4
2018–19	5.3	–1.6
2019–20	–2.4	4

Note: Figures are of the annual growth rate. Data for agriculture refers to crop production.
Source: Estimates of gross value added by sector published periodically by the National Statistical Office; see https://mospi.gov.in; accessed on 6 August 2021.

---

economists pointing out that the government has been adding portfolio capital to FDI to show inflated figures for inward capital flows, signalling the success of its policy. Their contention is that portfolio capital does not directly add to fixed capital formation, and therefore should be kept out of the calculation of foreign direct investment.

government. However, a deceleration sets in in 2016–17, and is unabated, with growth turning negative in 2019–20. As we know, 2016–17 was the year of the demonetisation, and it would be difficult to attribute the immediate decline in the growth rate to any other source. We see from the data on agriculture in the same table that the year was one of exceptionally high agricultural growth. Nor were there any shocks transmitted from the global economy during this period. Elsewhere, I have shown that, starting November 2016, for every subsequent month remaining of that financial year the monthly index of manufacturing output grew by less than it did in any of the previous seven months.[21] In fact, there was a progressive slowing. The cash crunch triggered by the demonetisation may be expected to have led to both lower supply and lower demand.[22]

Our evaluation of the "Make in India" initiative has been entirely quantitative. However, the response of manufacturing should also be judged qualitatively, in terms of the type of goods and their inherent quality. The qualitative response of the manufacturing sector after "Make in India" does not even come close to the explosion in the range and quality of consumer goods that was seen in the two decades after 1991. It would be interesting

---

[21] See Balakrishnan (2019).

[22] It is difficult to establish which of these two forces predominated in the Indian case, but this does not impinge on the argument being made here. Each of them, i.e. less supply and less demand, will contribute to less production, and would thus lower growth. The demonetisation in India also serves as a source of evidence pertaining to a classic question in macroeconomics, whether money affects output – see Romer (2016). It was a rare experiment in economics, and the evidence for what economists term the "real effect" of money seems to be strong.

to investigate the segments of manufacturing production that recorded most growth after 2014.

In the previous chapter I had established that the share of manufacturing in the economy has remained the same three decades after the reforms of 1991 that focused on this sector. An astute assessment of what it would take to raise it has come from an industry leader. In an interview with Piyush Pandey (2018), the head of Siemens India, Sunil Mathur, says:

> The PM has said that he wants to increase the share of manufacturing in GDP from 15% to 25%. GDP today is $2 trillion, and 15% of that is $300 billion. Let's assume that in 7 to 8 years, $2 trillion will become $4 trillion with 7–8% growth. So, 25% of $4 trillion is $1 trillion. So you got $1 trillion minus $300 billion, which is $700 billion of addition to GDP through manufacturing output. If you have to do an output of $700 billion, at least two times of that amount is the capex required which is roughly $1.5 trillion. That is my calculation. Right or wrong we can debate it. But I am saying that if we are to believe the vision of the PM, I have no reason not to believe it, the extent of the opportunity for manufacturing has got to be $1.5 trillion. But where is the money? Indian banks are having ₹10-lakh crore NPAs and most of the companies have stretched balance sheets and don't have the money to invest. The government have [*sic*] to invest to make infrastructure. You can't expect a GDP growth of 8% without having infrastructure. That is clear. You want steel. You are looking at cement, you are looking at electricity. If this has to come, you need steel companies to invest, you need cement companies to invest. You need a complete turnaround of the discoms. We know that and we need the transmission lines to be better, we need power generation to be more efficient. You know, 30,000–50,000 megawatt power plants are reaching end of life over 30 years. How do you replace them?

You can't replace them only with renewables. You need fresh power plants. That is a whole amount of capex that has to come into the system. So, you can't reach 8-plus percentage of growth unless you concentrate on infrastructure, which will drive industry.

Mathur's exposition of what it would take to raise the share of manufacturing has correctly identified both the need for investment and the source from which it may be expected to come. Infrastructure in the form of road networks and power generation have long gestation periods and require patient capital which the private sector may be reluctant to invest. It is for this reason that, globally, infrastructure has mostly been built by the state even in the market economies: prime examples of this would be the US Federal Highway System and the Chinese railways. In addition to the issues relevant to a large investment being undertaken under uncertainty, there is in India the reality of what may be termed "political pricing", with political parties encouraging an attitude of entitlement among citizens extending to the price at which they access services. This introduces an additional element of uncertainty for private investors who would need assurance that their bills will be paid. However, the main point made by Mathur is that taking the share of manufacturing in India to 25 per cent of GDP from its present 16 per cent would require very high capital expenditure. This condition appears to have been overlooked in the "Make in India" programme. It may be argued that this is not entirely true as the prime minister did make a pitch for FDI, and did succeed in attracting large amounts. However, FDI, being almost entirely private, is unlikely to flow into the building of physical infrastructure for reasons that I have already elaborated. And, in any case it is a small part of total capital formation in the economy.[23] The absence of any consideration given to the capital formation that must accompany any significant manufacturing transition in India renders the "Make in India" initiative somewhat naïve in its conception.[24]

Two further points may be made about "Make in India". First, it seemed to focus excessively on multinationals, while a large part of the manufacturing sector comprises small and medium enterprises. Continuing on a theme that I had brought to the discussion of the response of manufacturing to the reforms of 1991, not enough thought seems to have been given to their concerns, which are related to the regulatory regime and the infrastructure necessary for efficient production.[25] Arguably, starting with his long tenure as the chief minister of Gujarat, Modi

---

[23] National income statistics for the year 2019–20 show that it amounted to 5 per cent of total capital formation in the economy. It would be unrealistic to expect FDI to lead the transformation of the manufacturing sector of India in quantitative terms. It can, however, play a crucial role in transforming technology-intensive lines of production in manufacturing, raising product quality, and introducing global best practices in management – all contributing to higher productivity.

[24] But it is not inconceivable that the absence was ideologically driven. Recall the slogan "minimum government". An ideological approach to public investment was rife also in the capitals of the Western world after the collapse of the Soviet Union. As the Country Economist for Ukraine at the World Bank in the mid-1990s, I was astounded to hear economists demanding that plans for the rebuilding of Eastern Europe after communism should not involve public investment as all growth must come only from the growth of (total factor) productivity.

[25] The following media report is instructive: "R.G. Chakrapani, Secretary of the Tirumazhisai Industrial Estate, Chennai, said that there had been unscheduled power cuts and poor quality of power. He pointed out that there were no sub-stations or proper roads or an effective storm water drainage and adequate sewage treatment plants. Many MSMEs in Coimbatore, Tiruchi

has not given to India's small industrialists the same attention he has to big business. A quantitative transformation of manufacturing in India can only be achieved by including this segment in the government's outreach.

My second observation would be as follows. While Modi has correctly honed in on the importance of production, surely the economy comprises more than manufacturing. Data on agriculture has been included in Table 4.4 alongside the data on manufacturing to make precisely this point. Note that, in the Modi government's first term, crop agriculture registered a contraction in the majority of years. Despite talk of doubling farmers' income, there has not been any policy to address it. India's agricultural sector is more or less on par with manufacturing in terms of output but is far greater than the latter in terms of the population it supports. Till the Farm Laws were rushed through parliament during the COVID-19 pandemic, agriculture did not receive attention in relation to manufacturing nor the attention that it merits on its own.

The Demonetisation

Surely it is the demonetisation of 2016 that would count as the most dramatic economic policy move of the Modi government

---

and Madurai said skilling and training had really not helped the sector. Even now there was a huge shortage of labour they said. M.V. Ramesh Babu, President of the Coimbatore District Small Industries Association, said payments for orders catering to PSUs or government departments should be released to them within a month or 45 days. Smaller units in the sector said banks had never been considerate with them and most Central schemes did not reach them." "MSME Sector Flags Infra Issues", *The Hindu*, 20 March 2021.

so far. On the evening of 8 November, when it was abruptly announced, there had been frenzied shopping till midnight, especially in the upmarket malls. This suggests that some sections of the population had cash hoards from unaccounted economic activity and wanted to get rid of it while it was still legal tender. From the next morning on there was a rush to the banks to exchange the demonetised currency notes and deposit money into savings accounts. The experience of those attempting this was not a happy one. Newspaper reports spoke of long waits, scuffles, tellers favouring relatives when exchanging demonetised notes, and banks running out of cash. The government, including the monetary authority, were clearly unprepared for the consequences of their action. The visible turmoil, however, does not capture the extreme uncertainty that was generated regarding the immediate future of the economy. To convey a sense of it, I quote from an article I wrote soon after the event.[26]

> At dinner time on November 8, Prime Minister Modi announced that the 500 and 1000 rupee notes in circulation will no longer count as legal tender after midnight.[27] The quantitative significance of this is understood when we note that notes of these denominations accounted for 86 per cent of the total currency at that time. Demonetisation, as this move came to be known in India, is a standard tool in a government's bag of public policy instruments. However, that a policy has legal sanction does not it make it necessary in a given context. The demonetisation announced by the Prime Minister, in a speech relayed over All India Radio, did not contain particularly convincing economic reasons as to why one was

[26] See Balakrishnan (2016).
[27] Notes of these denominations accounted for 86 per cent of the total value of currency in circulation at the time.

necessary at this stage, but he did speak of it as an act of "purifying" the economy, and that it would check the growth of corruption.

A demonetisation that delegitimises a certain currency, even if only some denominations of it, would extinguish wealth held in that form. What we have seen in India, however, is a less extreme case. In this one, holders of 500 or 1000 rupee notes can exchange their notes or pay these into their bank accounts, to be done within a stipulated period. This does not extinguish wealth as much as it will potentially bring the hoards into the taxman's radar, for with the bank transactions there would be a record of them. So existing black money cannot be used to generate more of the same. To this extent the scheme is ingenious. Of course, it cannot be assumed that what is in a bank will necessarily be declared to the income tax authorities, but it becomes open to scrutiny in a way that it was not when money may have been stashed under a mattress.

What are some reasons why we may welcome such a move? First, the concealment of income with a view to avoid tax is a crime. So, in a constitutional democracy such as ours those who conceal their earnings deserve to be punished. Secondly, in order to evade the law, those with unaccounted wealth proceed to corrupt others, including representatives of the state. This criminalises the system further. If democracy is a way of actualising the public will, criminalisation of the machinery of government works against the ideal. So, the practice of tax evasion needs to be rooted out. To that extent this move of the government may be welcomed.

But how significant is demonetisation likely to be in the punishment it metes out to tax evaders and in its ability to control the generation of unaccounted wealth in the future? The efficacy of this policy move depends upon the extent to which unaccounted or "black" wealth is held in the form of currency notes of the specified denominations. One may presume of course that, for reasons of convenience, not much of it will be held in the form of notes of smaller denomination. If unaccounted money by Indians is held in the form of foreign bank accounts the present scheme can do nothing about it. These speculations would suggest that if unaccounted money is not held as 500 or 1000 rupee notes the demonetisation is pretty much useless. There is however the separate issue of counterfeit currency. If there is counterfeit currency circulating in the form of 500 or 1000 rupee notes the demonetisation will also extinguish it if the holder is reluctant to deposit it into a bank account. When counterfeit currency is actually used to de-stabilise the Indian Union, as has been claimed by the government, eliminating counterfeit money in circulation enhances national security. This would count as another reason to welcome the move.

Now to the question of whether the demonetisation will eliminate the black economy of the future. It should be obvious that it cannot by itself achieve this. For that to happen we would need a policy that checks the generation of black incomes at source. It would be a good surmise that much of the unaccounted money in India is generated in transactions related to the purchase and sale of gold and property. The markets for these assets are highly concentrated, with relatively few sellers exerting considerable control over supply. Market power, combined with the cultural significance of both a home and gold ornaments in India, empowers these sellers to insist that they are paid in cash, leaving many ordinary people in this country to have to abet criminal activity to even own a home. However, the very fact of real-estate companies, builders and jewellers being highly visible, and small in number, makes it that much easier for the long arm of the law to control the generation of unaccounted income by them. For this to take place, though, action by the tax authorities alone will not suffice. It would require the central government to step in and legislate that all transactions in gold and property must go through banks. The implication is that to prevent the generation of unaccounted income through these transactions a demonetisation was not necessary.

To sum up the argument thus far, we have no idea really how much unaccounted money hoards will be driven overground due to this measure, and can say with certainty that there is nothing in it to ensure that all the financial transactions of the future will be accounted for. What, for instance, will ensure that unaccounted income to be generated in future will not be held in the form of the new 500 and 2000 rupee notes to be issued by the RBI? Moreover, currency is not the only medium in which unaccounted income is held. Pulping the stock of money of certain denominations cannot stem the flow of unaccounted income to be generated in the future. Strict oversight of transactions in the areas of the economy where such income tends to be generated alone can achieve this result.

None of this even begins to explain why the demonetisation was necessary in the first place. Historically, demonetisations have been resorted to during hyperinflation, as in Weimar Germany, or periods when undeclared windfall profits were made, as in British India during the Second World War. No similar situation prevails in India today. Inflation is trending downwards for close to half a decade and the private sector is facing stressed balance sheets.

Finally, the government has only just closed a tax amnesty scheme that ended on September 30. When it was launched, dire threats had been held out then to those who would not come clean. Did this not flush out all the black money? If it did not, are we to understand that tax evaders will continue to dodge the tax administration and, therefore, demonetisation would have to be resorted to again sometime in the future?

It is difficult to escape the conclusion that the demonetisation has a political component. Surely the government is aware that data do not show anything of the kind of resurgence of the economy promised by it in May 2014, and we are almost exactly at the halfway mark of its tenure. This latest move could be a desperate signal of its determination to act, but there is no guarantee that the claims made for it will materialise.

The purpose of quoting from this particular article was to convey a sense of the uncertainty induced by the demonetisation when it was announced, coming like a bolt from the blue. What strikes me today is that I had not been able to foresee that it would trigger a declining growth rate. In Chart 4.1 we see that the rate of growth slowed in 2017–18, which commenced less than five months after the demonetisation and has decelerated ever since. In sectors of the economy in which production decisions are continuous, such as manufacturing, the rate of growth declined substantially in the year of the demonetisation itself. In fact the move set out a continuous decline in the rate of growth of manufacturing output which has lasted till 2019–20.[28]

On the possibility of the demonetisation ending corruption, though, my scepticism seems to have been justified. Within days of its announcement Gujarat's Anti-Corruption Bureau caught up with two officials of the public-sector Kandla Port Trust demanding payment for clearing a consignment of goods. The payment of close to Rs 3 lakhs was set to be made entirely in the newly issued 2000-rupee notes. Several instances of cash hoards being intercepted before elections continue to be reported a full five years afterwards, most recently in Kerala. Nothing, however, can match the sensational case of a perfume manufacturer

---

[28] See Table 4.4. Data on agricultural growth included in the same table imply that had agricultural output not rebounded to the extent that it did, growth of the economy would have slowed in 2016–17 itself.

in Kanpur being found with close to Rs 200 crores in cash in his premises.[29]

This points to two things. First, periodically changing the currency in circulation can do little to eliminate corruption at source, for which it is necessary to target the very generation of unaccounted income. For the latter, a re-engineering of the process of interaction between the government machinery and the citizen is necessary, with a public record and independent oversight of each such interaction.

This is not difficult to achieve. Two suggestions can be made right away. There must be a provision for the citizen to register with the government any demand for gratification made by the bureaucracy and of any attempt made to bribe its members. To ensure that frivolous or malicious allegations are not made, anonymous complaints ought not to be entertained and complaints should be made public. Secondly, as the largest generation of unaccounted income is believed to occur in the registration of the purchase and sale of property, details of all such transactions – including the names of the two parties and the value of the sale – must be entered on the relevant public body's website when they are concluded. With the capability enabled by information technology such transparency is easy to achieve.

The possibility of public scrutiny, as opposed to that by the income tax department in private, would make a difference to

---

[29] See https://www.ndtv.com/india-news/piyush-jain-kanpur-income-tax-raid-after-rs-200-crore-found-up-businessman-arrested-2672921, accessed on 9 February 2022. Clearly, neither demonetisation nor the subsequent introduction of GST, the hallmark of which is that it tracks payments made as part of production, has been able to root out the generation of unaccounted income and the practice of holding of it in cash.

the generation of black money. It should also provide some relief to citizens who are otherwise at the mercy of an unaccountable bureaucracy believed to extort payment for concluding transactions. If the Modi government is serious about ending corruption it must lay out a plan for ending the generation of black money in the interaction of the citizen with the government machinery, including the income tax department itself.

Then there is the issue of election funding. The prime minister has mooted public funding. The ethical basis of this proposal is contestable. In a democracy, it is not clear that citizens should be asked to pay for political parties often campaigning on sectarian agendas. However, there is a strong argument for the reform of present practices. First, the limits on spending should go, but so must the legality of anonymous donations to political parties. In fact, political parties must be brought under the provisions of the Right to Information Act. The argument that they are not public bodies does not carry credibility. They are unique private entities in that they are claimants to the government in the future. Since, if they come to power, they will oversee economic activity in the country, the citizen is entitled to know of their financial transactions even before they assume office. A demonetisation allegedly aimed at ending the generation of unaccounted income that has nothing to say about the funding of political parties is not credible. The Modi government has steadfastly refused to divulge the source of funding under the electoral bonds scheme of which, it is public knowledge, the BJP is the biggest beneficiary.

Demonetisation's potential in eliminating corruption is limited also for cultural reasons. Corruption thrives because surveillance and enforcement by public authority is weak. But while seeking to end corruption in India we cannot ignore the role of social norms. Corruption exists because it is tolerated by society. In India there is high socially sanctioned regulation of personal freedoms. This repression is justified by reference to religious sentiments and cultural traditions, seldom on ethical grounds. By comparison there is neither shame attached to the amassing of illegal wealth nor moral injunctions against the giving or taking of bribes. A bribe is seen as purely transactional and has no moral significance whatsoever. It would be naïve to ignore this aspect of Indian life. This leaves a role for civil society in ending corruption in the country.

The definitive indicator of the dubious consequence of the demonetisation is that close to 99 per cent of the currency stock that was demonetised returned to the banking system.[30] Well before this became known to the public – implying that the prime minister's claim that demonetisation would serve as a "surgical strike" against black money hoards was not actualised – the government changed the narrative. The demonetisation came to be rationalised as a move towards "less cash" in the economy rather than as aimed at corruption directly. The infrastructure for digital payments was boosted. The campaign for replacing cash with electronic money had international votaries, prominent among them being the economist Kenneth Rogoff.[31] Now, while the option of digital payments offers great convenience to individuals, a Rogoff-like labelling of cash as a "curse", with high-denomination notes seen to enable criminal activity, is contestable. Morever, legislating away the privacy that cash permits, and substituting it with electronic money, would constitute

[30] See RBI (2019).
[31] See Rogoff (2016).

a weakening of democracy in that it would give the state the power of surveillance over all economic transactions, not to mention the ability to shut its political opponents out of the payments system at will. The faint suggestion, part of the crusade against cash, that cash is somehow pre-modern and an impediment to wealth creation also remains open to question. Japan and Switzerland, among the wealthiest countries of the world, have had a high cash-to-GDP ratio historically. They are also shown to have less crime.

The demonetisation in India has received global attention. The leading economist Larry Summers stated that it counts among the "most sweeping changes in currency policy in the world in decades", that it was "unlikely to have lasting benefits", and that it has resulted in "chaos and loss of trust in the government".[32] Money is based on the confidence that its users have in it. It was recognition of this aspect that gave rise to the slogan "Debauch the currency and destroy capitalism!" attributed to the anti-imperialist Lenin. It is an irony of history that, over a century later, it was a government in India staunchly committed to capitalism that came close to enacting the communist's plan.

Why Modinomics Failed to Quicken the Economy

Embracing Fundamentalist Macroeconomics

The macroeconomic stability that the Modi government had taken credit for vocally in its first term came along with a certain

---

[32] Summers (2016).

fundamentalism in its policy-making generally, but in particular with respect to macroeconomic policy.[33] This could have played a role in restraining private investment despite Modi's image as a benefactor of the private sector. Economic policy-making may be described as "fundamentalist" when policies are adopted on ideological grounds, implying a lack of concern for the consequences. In the present context, an example of this would be the shrinking of government expenditure in relation to the economy, the fiscal counterpart of the maxim "minimum government". From the data in Table 4.5 we can see that central public expenditure as a share of GDP has been lower than it was in 2013–14 in every subsequent year. Interestingly, the years

Table 4.5

A Contractionary Macroeconomic Policy

Year	Public expenditure (% GDP)	Real repo rate
2012–13	14.2	–2.1
2013–14	13.9	–1.8
2014–15	13.4	2.0
2015–16	13.1	2.1
2016–17	13.4	1.8
2017–18	12.5	2.5
2018–19	12.2	2.9
2019–20	13.2	0.7

Source: Central government expenditure data are from http://indiabudget.nic.in; the real repo rate is calculated by the author as the difference between the repo rate and consumer price index inflation using RBI data from https://dbie.rbi.org.in.

[33] For a discussion of fundamentalism in macroeconomic policy, see Vickrey (1996).

of the sharpest decline were those that immediately followed the demonetisation. It should be easy to see why this is an example of fundamentalism in economic policy-making. With demonetisation, private consumption expenditure may have been expected to decline as households would have been cash-constrained temporarily. Equally, it may have been expected that private investment would decline due to depressed expectations. To reduce public expenditure at such a time, when private expenditure would have declined, surely is a case of fundamentalism in macroeconomic policy, reflecting a lack of concern for the level of aggregate demand and its consequence for output and employment.

But it is in the conduct of monetary policy since 2014 that a fundamentalism is most evident. In the very first year of the Modi government, the real repo rate turned positive, rising by a staggering 3.8 percentage points even as the inflation rate declined by 3.7 percentage points.[34] The hawkishness conveyed by the implied rise in the real interest rate was very likely intended as a signal of the resoluteness of the central banker rather than a response to any rise in the inflation rate. This approach was to reach its pinnacle in the years immediately following the demonetisation. Indeed, the real repo rate reached record highs. One is led to ask whether monetary policy in India was engaged in inflation targeting or whether it was targeting the real interest rate, with a view to keeping it elevated for reasons known only to the central bank. Generally, in the first term of the Modi government inflation declined substantially while the nominal repo

[34] See Table 4.5. The repo rate is the rate the Reserve Bank of India charges for overnight loans to the commercial banks. See the data on inflation in Table 4.1.

rate was lowered to a much lesser extent, confirming this suspicion.[35]

It should now be possible to see why the much vaunted macroeconomic stability that has characterised the economy since 2014 has not resulted in even steady growth, leave alone anything higher. The period has been one of contractionary macroeconomic policy all round. A fiscal policy that has shrunk government spending in relation to the economy and a monetary policy that has been unusually tight by historical standards may be expected to have slowed the growth of aggregate demand. Standard macroeconomics prescribes that these two levers be moved in an offsetting way.

For instance, the prescription for a government intent on lowering the fiscal deficit, likely to shrink aggregate demand, is that it should slacken monetary policy, expected to raise aggregate demand. Instead, for much of the period since 2014 macroeconomic policy has been firing on both cylinders to restrain demand growth. It should not come as a surprise that growth slowed and private investment did not take off. Macroeconomic policy was uniformly contractionary. It bears repeating that it is in the hardening of an already contractionary stance following the demonetisation that the macroeconomic policy of the Modi government comes across as inexplicable. A loss of momentum in the economy was now inevitable.

To the extent that macroeconomic stability did little for private investment, an important tenet of the Washington Consensus – to which policy package the Modi government has shown an affinity – has been shown to be questionable. However, there is

---

[35] For the contemporaneous movements of the nominal repo rate and inflation during this period, see Balakrishnan (2019).

one element of the Consensus that the government has shown scant respect for. This was the recommendation for "switching expenditure in a pro-growth and pro-poor way, from . . . non-merit subsidies to basic health and education and infrastructure."[36]

From Table 4.6 we find that since 2014 the share of health and education in the total expenditure by the central government has declined, and so has the share of subsidies, while the share of capital spending has remained stable.[37] The inescapable conclusion is that the fiscal consolidation has not led to a shift in spending in a pro-growth and pro-poor direction. It has merely led to a quantitative lowering of the fiscal deficit, which has gone with a reduction in the expenditure on health and education. The Modi government has been guided by the goal of reducing both public expenditure and the fiscal deficit without concern for the capacity of such a policy to do damage.

Finally, the point of including the share of each item of public expenditure being considered in Table 4.6 is to give an idea of how it is structured in India. Subsidies amount to one and a half times the expenditure on health and education and to three-quarters of the capital expenditure. It is questionable whether India should spend more on subsidies than on health and education together, as they also reflect inefficiencies in the functioning of the public sector.[38] Though the present structure

---

[36] Williamson (2004).

[37] Note that the items "Health and Education" and "Capital Spending" are not fully independent as the former contains capital expenditure on health and education. However, both of them may be compared to the item "Subsidies", which does not include capital spending.

[38] If, for instance, the Food Corporation of India, which is responsible for

Table 4.6

Expenditure Priorities of the Modi Government

Item	Direction of change	Share in total spending (2019–20)
Health and Education	Reduction	5.7
Subsidies	Reduction	9.5
Capital formation	Stable	12.7

Note: "Direction of change" refers to the difference in the share of the item of expenditure over 2013–20.
Source: Calculated using data from https://www.indiabudget.gov.in.

of public expenditure in India pre-dates the arrival of Modi and subsidies have been lowered since 2014 (enabled by the decline in the global price of oil), no restructuring of public expenditure has taken place in the close to two decades since the enactment of the FRBM Act of 2003. The Act has exclusively focused on fiscal consolidation, a reduction in the fiscal deficit without any fiscal correction. The Modi government has shown enthusiasm for the first injunction on fiscal discipline of the Washington Consensus but refrained from recognising its second one.

Economics, indeed the social sciences in general, cannot proceed as the experimental sciences do. In the practice of the latter we can simulate alternative scenarios, but we cannot in the case of economics, having to rely instead on historical data. The history of the Indian economy since 2014 is an important test case for the conduct of macroeconomic policy. In the 1980s,

---

managing the supply of foodgrain for the public distribution system, procures grain and lets it rot due to faulty storage practices, it would show up as an increase in subsidies according to the Government of India's budgeting practice.

much of the advice to developing countries from the multilateral agencies, then far more powerful than they are today, was to "get the prices right". The advice was addressed particularly to the management of the exchange rate. This is quite unexceptionable. You don't want an overvalued exchange rate, which could arise from the protection of domestic industry. But at the same time you do want a supportive macroeconomic environment. Aggregate demand matters for growth. So, "getting the macroeconomics right", as it were, is as important. The mistake of the Modi government seems to have been to assume that macroeconomic stability would be sufficient to take care of aggregate demand. But private investment never revived, and the government stubbornly refused to maintain the level of aggregate demand via an increase in public investment.[39] Ideological commitment can be a barrier to seeing the economy for what it is.

Mistaking Architecture for Force

I now address a second error of judgement made by the Modi government in its approach to the economy. Underlying its failure to raise the growth rate in India is a flawed understanding of what drives the economy. At the core of this misunderstanding is an inability to distinguish between architecture and force. The error is to imagine that a particular policy configuration or "architecture" assures economic dynamism or "force". The latter comprises the forces of demand and supply that make for expansion or contraction of an economy, as the case may be. Now, architecture can be a force multiplier but it cannot produce

---

[39] As may be seen in Table 4.2.

force.⁴⁰ At a macroeconomic level the best example of force would be investment. Investment actually impacts the economy from both its supply and demand sides. By raising the capital–labour ratio it increases the productivity of labour from the supply side, by adding to total expenditure it boosts the economy from the demand side.

Three policy moves by the Modi government indicate what it imagined are elements of a desirable architecture for the economy, namely, a digital payments network that would replace cash, a unified indirect tax regime, and less government. The government has had some success in moving the economy towards such an architecture. The demonetisation, initially spoken of as a "surgical strike" on black money hoards, was later rationalised as nudging Indians towards adopting a digital payment mechanism. The resultant formalisation of the economy was to lead to more tax revenue for the government, enabling greater spending on infrastructure. Next came the launching of the GST. This certainly had merits, such as the associated removal of inter-state barriers to transportation of goods, but above all as a super value added tax. Also, GST ended the "cascading" of taxes, an attribute of the Indian system hitherto. The government cannot claim all the credit for this move, though, as a restructuring of the indirect tax regime has been on the books, if not in the works, since the 1970s, and there has been a high degree of participation of the states in its launching. The third element of the new architecture was the actualisation of the slogan from the 2014 election,

[40] My thinking on this issue has been influenced by the work of Kentaro Toyama (2015) on the potentiality of information technology to bring about social change. Toyama's conclusions are based on fieldwork in Bengaluru.

"minimum government". This took the form of a lower share of the central government's expenditure in the economy. So the government has been able to achieve much of the economic architecture that it aspired to.

Arguably, the government's macroeconomic policy, discussed in the previous section, too may be seen as an extension of the approach to place centrestage a suitable architecture. Accordingly, there was the move to a "modern monetary policy framework" in 2016. This meant that henceforth the sole objective of monetary policy would be inflation control. And fiscal policy has been guided by "fiscal consolidation" or the objective of deficit reduction. As we have seen, inflation has steadily declined, and throughout the first term of the government fiscal consolidation has proceeded apace, leading Finance Minister Jaitley to remark at the end of its first term in office that the government had achieved macroeconomic stability and that this was the best period ever for India's economy.[41]

A significant part of the promise of demonetisation and the introduction of the GST, namely higher public revenues from formalisation, has not materialised. On the other hand, though digital payments have increased considerably, a progressively declining growth rate set in soon after the demonetisation and has not been reversed since. If architecture alone matters for growth, then presumably the impact of the demonetisation would have been reversed soon, as the money supply was restored to its previous level fairly quickly. The fact is that throughout the

---

[41] See https:// www.thehindubusinessline.com/ economy/ budget/ macro-economic-stability-2014-19-perhaps-the-best-performing-period-for-india-says-jaitley/article26155505.ece, dated 1 February 2019, accessed 17 August 2021.

Modi government's tenure the *force* necessary to move the economy to a higher growth path has been lacking. The private investment rate has not risen and the government has shown itself unwilling to make up for this by expanding it own expenditure, perhaps out of its commitment to a certain architecture.[42] The discussion in the preceding section was meant to show how this can be understood. Slowing growth combined with a contractionary macroeconomic policy does not augur well for future profits, negating the benefits, if any, of the architecture that has been put in place by economic policy. There are times when a government must anchor profit expectations. A dogmatic belief in the growth-generating powers of a certain economic architecture meant that this was not even recognised.

The above account is that of the first six years of the Modi prime ministership. In 2020 India was struck by the COVID-19 pandemic. As an *exogenous* event, i.e. an external influence on the economy, it would be proper to address what followed separately.

COVID-19, and the Lessons Learned

Though the first case of COVID-19 in India was identified in December 2019, its presence in the country was officially acknowledged by the Government of India in March 2020. Perhaps no other epidemic has caught the imagination of the public, mainly in terms of the fear of contagion, as much as this one. The plague in the nineteenth century and the Spanish flu of the early twentieth had resulted in deaths too, but the deaths were more localised as transportation networks were far less developed.

---

[42] Finally, in the union budget of 2022, the government appears to have veered away from this stance.

The port city of Bombay was at the time, in today's language, a "hotspot", but the rural areas were relatively protected. This time, originating in the parts of the country which had greater international connectivity through travel, the virus spread to the interior. No part of the country has been spared, including the north-east, which had shown a far slower growth of infection in the early days of the spread of the virus. Finally, in a major difference from the history of the earlier epidemics in India, the strong presence of the media and the technology for image transmission has meant that information on the growth of the infection and the resulting mortality has been available in real time across the entire country.

India's early experience of the epidemic seemed subdued in a global comparison. Then the hotspots were elsewhere, in northern Italy and in the UK and New York. By February 2021, it seemed that the virus was under control in India. There came a second wave, however, in mid-March 2021. This time the experience was qualitatively different. The severity of the virus attack was greater, reflected in a spike in infections and deaths. It has been described as a tsunami in terms of the surprise factor and the devastation.

The country's health infrastructure was found to be utterly inadequate to handle the epidemic. A shortage emerged in almost every department, from hospital beds to ventilators and oxygen itself. The visual media relayed horrific scenes of the sick lying on hospital floors, dead bodies piling up in the corners of wards, and people queuing with empty cylinders in the hope of finding oxygen for their families. The collapse of the health system was complete.

Further, having failed to secure their lives, citizens were unable to even take the bodies of departed family members to their final resting place in a dignified manner. In Delhi, crematoria were either full or often not capable of functioning at full capacity due to faulty equipment. In UP, bodies were found floating in the Ganga. This was deeply demoralising, for while Indians are used to seeing death around them, being unable to conduct the last rites for the departed in accordance with tradition was traumatic for many. Scenes of makeshift funeral pyres in India inevitably reached the rest of the world via the global media, denting the image of a rising India that had been projected by the Modi government ever since it came to power. A relatively independent media has meant that there is little that the public did not get to know about the unfolding of the epidemic and its ghastly consequences. But there was a pattern to the impact of the virus that I shall describe and account for, which may have been missed. Understanding what underlies this pattern is essential for us to move closer to securing our health in India in the future.

The Importance of a Public Health System

Underlying the large number of COVID-19 deaths in India is the feature that there is a significant inter-state variation in the death rate. For instance, on 31 March 2021, at the two ends of the spectrum, the death rate was 10 deaths per million population in Mizoram, and 463 per million population in Delhi.[43] This needs explaining. Sreenath Namboodhiry and I have established a pattern between the death rate and certain

[43] Authors' calculation from mortality data in "*COVID-19 State-wise status*", https://www. mygov.in/corona-data/covid19-statewise-status, accessed on 1 April 2021, and state-level population data in MHFW (2019).

attributes of the states of India.[44] Our first finding was that the states recording a higher death rate also had a higher per capita income. This came as a surprise to us. In any case, it shows that wealth, to which income may reasonably be assumed to be related, has not acted as a shield against death during the epidemic. So, what is the factor that may have shielded the populations of some states to a greater extent? To get a handle on this, my co-author and I compared state-wise data on death from COVID-19 to state-wise data on health infrastructure in the public sector and public expenditure on health. Of the three measures each of infrastructure and expenditure, respectively, only one was statistically significant. This was the ratio of public health expenditure to the state's GDP, in our view a measure of how well funded a state's health system is. The rank correlation coefficient for the data was -.42, indicating a negative relationship, i.e. states that spent more of their GDP on a public health sector had lower mortality from COVID-19. As the statistical exercises that underpinned this finding may be read in our published paper here, we present only the relevant graph in Chart 4.3.

To confirm our result regarding the importance of the public health system, we tested for the role of private health infrastructure, including equipment directly relevant for COVID-19 treatment such as ventilators, and found that it did not have an impact on mortality once public spending on health had been taken into account. The significance of this result is that public expenditure on health matters, however good the privately provided system may be.

[44] See Balakrishnan and Namboodhiry (2021). The pattern is established through an extensive statistical examination of the data, details of which have been excluded here. Interested readers may consult the original study.

Chart 4.3
The Inter-state Variation in COVID-19 Mortality

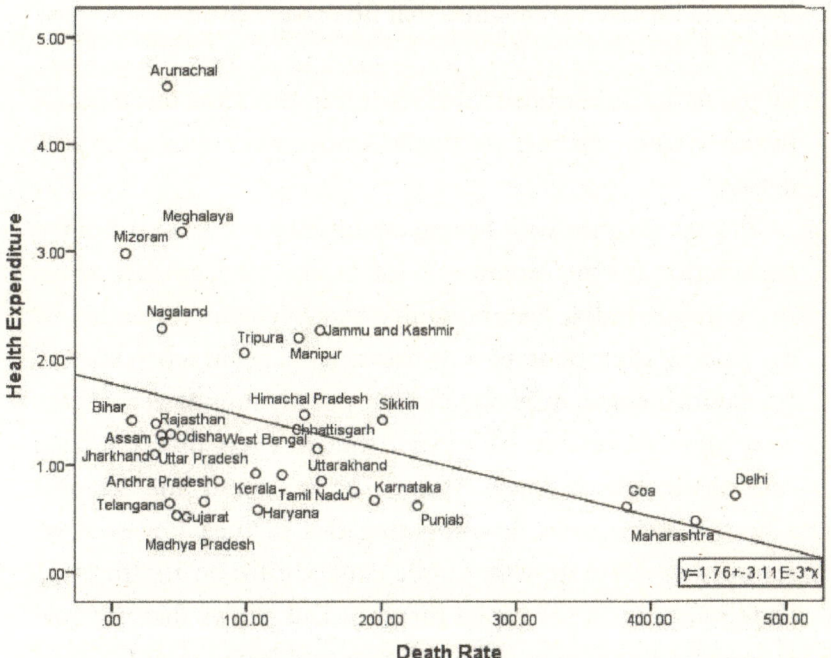

Notes: Variable definition and data sources are stated in the text.

Further, it is important to note that the result obtained is for public spending on health and not for the availability of infrastructure in the public health sector, suggesting that what may be being captured is the role in the prevention of death of a whole complex, so to speak. This complex would be the public health "system" which, at the time of an epidemic, would be responsible for all aspects of its control, including surveillance, testing, detection, containment, and the co-ordination of treatment. Co-ordination becomes particularly crucial when the physical infrastructure of a state is geographically dispersed. The effectiveness of a health system is determined by more than just the medical infrastructure in place and is therefore related to the funding it receives.[45] It is the magnitude of this funding that this variable, the ratio of health expenditure to GDP, measures. It should be easy to recognise that no private entity would have either the capacity or the legitimacy to undertake the tasks assigned to the public health system. It is in this sense that a public health system assumes particular importance during an epidemic.

Though satisfied with having established at least a part of the explanation for the variation in the COVID-19 death rate across the states of India, Namboodhiry and I remained puzzled by the finding that the state-wise mortality is positively related to per capita income, implying that the populations of richer states were more vulnerable. This experience was very different from that of the rest of South Asia, or, as we found out, for over a hundred countries. Investigating this further, however, we found that the state-wise public expenditure on health is inversely related to per capita income. This shows that the governments of the richer Indian states spend less of their GDP on their public health systems than the poorer ones. In the light of this finding, what had first appeared puzzling was no longer so.

Noting the importance of public health expenditure for mortality, we now studied the allocation for health in the budgets of the state governments. According to the Constitutional distribution of responsibilities between the central and state governments in India, health is a State Subject. Therefore, the expectation is that the state governments will bear the greater part of the public expenditure on health. From data assembled by

---

[45] This has been suggested by health specialists at the World Health Organisation. See Kandel, *et al.* (2020).

PRS Legislative Research, an independent body aiming to make the Indian legislative process better informed, more transparent and participatory, we found that for the year 2018–19 on average the states allocated 5.1 per cent of the total budgeted expenditure to health.[46] While there is no absolute standard, it would appear that a share of less than 5 per cent would be low, given the state of health infrastructure in India. Half the states of India fall into this category. It is also noteworthy that almost half of them spent very close to the same amount or more on the police than they did on health. The largest among them – namely, Bihar, Jharkhand, Punjab, Haryana, UP, MP, Chhattisgarh, and Maharashtra – account for a very large share of the Indian population. Thus, for a significant section of it, the public expenditure on law and order exceeds that on health.

Apart from Maharashtra, these states are located in the north of the country, and share a certain culture and history, which has a bearing on public policy. It must be pointed out that some of the north-eastern states and the erstwhile state of J&K too spend more on the police than on health. But these are also states with a higher than average level of public spending, ensuring that health expenditure remains elevated in relation to GDP. In fact, for every north-east state the ratio of health expenditure to GDP was greater than the Indian average. On the other hand, for most of the eight centrally located states mentioned earlier this ratio is lower than the national average. The exception is Bihar, where the health expenditure is on par.

[46] Authors' calculation from state-wise expenditure data assembled by PRS Legislative Research; see https://www.prsindia.org/parliamenttrack/budgets/state?field_state_tid=All&field_session_year_value[value]&page=1; accessed 7 September 2020.

Finally, special note may be taken of the case of Maharashtra, the state which on 31 March 2021 had registered the highest number of deaths and the second-highest death rate. Maharashtra allocates less of its budget to health than the national average, which, when combined with low overall public expenditure in general, resulted in a health expenditure to GDP ratio of less than half of 1 per cent.[47] The state is by far the richest in India in terms of GDP. The consequence of the low spending on health is reflected in this state's health infrastructure; only two other Indian states have less hospitals, only three have less (allopathic) doctors, and only eight have less hospital beds per head of the population than Maharashtra does.[48]

There is a lesson to be learned from the Indian experience with COVID-19 for those concerned with the health of its population. While health may be a State subject, implying that the states are expected to do the bulk of the providing for the health of their populations, they do not have to spend on Defence, Communications, National Highways, and External Relations. Yet some of them devote a lower share of their budget to health than the central government. We were able to see the importance of investing in a public health system when COVID-19 struck, in that states which spent more on the public provision of health services experienced lower mortality. It would be reasonable to assume that the inverse relationship carries over to the health status of a population more generally. Given the very low level of spending on health out of their budget in some states of India at present, assuring health security to the Indian population will require a radical restructuring of spending priorities.

[47] See Balakrishnan and Namboodhiry (2021), Table 8.
[48] MHFW (2019).

Fiscal Restraint Is Not Always Prudent

The Indian government's initial response to the pandemic was in March 2020, when a lockdown was imposed on the country as a whole. The move elicited strong criticism on grounds ranging from the very short notice of just four hours that was given, to the fact that the central government did not consult the states. Both are serious criticisms on political grounds. The extremely short notice given has also attracted the criticism that it resulted in hardship and mental stress for migrant labourers far from their home, but it is not obvious how much less the longer-term hardship would have been if more notice had been given without assurance of economic relief measures. Be that as it may, the lockdown lasted for approximately two months, the period first announced having been extended more than once. Since then the central government has not announced any nationwide lockdown, leaving it to the state governments to announce a lockdown in their territories if they so desire. Most states have since announced lockdowns in line with the progress of COVID-19 infections, or have imposed some restrictions on travel. Well over a year after the central lockdown was lifted, there was no complete restoration of economic activity. The economy contracted by approximately 7 per cent in 2020–1. An incipient recovery by the end of that year was thwarted by the unexpected appearance of the second wave of the pandemic in the early part of the next one.

The stringency of the central government's lockdown – in terms of a total clampdown on movement and economic activity – which received international attention, was not matched by its economic response. An appropriate policy response in the situation would have had two components, namely relief and revival. The first of these is necessitated by the loss of livelihood during a lockdown. The second is motivated by the macroeconomic consideration that the loss of output during the lockdown sets in motion loss of demand which may not revive fully even after the lockdown is lifted. The economy now contracts. If the economy were to remain depressed long enough, private investment may be affected and the recovery indefinitely delayed. We would end up in a Keynesian demand-constrained equilibrium and only increased public spending, referred to as a stimulus, can take the economy out of it.

The government's first response has been largely in the form of increasing the food entitlements for the poorer households through the public distribution system. In addition, some extremely meagre cash transfers were made to women in poor households. The government's economic recovery plan was to come much later, over May–June 2020. First the prime minister announced on television that the stimulus would be of the order of approximately 20 lakh crore rupees, amounting to 10 per cent of GDP. However, when the finance minister came to announce the details, it was found that the direct injection of purchasing power via greater public spending was to amount to little less than 2 per cent. The rest was to take the form of a financial backstop, with the government guaranteeing loans made by the banking sector. In addition, the RBI announced that it would provide adequate liquidity.

The stimulus to the sagging economy by the government was weak. Assuming that the two-month-long initial lockdown in 2020–1 would have shaved off about a sixth of the GDP, taking the approximately 200 lakh crore rupees in 2019–20 as the benchmark, the loss of income would have amounted to 33.3 lakh crore rupees. With a multiplier of 1.5, a stimulus in the form of additional public expenditure of 22 lakh crore rupees would have been needed to generate an equivalent income. However, as of 17 March 2021 the central government's stimulus – being the additional budgetary spending and forgone revenue – amounted to only 6.5 lakh crores.[49] It had fallen short of the estimated requirement by more than two-thirds. This could not but have had an impact on economic activity. This can be seen in Table 4.7, in which are assembled the relevant data for India, the rest of the BRICS countries, and the United States.

The numbers tell a definite story. Across these countries, the decline in output in the year the epidemic struck, i.e. 2020, was inversely related to the extent of the stimulus, though not

Table 4.7

The Macroeconomic Policy Response to COVID-19

Country	Stimulus/GDP	GDP growth (y-o-y)		
		2019	2020	2021
India	3.3	4.0	-7.9	12.5
Brazil	8.8	1.4	-4.1	3.7
China	4.8	5.8	2.2	8.4
Russia	4.3	2.0	-3.1	3.7
South Africa	5.9	0.2	-6.9	3.1
United States	25.5	2.2	-3.5	6.4

Source: "Stimulus" is the additional spending and forgone revenue as on 17 March 2021, reported in IMF (2021a); GDP growth data are from IMF (2021b); the figure for 2021 is the IMF's forecast.

[49] See IMF (2021a).

proportionately. In particular, the contraction was highest in India, which undertook the smallest fiscal stimulus. This cross-country data suggests that so large a contraction may have been avoided by the government undertaking a larger stimulus. The refusal to do so may have caused an avoidable loss of output. Finally, the high forecast growth rate for India in 2021 must be read in conjunction with the fact of a negative growth rate in 2020. To place matters in perspective, by the end of the first half of 2021–2, real output (GDP) was yet to regain the level in the corresponding period of 2019–20, the pre-pandemic year.[50] Also, the Indian government's first estimate of the economy's growth rate in 2021–2 is far lower than that of the IMF.[51]

It is difficult to fathom the economic policy response of the Modi government. The proposition that public spending should rise when an economy experiences a negative aggregate demand shock is no longer controversial among reasonable economists. Surely the Indian government was watching how the United States Congress had closed ranks and plumped for a 2 trillion dollar fiscal stimulus as soon as the epidemic struck their country? The biggest stimulus to be implemented in the history of that country, it was a bold and timely response to the situation. Many Indian economists, including myself, had very early on in the lockdown written in the media that India needed a strong fiscal stimulus if it were to avoid output loss.[52]

However, the Modi government's reluctance to provide one was evident in its actions. During the course of 2020, when everything was pointing to a continuing contraction of the economy,

[50] See MOSPI (2021).
[51] See MOSPI (2022).
[52] See Balakrishnan (2020).

the government, while it did finally increase spending over and above what had been budgeted, was already giving out assurances that fiscal consolidation was not being abandoned. And it gave direct evidence of its intent when in the budget for 2021–2 it kept expenditure almost unchanged over the revised estimate for 2020–1. At a time when there was no certainty of a recovery to the previous level of output, or at least of a revival in private investment, this could not but have delayed the recovery. If keeping the total budgetary expenditure unchanged was unwise, the actual reduction in the expenditure on health before the epidemic had substantially abated was downright irresponsible.[53]

The Modi government's economic management during the epidemic provided neither significant relief to those likely to have lost their livelihood due to the initial lockdown nor support to aggregate demand on anything like the scale necessary to bring about a quick recovery. On the scale of the response itself, a misunderstanding often encountered is reflected in the plea that India could not have afforded a bigger stimulus as it is a poor economy compared to the economies of Europe and North America. This misses the point that the stimulus is to be evaluated in relation to a country's GDP and not some absolute standard. In any case, India has the world's third-largest economy when GDP is measured in purchasing power parity terms.

It is important to note that the provision of relief and a boost to economic activity via the budget are not acts that need be confined to the central government. The states have a role to play, and are not without resources, even though they face greater

---

[53] See the figures reported in MinFin (2021).

restriction on borrowing compared to the central government. While we do not have comparable data to analyse the response to the economic fallout from COVID-19 by India's states within a unified framework, the governments of the larger states of India have not shown much initiative in crafting a recovery.

Conclusion: When the Market Met Its Match

Narendra Modi came into office in 2014 after an electoral campaign that placed the management of the economy centrestage. He had inherited an economy with accelerating growth and decelerating inflation. At the end of his first term in office, growth had been decelerating for three years and inflation was accelerating. More importantly, the unemployment rate had mostly been higher than before. Modi has been able to create far less jobs than he promised. Egregiously, Modi's reputation as a pro-business politician has not led to a rise in the private investment rate, though some leading capitalists from his home state may have seen their assets rise. Modi has not enthused India's private sector. Perhaps out of ideological commitment, his government has shown a stubborn refusal to raise public investment when it was most needed.

Under Modi, the economy's growth began slowing well before COVID-19 struck in 2020. The loss of momentum may be seen as a case of the economy's response to the government's policies. Data suggest that the immediate cause for the slowing of growth since 2014 was the demonetisation, implemented exactly midwaythrough Modi's first term in office. But other aspects of policy may have provided the deeper underpinning of the slowing, namely, a contractionary macroeconomic stance, and the heavy-handed use of the state apparatus to unearth imagined illegal financial transactions. Of these two, the chilling impact on economic activity of unleashing the tax and economic enforcement authorities on India's entrepreneurs works in a more subtle way.

In the inability of the Modi government to enthuse the private sector to invest we may also be seeing the impact of such intimidation over and above the depressed long-term expectations of investors. These expectations may well be rational, being based on the observation that the government has no credible strategy for keeping the economy buoyant in the future. In the absence of any obvious external factor that lowered India's growth prospects, much points to the Modi government's hand in bringing about a loss of momentum.

There is in this a certain similarity with Indira Gandhi's leftward lurch, leading to an immediate collapse of private corporate investment for close to a decade from the late 1960s onwards. However, Indira Gandhi was able to quickly correct her toxic policies to bring about a recovery. At present it is not clear whether we can expect the same of Modi, who seems to have privileged his political and cultural agenda over the economic, with predictable consequences for the economy. In fact, India's economic evolution after 2014 may be seen as the collateral damage.

5

An Unfinished Journey
Modernisation
Without Development

INDEPENDENT INDIA'S economy is completing a 75-year-long journey. It has been a remarkable one too. Agricultural production has grown considerably and stabilised. We have not faced food shortages for over half a century. From its import-dependent status, Indian industry has transformed itself into one with a highly diversified product mix. Services produced here no longer mean just an Ayurvedic massage or the rope trick but high-end software solutions delivered onsite to the leading corporations of the world by young Indian engineers. Clearly, the economy has modernised in some significant ways.

However, heart-warming as these achievements may be, after seventy-five years India's economic journey must be gauged by the goal that was set at its beginning. I began this book by arguing that the goal of Indian independence, as visualised by its founders, is best reflected in Nehru's observation that India was embarking on a journey to end "poverty and ignorance and disease, and the inequality of opportunity". As these outcomes may be expected to be partly dependent on the economic progress made, this is why I have narrated the story of India's economic journey over these seventy-five years. I end this book with an evaluation of the extent to which political democracy, embraced wholeheartedly in 1947 and the procedures of which have been retained, has succeeded in delivering the goal envisaged for it.

Democracy and Development

Everyone in India has a certain understanding of what is meant by democracy. The same cannot be said about development, though it is a term that appears often in the public discourse. The leading political parties of India all claim to be working for development. Thus, the government of Narendra Modi at the centre started out with the slogan *sabka saath, sabka vikas*. India's state governments seem not to be lacking in zeal either. In Maharashtra today, the ruling coalition, which includes prominent national parties, calls itself the *Maha Vikas Aghadi* (loosely, Maharashtra Development Front). But what are we to understand by their use of the term "development" to describe what they claim to be bringing about in the country?

Amartya Sen redefined development as the expansion of freedoms.[1] The concept of freedom at stake in this definition is the freedom to do or to be. For Sen, in the pursuit of freedom, individuals are constrained by their "capability" to achieve certain "functionings". These functionings are the "beings and doings" that the person values. Thus, capability reflects a person's freedom to lead one type of life or another.[2]

---

[1] Sen (1999).
[2] For definitions of "functioning" and "capability", see Sen (1992).

This view of development also provides a standpoint from which to understand marginalisation in a society. The marginalised can now be seen as the unfree, as they are not free to achieve the functionings they value. Now, working backward from the conception of development as freedom, marginalisation can be located in the absence of what Sen referred to as "basic" capabilities, i.e. it reflects "basic capability (in)equality".[3] Of significance for practice is the implication that so long as these capabilities are not inborn, society can endow all its members with the capability set deemed basic, provided that it can muster the resources and the political will.

It is important when trying to understand marginalisation that the numerical factor is redundant. The marginalised can well be the majority in a society, and it is not necessary to revisit apartheid-era South Africa to encounter such a situation, some may argue that this is the case in India today. While it would be impossible to outline to the last detail what will lead to the expansion of individual freedom in every case, it would be reasonable to assume that it is education that contributes most to the functionings a person can achieve. Again, this has an implication for practice. Beyond its clear economic potential, education in the form of uniform schooling has the capacity to neutralise what has been recognised as *cultural* capital by Pierre Bourdieu.[4] Those familiar with the Indian reality would recognise the role of cultural capital in reproducing marginality in its society in the past. Once basic capabilities have been equalised, mainly through fairly uniform education, any inherited cultural capital should hardly matter over a wide field of human interaction.

[3] Sen (1980), p. 219.
[4] Bourdieu (1986).

Apart from education, health too matters in determining capability. Given the educational level attained, the individual's health will determine how effectively that education can be utilised to achieve the functionings that are valued. Adopting the premise of "development as freedom", it can be seen that the distribution of freedom in a society is closely tied to the distribution of capabilities. Overlooking this has consequences when evaluating social arrangements. For instance, societies with a fairly equal distribution of goods, achieved through welfare programmes, could yet remain ones where capabilities are unequal, implying that not everyone has the same extent of freedom. Anticipating what follows here, public policy in India, with its emphasis on the distribution of goods, has tended to overlook this feature.

To an extent, Sen's view of freedom derives – as noted at the start of this book – from the work of Isaiah Berlin. Clarifying that he used the terms "liberty" and "freedom" interchangeably, Berlin had imagined two concepts of liberty: freedom from interference by others and the freedom to do. As noted earlier, the first he termed "negative" freedom and the latter "positive" freedom. For Berlin, the notion of negative freedom was best understood as follows: "I am normally said to be free to the degree to which no man or body of men interferes with my activity. Political liberty in this sense is simply the area within which a man can act unobstructed by others."[5] On the notion of positive freedom, Berlin said that it

> derives from the wish on the part of the individual to be his own master. I wish to be somebody, not nobody; a doer – deciding, not being decided for, self-directed and not acted upon by external nature or

[5] Berlin (1969 [1958]), p. 3.

by other men as if I were a thing, or an animal, or a slave incapable of playing a human role, that is, of conceiving goals and policies of my own and realising them. I wish to be somebody, not nobody; a doer . . . conceiving goals and policies of my own and realising them.[6]

Berlin's work proved to be foundational to the discourse on rights, justice, and well-being in the Western intellectual tradition. We are now able to see that – as there cannot be individual freedom to act so long as there is interference by other men – for Sen's idea of development to be actualised, both the concepts of liberty are essential. Negative and positive freedoms are, as it were, the "necessary" and "sufficient" conditions, respectively, in the space of development. Each of the two notions of freedom comes with its own implicit role for the state. For negative freedom to prevail in a society, the state must act as a "nightwatchman" or "traffic policeman" to ensure that the liberty of the citizen is not encroached upon by others. Indeed it is absolutely essential, for individuals cannot realise their goals if they are restrained, not just by the state but also by convention.[7]

Yet Berlin did not engage with the question of the role of the state in the case of positive freedom – on the grounds that the idea of positive freedom has been used to rationalise authoritarian regimes in history. It is apparent, though, that to endow individuals with capability, the state would have to be more than merely a night watchman or traffic policeman. In the presence of ideological commitment, agreement on the role of the state

[6] Ibid., p. 8.
[7] The role of convention, at times enforced through violence, has played a central role in the social control of the lives of women and the lower castes in India.

in development is unlikely to be attained easily. It is perhaps this that led Berlin to jettison the idea of positive freedom, alluding to its use by those "great, disciplined, authoritarian structures" to debase liberty by requiring individuals to conform in deference to the goal of achieving a rational society. However, he appears to be self-contradictory here, having started out by arguing that the notion of positive freedom derives from the individual's wish to be "self-directed" or, in effect, "his own master".

Further, as pointed out by Macpherson, there is nothing immanent in the idea of positive liberty that lends itself to the assertion that liberty must be curtailed to ensure its attainment, as Berlin had feared.[8] The route taken by Macpherson was to show that positive freedom implied negative freedom, thus weakening the distinction between the two made by Berlin, but, more importantly, rendering the denial of negative freedom in the name of advancing positive freedom an incredible project.

If development means the expansion of freedoms, and freedom is capability, identification of the basic capabilities is necessary. Sen himself desisted from drawing up such a list. He thought of the notion of basic capability as quite a general one, and allowed for its implementation to be culture-dependent, especially in the weighting of different capabilities. Other philosophers, such as Martha Nussbaum, while subscribing to Sen's capability-based approach to development, have taken the view that a list is indispensable.[9]

---

[8] See Macpherson (1973).

[9] See Nussbaum (2007). However, Sen and Nussbaum seem to converge on the position that it is education that is central to capabilities.

While Sen may have refused to be tied down to any particular set of capabilities, he provided an important insight into the question of how to deal with marginalisation. As individuals do not come into the world rigged with capabilities, and resources are needed to equip them, extending the basic capabilities across the population would require a collective commitment to the expansion of individual freedom. Despite its idealistic ring, this is actually a most practical suggestion. Collective action is needed to equip individuals with capabilities, for if individuals could simply endow themselves with capability, they would not remain marginal in a society. This implies that empowering individuals requires what Sen has referred to as "public action", being a collective effort that may be undertaken either by the state or by civil society groups. To summarise, while capabilities ultimately reside in individuals, when barriers to attaining them exist, a social programme to equipping them with the basic capabilities is needed.

With this recasting of the idea of development as the expansion of freedoms, the focus of attention shifts from goods to human capabilities and from national aggregates to individuals. From the point of view of public policy, we become less interested in the total value of production and more interested in distribution of the endowment of health and education in a population. Development now becomes synonymous with *human* development.

As India is a democracy, the case for human development as its ultimate goal emerges inexorably. Macpherson points out that the claim for liberal democracy – that it maximises men's powers – is based on the proposition that the end of man is to use and develop his uniquely human attributes or capacities. To quote him, "His potential use of and development of these may be called his human powers. A good society is one which maximises or permits and facilitates the maximisation of these powers, and thus enables men to make the best of themselves."[10] The claim is that liberal democracy maximises each individual's powers in the sense of maximising his or her ability to use and develop their essentially human capacities. With this, on its seventy-fifth anniversary, India must be judged by the extent to which it has advanced human development.

Building Capability

Education has been identified as the single-most important input into the building of capabilities of a human being. To education may be added health, as there is clinical evidence that learning is thwarted by poor health, malnutrition in particular having been identified as an example of this.[11] Research in the field of education points to three features. First, learning is a function of the stock of knowledge already in the possession of the individual, therefore the initial educational inputs influence the productivity of subsequent ones. Second, early childhood education is crucial, for it is at this stage that the brain is most receptive to environmental influences. Third, a part of mental development is believed to be even prenatal and therefore related to the health of expecting mothers. All of this adds up to the implication that some parts of an individual's capabilities are developed at a very early stage in their life cycle. This, in turn, has implications for educational policy, particularly

---

[10] Macpherson (1973), pp. 8–9.
[11] See Jukes (2005).

for how public spending should be distributed across levels. It may come as a surprise that studies from the United States have shown that the rate of return to public spending is highest at the pre-school level.[12]

Education has long been identified as the medium for the development of cognitive skills. However, while cognitive skills may be paramount, there are also non-cognitive skills such as tenacity and perseverance, not to mention attributes of the personality such as motivation, the inculcation of which should be considered one of the tasks of education. Randomised control trials conducted in the United States have shown that special school programmes can make a difference in these areas. But there is a third dimension to be considered. Formal education, including time spent in playschool, takes place during the period in a child's life when values such as empathy develop. Skills, both cognitive and non-cognitive, gained through spillovers, and values such as empathy inculcated at school, contribute to social cohesion. Social cohesion may be thought of as a public good.

We know from economic theory that in the presence of externalities and when it comes to public goods, private provision may be expected to be suboptimal. This in turn suggests that there are sound reasons for the government to take a lead in such instances. It is very likely that it is due to this awareness that education is believed to generate externalities. Education has been largely publicly provided in Western Europe and the United States since at least the nineteenth century. Additionally, in the United States the reliance on public schooling may have also been motivated by a strong ideological commitment to equality of opportunity among the settlers.

---

[12] See Heckman (2006).

Acemoglu and Robinson (2012) argue that one characteristic of successful nations is a relatively equal distribution of power. Surely this is not unrelated to publicly provided, and fairly uniform, compulsory education. This arrangement ensures a degree of equality of opportunity, and through the equalisation of capability brings about a sense of social cohesion, thus widening the cohort of stakeholders in a country. Of course, the movement towards a more egalitarian provision of education, without sacrificing quality, may require a certain social transformation. This can be seen in the fact that the United States, France, and Russia, each in a widely differing region of the world but sharing a fairly egalitarian school system, are united by a history of revolutionary change, though of widely differing forms. In the United States, the transformation perhaps commenced even before 1776, the settlers having rejected the values of the mother country in the very act of migration to a distant land. I shall return to a discussion of the role of social transformation in the spread of equal opportunity in India.

Public Policy and Human Development in India

The ending of colonialism and the adoption of political democracy did usher in an important freedom to Indians. They were no longer constrained by a foreign power and, at least in principle, were free of arbitrary rule. But surely the founders of India had more in mind for their compatriots. Actually, it is possible to argue that when Nehru spoke about ending poverty and ignorance and disease and the inequality of opportunity, he had in mind the need to endow Indians with the capability that would enable them to lead a fulfilling life.

For a comparative assessment of the progress India has made towards the ending of poverty and ignorance and disease, we may turn to the data in Table 5.1. The data tell a definite story. In 2020 Indians had an income that was only one-third of the global average per capita income. Related to this, over a fifth of the population was in a state of what the World Bank terms "extreme poverty". This is more than twice the global poverty rate. There is also far greater undernourishment in the country and greater illiteracy. The only metric by which the Indian population is not far from the rest of the world is life expectancy. These data together imply that while Indians live almost as long as everyone else on the planet, a sizeable section of them lead a life of deprivation. In a significant contrast, poverty, illiteracy and undernourishment have been almost eliminated in China. On every

Table 5.1

Human Development in India and the World

	India	China	World
Income	6454	17,312	17,110
Poverty	22.5	0.5	9.3
Adult Literacy	74	97	86
Life expectancy	70	77	73
Undernourishment	14	3	9

Notes: "Income" is GDP per capita in current international dollars. "Poverty" is the percentage of the population living on less than 1.90 dollars (2011 PPP) per day; "Adult Literacy" is the proportion of literate adults in a population; "Life expectancy" is the life expectancy at birth; "Undernourishment" is the percentage of the population with unmet dietary energy consumption.
Source: The World Bank, https://data.worldbank.org/indicator; accessed on 13 September 2021.

one of the indicators in the table, China does better than the world and India does worse than China. In terms of the most basic indicators of development, India has very far to go to reach the global standard.[13]

The point of comparisons such as the one just made is to assess the gap that may exist between countries on the indicators of interest. This does involve the assumption that the benchmark used is attainable by all the countries included in the exercise. A good reason for comparing India's achievements with those of China is that they were more or less on the same level economically and had a similar social structure in 1947. Our comparison shows India well behind China. However, it is often asserted that comparing India and China is not valid as one of them is an authoritarian state and other is a democracy.

This is a flawed understanding of the reasons for India's condition. Her relatively poor performance on standard human development indicators can be understood by reference to public policy. In my discussion of the mortality from COVID-19 in Chapter 4, I pointed out that the death rate across India can be explained in terms of the varying investment in a public health system, measured by the share of GDP that is devoted to public expenditure on health. As health is a State Subject in India, the analysis was based on the expenditures of state governments. This showed some of them spending less on health than they do on the police. The state of Maharashtra had stood out as one that spends less than 0.5 per cent of its GDP on a public health

---

[13] I have stopped at a comparison of India and China, as it suffices for my purposes. For a comparison of India with its neighbours in South Asia, see Dreze and Sen (2013), which provides a comprehensive evaluation of the progress of health and education in India.

system. During the first wave of COVID-19 it was the site of the worst form of the health crisis in India, with overflowing hospitals, limited health personnel, shortage of ventilators and oxygen – and with the highest death rate among the states of India at that stage of the pandemic.[14] No more evidence is needed to confirm the close relation between health outcomes and public policy.

As evidence on the connection between health outcomes and public policy has already appeared in this book, I will here confine myself to the case of education. In Table 5.2 we can see the level of public spending on education in India and its consequences. Public expenditure on education as a share of GDP

Table 5.2
Public Spending and Educational Outcomes Across the World

	Public Expenditure on Education as Share of GDP	Adult Literacy Rate	Share of Tertiary Sector (%) in Spending	Pupil-Teacher Ratio (Primary)	Secondary School Enrolment (per cent)
World	4.5	86	22	23	66
North America	5.0	99	28	14	93
Europe and Central Asia	4.8	98	21	15	90
Middle East and North Africa	4.5	79	23	21	73
East Asia and the Pacific	4.2	96	16	18	79
Latin America and the Caribbean	4.5	94	21	21	78
Sub-Saharan Africa	4.3	65	21	37	36
India	3.8	74	29	33	62

Source: The World Bank; https://data.worldbank.org/indicator, accessed on 3 September 2021.

[14] See Balakrishnan and Namboodhiry (2021).

is lower in India than in every other regional grouping of the world. Commensurately, the outcomes in terms of literacy and schooling are, mostly, worse. As spending here is lower than even that in sub-Saharan Africa, a region of the world with lower per capita income, it cannot be said that low spending on education reflects the capacity to spend. For India, it appears to have been a matter of priorities in public policy. Its consequence has been persisting illiteracy.

Interestingly, we find that public expenditure on education is much higher in the United States, a country committed to free market capitalism, while India's Constitution declares the country is a socialist republic. As seen in the table, the former socialist republics of Europe and Central Asia spend substantially more on health and education than India does, and this is reflected in the superior human development indicators in these countries. In the case of India, a further bias can be seen within the already low level of spending on education; notice that the tertiary or university sector here receives a higher share of the public spending on education than in any other major regional grouping, higher than even North America. India spends relatively more on higher education than the rest of the world while the number of pupils per teacher in its primary schools is higher and enrolment in secondary schooling is lower by comparison.

It is difficult not to conclude that there is a class bias in this pattern of expenditure as public education is availed of only by the poorer classes. Whatever the underlying reason, it could not have been without wider-ranging consequences for the country. India's children may not be receiving the attention they need at the time when they need it most – that is, while at school. In any case, India's poor performance on health and education can be understood in terms of the meagre public outlays on these foundational inputs into the capability of a population. It is the nature of its public policy alone that accounts for India's disappointing human development record.

Comparisons such as the one just made help us see how much behind the rest of the world India is when it comes to development even seventy-five years after it became a democracy. This distance is often substantial even in relation to the global average, leave alone the world's best-performing countries, implying that a significant section of the Indian population is yet to attain the global standard in development. Is this inevitable? This is the question to which I now turn.

India is a vast and diverse country, and the national average can turn out to be a misleading representation of the state of affairs across it. To check the extent to which this is so, I present in Table 5.3 information on a standard set of development indicators for a group of the larger states of the country, one each

Table 5.3

Regional Variation of Development in India

State	Per capita Income (in current rupees)	Multi-dimensional Poverty (Headcount Ratio)	Under Five Mortality (per 1000)	Life Expectancy (at birth)	Adult Literacy Rate (per cent)	Secondary School Enrolment (per cent)
Gujarat	213,936	21.7	31	69.9	78	41.2
Kerala	221,904	1.1	10	75.2	94	80.3
Uttar Pradesh	65,704	40.8	47	65.3	68	46.1
West Bengal	113,163	26.3	26	71.6	76	51.7
India	180,583	27.9	36	69.4	73	50.1

Sources: Income, Life Expectancy, and Literacy – Reserve Bank of India, https://m.rbi.org.in, accessed 17 March 2022; Poverty, Under Five Mortality, and School Enrolment – NITI Aayog (2021).

from its four regions. The states represented are Gujarat, Kerala, West Bengal, and Uttar Pradesh.

This comparison points to a considerable divergence in human development across India. As is often pointed out, the states of the south and the west have a higher income per capita than those of the north and the east. Uttar Pradesh, India's largest state, has a per capita income far lower than the Indian average, let alone the top state in the sample.

This pattern carries over to poverty, but not proportionately. For instance, Gujarat, one of the richest states, has only a little less poverty than West Bengal, which has far lower per capita income. However, the divergence in poverty between Kerala and UP is particularly striking, with the former showing next to no poverty. A divergence is evident also when it comes to the indicators of health and education. Income matters less for development, it would appear, as West Bengal has superior outcomes also in health and, in one of two dimensions of, education than Gujarat despite the higher per capita income of the latter.

All in all, a look within India shows a wide variation across its regions. Viewing the information in Tables 5.1 and 5.3 together we would also see that there are states in India, such as Kerala, which do better than the world in terms of some development indicators. The implication is that there is nothing inevitable about the low levels of capability development in parts of the country. States with better social indicators, such as Kerala and Tamilnadu, are known to have devoted more of both attention and public funds to human development over a long period.

Data presented so far pertain to the population as a whole. I now assess the extent to which development in India has extended to its women. From the indicators in Table 5.4, we find that there is considerable regional variation in this too. What is most

Table 5.4
Gender in Development

State	Prevalence of Anaemia (%)	Female Literacy Rate	Ratio of Female to Male Labour Force Participation	Crimes Against Women (per 1 lakh)	Women Legislators (%)	High Court Judges (%)
Gujarat	54.9	69.7	0.28	27.1	7.5	16.7
Kerala	34.3	92.1	0.45	62.7	5.7	13.3
West Bengal	62.5	70.5	0.28	64	13.6	15.2
Uttar Pradesh	52.4	57.2	0.19	55.4	10.6	6.8
India	53.1	64.6	0.33	62.4	8.4	11.6

Sources: Anaemia (2011) – NFHS 4, http://rchiips.org/nfhs/NFHS-4Report.shtml, accessed on 17 March 2022; Literacy (2011) – "Census of India", http://www.dataforall.org/dashboard/censusinfoindia_pca/ – accessed 2 February 2022; Labour force participation, Crimes Against Women and Women Legislators – NITI Aayog (2021); Judges – calculated from data in "Judges in the High Courts as on 1/11/20", Department of Justice, https://doj.gov.in/sites/default/files/HCs-01.11.2020.pdf, accessed on 2 January 2022.

noticeable is that Kerala's generally superior development performance has not resulted in women's empowerment. Though Kerala has more women than men in its population, with a sex ratio close to the highest achieved in the world, its record of furthering women's agency is poor.[15] At 45, the ratio of the female to male labour force participation rate in the state is far lower than the global average of 65.9, and crimes against women are higher in Kerala than is the national average.[16] But it is in governance

---

[15] For the sex ratio of Indian states, see Census of India – http://www.dataforall.org/dashboard/censusinfoindia_pca/; accessed on 17 March 2022. For the sex ratio of the World see World Bank – https://data.worldbank.org/indicator; accessed on 17 March 2022.

[16] See NITI Aayog (2021) and World Bank – https://data.worldbank.org/indicator, accessed on 17 March 2022, respectively, for data on gender dif-

that gender inequality is most evident. Less than 6 per cent of the legislators and less than 15 per cent of judges in Kerala are women. This when women outnumber men as participants in elections by over 10 per cent.[17] Women's active participation in the democratic process has not been rewarded by a place at the high table of governance, virtually reserved for men. While the "Kerala Model of Development" has received high acclaim internationally, this aspect has mostly gone unrecognised.

The relative absence of women in the highest governance positions in Kerala is matched by the almost generalised marginalisation of women in India. In a global comparison, the national sex ratio is lower than the global norm and so is the female labour force participation rate.[18] Particularly disturbing is that a third of the female population is illiterate and more than half is anaemic. And the absence of women in governance is almost complete.

We see the continued existence of gender inequality in India's democracy. The other axis along which India's population is aligned is caste. Caste as a system of social stratification, whereby individuals are assigned an immutable place in society based on birth, is unique to India. This can render some aspects of economic models constructed for other parts of the world irrelevant in their assessment of the challenge in this country. For instance,

---

ference in labour force participation in Kerala and globally. See NITI Aayog (2021) for data on crimes against women in India.

[17] https://eci.gov.in/files/file/3767-kerala-general-legislative-election-2016.

[18] The female labour force participation rates for India and the World are 20 per cent and 45 per cent, respectively; see https://data.worldbank.org/indicator; accessed on 17 March 2022.

as caste can restrict equal access even to public goods, public policy would have to be designed in such a way that historically deprived groups are not prevented from benefiting from its interventions. This naturally raises the question of how the presence of caste inequality in India should define public policy, and even politics more generally. I address this question briefly after presenting some data on caste-based inequality in development.

In Table 5.5 are gathered data on some basic indicators of health, education, and economic status for the entire population, and for the scheduled castes, respectively. These show the scheduled castes of India to be behind the general population on all of the metrics considered even after sixty years of Indian independence. They show a lower literacy rate, higher child mortality, less consumption, and greater poverty.[19] A persisting influence of caste is visible, implying that India's democracy has

Table 5.5
The Imprint of Caste

	Literacy rate	Under-five Mortality (per 1000)	Consumption Per Capita (current rupees)	Poverty Rate (headcount)
All Groups	72.9	49.7	1804	27.5
Scheduled Castes	66.1	55.9	1494	37.8

Sources: Literacy (2011) – MTA (2015); Under-Five Mortality (2011–15) – NFHS 4 –http://rchiips.org/nfhs/NFHS-4Report.shtml, accessed on 17 March 2022; Consumption (weighted average of rural and urban 2011–2) – MOSPI (2015); Poverty (2004–5) – MTA (2015).

[19] The distances would be greater if we had substituted the scheduled tribes for the scheduled castes, which I have not done as the latter are much greater in number.

not been able to erase it. As with the uneven spread of human development in India, the condition of the scheduled castes too has varied across the country. The scheduled castes of southern India have social indicators and consumption levels superior to that of the scheduled castes in the rest of the country.

Given the uniqueness of the caste system to India, it is often argued that in this country political mobilisation along caste lines is essential to reduce inequalities between social groups. One route to testing this hypothesis would be to compare political mobilisation and development outcomes in Kerala and Tamilnadu. After 1947, while Kerala's communists initiated a political programme associated with European social democracy – though not, it may be clarified, European communism – the Dravidian parties of Tamilnadu undertook political mobilisation based on ethnic nationalism. I am currently engaged in a study of the impact of these divergent political programmes on the historically disadvantaged. Two findings emerging from this research may be flagged. First, while the gap between the scheduled castes and the total population for consumption is greater in Kerala than in Tamilnadu, the gap is less in the former when it comes to literacy and child mortality. Secondly, the scheduled castes of Kerala have achieved superior levels for all these three variables compared to the scheduled caste population of Tamilnadu.

We are inevitably left to arbitrate between the development strategies of the two states in this example. One approach would be to take the Rawlsian route to choosing between social arrangements. Now, according to the "maximin principle", we should be maximising the position of the worst-off in a society. By this criterion it is Kerala that would be chosen as the more successful as it has the better outcomes for the socially most disadvantaged.[20] Though we would need more analysis and the use of controls to arrive at a definite conclusion, this evidence suggests that caste-based political mobilisation may not be as effective in all instances as one based on the goals of social democracy.

Finally, the presence of gender inequality remains even after disaggregating the development indicators by caste. We would find that, on indicators such as literacy and infant mortality, females do worse than their male counterparts in every caste group across the country.[21] Consumption and poverty estimates are not available by gender but we may safely infer from the fact of a lower female labour-force participation rate that women have less autonomy over their consumption. The feature that gender inequality exists in every social group in India shows that it is the most pervasive inequality in the country. It is striking, then, that in its public policy, affirmative action for women does not match that for social groups, pointing to an unwillingness to address the issue.

As I had pointed out, international comparison of economic development indicators is often met with the criticism that we could be comparing across political regimes. However, this is irrelevant in a comparison within India where the states are all

---

[20] A clarification is in order here. Note that the point emerging from the discussion is that, though located in India, Kerala has succeeded to a greater extent in building the capabilities of the population. This does not by itself translate into a higher human development. Kerala has been far less successful in generating employment and has allowed the rampant destruction of its natural capital, both of which stand in the way of human development. On these counts it has much to learn from the rest of India. See Balakrishnan (2015).

[21] For data on gender inequality among the scheduled castes and scheduled tribes, see MTA (2015).

under the umbrella of one governance system, namely political democracy. What we found in such a comparison is that a wide variation in human development exists. While at least some states appear to be inching towards the global standard of development in some dimensions, democracy in India coexists with low human development in states accounting for a large part of the country.

In a country as large as India, some regional variation may be expected. However, the divergence can be considerable and has been long-lasting, not having been erased in seventy-five years. As all states function under a common set of rules, there must be something unique to the states that differences of such magnitude persist into the twenty-first century. Why is it that democracy has not been able to eliminate basic deprivation in large parts of India?

A clue may be found in the disquisition on democracy by the sociologist Barrington Moore, who has studied the transition to democracy across the world. Moore sees the prior revolutions that took place in Europe and the United States as crucial in the transition to a democracy there. When it comes to India, he says: ". . . the nationalist movement did not take a revolutionary form, though civil disobedience forced the withdrawal of a weakened British Empire. The outcome of these forces was indeed political democracy, *but a democracy that has not done a great deal toward modernizing India's social structure*. Hence famine still lurks in the background."[22] Strangely, when it came to India,

---

[22] Moore (1966), p. 416, italics mine. The reference to famine needs explanation. For Moore modernisation meant the transition to "a modern industrial society" which includes a dynamic capitalist agriculture. By this account, famine would signify a pre-modern society. At the time of Moore's writing, there was food shortage in India, but no famine.

Moore seems to have inverted his thesis to suggest that democracy can alter the social structure, presumably through parliamentary means.

However, his general thesis, that a social transformation is essential for democracy to attain its potential, is useful in understanding the regional variation that we observe in India. Arguably, the regions of India that have seen the most development, including the elimination of illiteracy and extreme poverty, are regions that have witnessed social transformation that eliminated the old order. This is most pronounced in the case of Kerala, where as early as 1957 an elected communist government initiated a process of improvement of the conditions of life for the mass of the population. This mainly involved the spread of health and education, resulting in a social emancipation of the lower orders of its society. A significant event in this transformation was the land reforms initiated within weeks of the installation of the government. This led to the ending of landlordism and the associated suppression of the labouring classes. So the social structure was altered, awareness grew, and with it an unstated but recognisable demand for a better life. Competing political parties had no option but to respond with policies that enhanced human capabilities if they were to survive. Though the culmination of the social transformation in Kerala was the installation of a communist party, the transition was long. Having commenced in the late nineteenth century, it had involved a caste-reform movement that initiated social mobility, the work of Christian missionaries that spread literacy, and an enlightened public policy of the princes who had ruled a large part of what is now Kerala.

A transformation of a kind took place in Tamilnadu too, though its origin was a caste-based movement aimed at eliminating the hegemony of the Brahmins. However, it could come to power only by riding on ethnic nationalism fuelled by the attempt to impose Hindi as the sole official language of the country. Since then the "Dravidian movement" has had great political success and parties that draw inspiration from it have now been in power in the state for over half a century. As with the rise of the communists in Kerala, so too has the Dravidian movement left its imprint on society. Tamilnadu has achieved relatively good development indicators, though they are yet to reach the levels achieved in Kerala.

No social change comparable to that in Kerala and Tamilnadu has taken place in the three other states in our sample in Table 5.3. Not even Zamindari abolition in UP and the land reforms of the Left Front in West Bengal seem to have achieved a similar success in the social sphere, necessary to bring about development in the sense that we use the term. These states have higher poverty and poorer social indicators than Kerala, the shortfall in women's literacy being particularly noticeable. The case of Gujarat suggests that overall economic prosperity may be insufficient to bring about the expansion of freedoms of the population. We saw in Table 5.3 that though it is one of India's richest states, it harbours significant poverty and its social indicators are not much better than the national average. A change in social structure that redistributes power appears to be essential to widespread development in a society, including the elimination of poverty.

Interestingly, in his final speech to the Constituent Assembly, Ambedkar had recognised the role of the social structure in perpetuating social and economic inequality when he pointed out that, in the India that was to come,

In politics we will have equality and in social and economic life we will have inequality. In politics we will be recognising the principle of one man one vote and one vote one value. In our social and economic life, we shall, by reason of our social and economic structure, continue to deny the principle of one man one value. How long shall we continue to live this life of contradictions? How long shall we continue to deny equality in our social and economic life? If we continue to deny it for long, we will do so only by putting our political democracy in peril.[23]

Ambedkar was prescient in seeing that political democracy is no guarantor of the expansion of freedoms, an insight that is crucial to our understanding of the history of both democracy and development in India.

Quite often, when it is suggested that India's democracy is diminished by the presence of deprivation on so large a scale, it is asserted that democracy is really a form of government by discussion, and expecting it to deliver human development is to see it merely as an instrumentality. An antidote to this line of argument is offered in Moore's recounting of the history of democracy. He sees its development as "a long and certainly incomplete struggle" to do three related things: (1) to check arbitrary rulers, (2) to replace arbitrary rules with just and rational ones, and (3) to obtain a share for the underlying population in the making of rules.[24] He sees the ending of monarchy, the efforts to establish the rule of law and the power of the legislature, and, later, use of the state as an engine of social change as the best known aspects of these three aims.[25] The definition of democracy as

[23] Ambedkar (1949).
[24] Moore (1966), p. 414.
[25] The author had used "welfare" whereas I have used "change", considering it to be more appropriate in the context.

"government by discussion", attributed to Bagehot, may well reflect a consensus on how it was intended to function, but remains ahistorical, and leaves us blind to its potential to improve the conditions of life for the mass of the population, a matter of urgency in India.

Democracy in India has received worldwide attention, especially from observers based in Western democracies. The cynic might observe that the admiration has turned particularly vocal ever since India's economy has billowed out. Some recent congratulatory reviews of India's democracy emanating from overseas have been those by Mathews (2015), Shani (2017), and Desai (2017). These observers have generally marvelled at one or the other of two features of Indian democracy – such as that a country of such great diversity has held together. Others have remarked upon not only the successful conduct of elections but also the peaceful transition once they are completed, both quite remarkable in a poor country which till recently had very low levels of literacy.

Surprisingly, none of them has wondered why poverty is tolerated to such an extent in India's democracy. It is understandable that some in India should feel elated by the praise but it should also leave us circumspect. Is democracy about procedural routines such as elections and guidebooks such as written constitutions, or is it about the transformations wrought after its adoption as the form of government? To paraphrase Moore, how much has democracy done for India? The evidence on human development in the country implies that the praise needs to be tempered. Significant deprivation exists in the country even after seventy-five years of its formation. This has not received as much attention, but it is high time it does. Few democracies have tolerated so much deprivation for so long. The substantial divergence in the progress of human development across the country implies that it is possible to eliminate its worst forms through public policy. I conclude by asking to what extent India's impressive Constitution can advance this outcome.

Formal Rights and Substantive Freedoms

India's Constitution reflects the high-mindedness of its founders. Its well-meant constitutional provisions, however, have failed to bring human development to a substantial section of the population. Viewed through the framework expounded here, this is not entirely surprising. Even though the founders were alert to the importance of negative freedom, these constitutional provisions could not by themselves ensure a significant project to advance positive freedom for the many. For example, of what use is the right to property when one does not have the opportunity to earn a livelihood, or earns so low a wage as not to be able to save to acquire any? Equally, the constitutional provision of the freedom of expression cannot be fully acted upon by the poor and the illiterate, or even the poorly educated.

India's founders did not completely overlook these possibilities and had imbued the Constitution with "Directive Principles of State Policy".[26] These were meant to serve as a guideline to the state in the making of policy. They include the goals of social justice and economic welfare, and explicitly refer to the provision of free education and the improvement of public health. The principles, however, are not justiciable and, therefore,

---

[26] The distinction between "fundamental rights" and "directive principles", and the tension that can arise when they are invoked at the same time, is central to understanding India's constitutional provisions. For a concise contemporary introduction, see Khosla (2012).

of little use when citizens are faced with political parties devoted to maximising the "private" welfare of their members as opposed to "social" welfare, howsoever construed.

It is now possible to see that India's constitutional provisions, whether in the form of the Directive Principles or of Fundamental Rights, have proved inadequate to the task of advancing human development. Even when the rights are justiciable, in that the violation of these rights may be challenged in courts of law, they may not be sufficient to advance positive freedom. The Directive Principles may be heeded by the state to build capability, but they are not justiciable. Thus, if the Indian state, captured alternately by one or the other of its political parties, cannot be made to go in the desired direction, the Directive Principles are not of much use to the marginalised.

This is a version of what economists have recognised as the "principal-agent problem". The principal-agent problem can readily emerge in the governance of as vast and diverse a society as India's. The idea and its implications are most easily understood in the context of corporate governance. Under contemporary capitalism, shareholding is widespread and firms are run by managers. This feature, as Robin Marris observed, effectively separates ownership from control.[27] Marris identified this form as *managerial* capitalism, as opposed to the *entrepreneurial* capitalism of the nineteenth century. The implication of managerial capitalism is that there is now no guarantee that the managers, who are the agents, will manage the firm in the interest of the principals, who are the shareholders.[28] Under actually existing

[27] See Marris (1964).
[28] Marris' insight was to be vindicated some four decades later when managers of the financial sector came close to wrecking the global economy by taking excessive risk in the pursuit of personal reward. See Krugman (2009).

democracy, as opposed to some idealised form, the principal-agent problem is an ever-present possibility. In a parliamentary democracy, citizens own it, so to speak, but it is the executive that governs the country via a permanent bureaucracy, which in theory is accountable to parliament but in reality remains ungoverned. The conundrum *Quis custodiet ipsos custodes*? (Who will guard the guards themselves?) captures the implication of such an arrangement. Coined even before the beginning of the Common Era to express the challenge of enforcing marital fidelity, it has a direct bearing on the issue of governance in a democratic polity.

While there is no universally accepted measure of capability, we do know that poverty remains very high in India. That at least a quarter of its population is considered to be poor according to a low poverty line indicates that a substantial proportion of the population remains marginalised. This is so despite the claim that the rationale of economic policy is the eradication of poverty. It is now over half a century since Indira Gandhi's slogan *Garibi Hatao* (Eradicate Poverty), conveying the intent of the policies her government would adopt if it were to come to power. While the economics of this failed experiment needs to be understood, the capability approach would have served to predict the outcome. The means adopted by Indira Gandhi were mainly draconian controls on the private corporate sector combined with an extortionate tax rate, rationalised as "socialism". This by itself could do little to lift the poor out of poverty. In fact, as shown in Chapter 2, the economy promptly contracted as private investment declined, worsening prospects for the poor. As we saw, the reduction of poverty in India had to await the onset of faster agricultural growth. While the controls effectively restricted the liberty of the capitalists, they did little to build a healthy and productive workforce that could have lifted itself out of poverty.

India's experience of dealing with marginalisation should hardly be surprising. In a market economy, individuals have two livelihood options: to either work for others or be self-employed. While peasants are self-employed, this option is available only to those who own land. On the other hand, the landless must seek employment or become entrepreneurs. Capability built through education underpinned by health is crucial to whether they will be able to earn their livelihoods as successful entrepreneurs or as productive labourers for hire in the market. The persistence of poverty in India reflects the underinvestment in building the capability of the population that has characterised public policy in India for over half a century. I now turn to a brief appraisal of the approach that has mostly been taken towards marginalisation during this time.

Historically, there have been two approaches to dealing with poverty or marginalisation in India. The first was prevalent in the 1950s, when policy-makers simply assumed that a growing economy would lift the poor out of poverty. While the idea that growth is a necessary condition for poverty alleviation made good sense, the strategy could not succeed fully without the expansion of education and the upgrading of skills among the poor. More recently, the approach appears to have altered. Now the keyword is "inclusion", chosen to reflect the intent of public policy to mainstream the marginalised. What is meant by "inclusive growth" is revealed in the state's increasing resort to transfer payments of various kinds that have come to represent public policy. There has also been a proliferation of so-called rights promulgated through acts of parliament such as the Right to Work or even the Right to Food. Apart from the fact that it is not yet clear whether these rights are justiciable, if marginalisation is understood as unequal capabilities these proclamations do not even address the problem for they leave the capabilities of the population untouched.[29] This then not only smacks of paternalism but, more significantly, it implies that the poor may never be enabled to go about on their own, being permanently on a state-sponsored drip, as it were.

A particular version of the approach may be found in a speech in 2008 by the then finance minister, P. Chidambaram: "India must touch a 10 per cent growth and sustain it for 10, 20 and 30 years" to make poverty part of history. The minister went on to say that growth was not an end in itself but part of a strategy to "raise resources and acquire the capacity to spend more money on the provision of goods and services that will mitigate the hardship of millions of poor people and bring some cheer into their lives."[30]

This is perhaps the clearest articulation of the rationale of the Indian state in the early twenty-first century. Welfarism, as such an approach may be described, cannot be expected to eliminate marginalisation through the building of capability.[31] It is also likely to be self-defeating: as the government spends an increasing share of its revenues on subsidising consumption, there is little

---

[29] For an assessment of the difference these rights have made for the poor in India, see Das (2013).

[30] Excerpt from a speech outlining the policies of his government delivered in Singapore, quoted in Rajamohan (2013).

[31] The following comment on the consequences of a welfarist approach by the Yogi Adityanath government in Uttar Pradesh illustrates this: "the flip side of lavish spending on cash transfers has resulted in an abject neglect of public goods such as education and health . . . There is also little room to expand the state sector to ameliorate the unemployment crisis . . ." Ali (2022). Health, education, and employment were the three original pillars of the post-war European welfare state.

left for capital formation. The growth of the economy is now bound to slow down, and with it the growth of revenues necessary to feed the government's welfare schemes, not to mention the impact that slowing growth can have on the generation of employment.

Though based on a study of the state of Tamilnadu, Lakshmanan and Venkatanarayanan (2021) have made an observation with wider applicability on the distinction between what may be considered legitimate practice in a genuine welfare state and the welfarism practised in India:

> Theoretically, there is a qualitative distinction between subjects in an authoritarian regime and being citizens in a democratic polity. Unsolicited freebies cultivate a patron–client syndrome and encourage personality cults in a democratic polity. Providing freebies is to treat people like subjects, whereas citizens are entitled to constitutional guarantees. Welfare initiatives are an embodiment of civil rights, whereas unsolicited freebies show benevolence at best and apathy at worst towards the poor by the ruling parties.[32]

Given its more or less similar starting point in the early 1950s, the experience of China in addressing poverty is relevant to India. China spent public funds on health and education but made sure to maintain a high rate of public investment necessary for growth. Of course, present-day China fails the test when development is defined as the expansion of freedoms, for the civil liberties of the population have never been acknowledged by its political leadership – propped up by the military. At the same time, any nationalistic pride in India's democracy would have to engage with Macpherson's claim: "[W]e must

[32] Lakshmanan and Venkatanarayanan (2021).

weigh not only political and civil liberties but all the other freedoms which ... make up the total opportunity each man has to develop all his natural capacities."[33] This observation helps us see the role of a Constitution in perspective. Constitutional provisions act as a check on the powers of the state. However, whether the state will adopt a programme of human development as capability formation and implement it effectively depends on whether the alignment of social and political forces impinge upon it to do so.

It is possible to conceive of two ways of neglecting a problem. A problem may be neglected by not placing it on the policy radar. Or it may be neglected by starving its solution of the necessary resources. It could be said that, for about half a century after 1947, there was neglect of human development on both counts, that is, it received neither sufficient resources nor attention. For about a decade now, with faster growth and, in the case of education, some external funding, there has been a substantial increase in public spending on the social sector but no visible improvement in outcomes, possibly due to worsening governance.[34]

If marginalisation is to be addressed, staying focused on the building of capability via effective – and continuing – education is a must. Two considerations may be flagged. First, the world is far more complex today than it was in the 1950s, when India started out on its journey. Today, early education has to go well beyond the "3 Rs". In the context of the challenges posed by globalisation, rapidly changing technology, emerging ecological

[33] Macpherson (1973), p. 15.

[34] For an evidence-based account of how indifferent governance may account for poor outcomes in three widely differing public programmes in India, see Balakrishnan (2010).

constraints, and making democracy work, learning to learn continuously must be part of the capability set of citizens. Secondly, in as much as marginalisation may be understood as inequality of capability, the move towards a certain degree of uniformity, at least at the level of primary and secondary education, has to be contemplated. The diversity of school boards, and their varying degree of prestige, is too large in India today. As already observed, uniformity of schooling can also contribute to social cohesion.

Conclusion: Journeying to the Valuable Economy

India is no longer a poor economy when taken as a whole. In 2011 it overtook Japan as the third-largest economy of the world when output is measured in purchasing-power parity terms. The material resources needed to spread human development and permanently end exclusion is no longer a constraint. Then what is? As India is a democracy it should be clear that the working of its democracy is where we should be looking for the answer to this question. From an economic point of view, democracy may be seen as a case of individuals combining to solve the co-ordination problem that results in the absence of public goods in a society. Or, to put it positively, citizens give themselves a democratic form of government mainly to ensure that they have access to the goods, public and private, that allow them to lead the lives that they value. The Westminster model with the political parties that populate it were meant as a mere instrumentality in achieving this. This tends to be overlooked in Indian democracy, where the political parties have come to be more prominent than the people.

In India, an acute case of the principal-agent problem has come to mean that democracy first benefits the political parties, whose main objective, it seems, is to capture the state apparatus to enrich their members. The extraordinary increases recorded in the assets of politicians while they are in power reflect this. All the parties of India govern in the name of the poor but most of them do very little for human development once elected. The present state of affairs may be expected to continue in India so long as a substantial section of the population is ill-educated and remains in poor health, leaving it unable to control the actions of its elected representatives. Significant sections of India will remain marginalised as long as the development of their capability remains incomplete.

In its seventy-fifth year, Indian democracy must acknowledge a deep deficit when it comes to human development. Over the past few years, a long-term neglect of this first task of democracy has been joined by an erosion of civil liberties. Freedom of expression is under threat, the independent press has faced restrictions, and religious minorities feel threatened. This has not gone unnoticed globally, with democracy watchdogs marking down their rating of Indian democracy. If social progress is viewed as the expansion of freedoms, the project has suffered a setback. This has already had an impact on its economic prospects and leaves in balance the hope of advancing human development, the goal set for democracy in India.

My hope is that this book has succeeded in showing that the promise of Indian independence was the human development of its population. India has made significant advances since 1947, but these have been more in the nature of growing the economy while modernising it than in bringing human development to the population. In its seventy-fifth year we must recognise that we yet have a great distance to travel to achieve the latter. While the global discourse on human development has focused closely on education and health, the importance of which we have come to realise during the COVID-19 pandemic, India is also beset by an infrastructure deficit and threatened by ecological decline, both of which matter for human development. These conditions define the kind of economy that we need. An economy is valuable only to the extent that it caters to our everyday needs and leaves us prepared for contingencies of the future. Yet it must enable something greater. A valuable economy is an ecosystem not just for living but for human beings to flourish, i.e. to lead the kind of life they value. Economic policy in India must reorient itself to the task of creating such an ecosystem. This gets overlooked when the focus is exclusively on quantitative goals such as achieving a 5-trillion-dollar economy by 2025. Oscar Wilde went to the heart of the matter when he said that it is possible to know the price of everything but the value of nothing.

Bibliography

Acemoglu, D., and J. Robinson (2012). "Why Nations Fail: The Economic Origins of Power, Prosperity and Poverty", Cambridge, Mass.: MIT Press.

Ahluwalia, M. (1978). "Rural Poverty in India, 1956–57 to 1973–74", in Montek S. Ahluwalia, John Wall, Shlomo Reutlinger, Robert Cassen, and Martin Wolf, *India: Occasional Papers*, Washington, DC, World Bank Staff Working Paper No. 279.

Ali, A. (2022). "In Uttar Pradesh, the Crux of Welfare Politics", *The Hindu*, 14 February 2022.

Ambedkar, B.R. (1949). "Concluding Remarks in the Constituent Assembly (on) the Constitution (made) on November 25, 1949", https:// prasarbharati.gov.in/whatsnew/whatsnew_653363.pdf, accessed 30 January 2022.

Ambirajan, S. (1976). "Malthusian Population Theory and Indian Famine Policy in the Nineteenth Century", *Population Studies*, 30: 5–14.

Aron, L. (2011). "Everything You Think You Know About the Collapse of the Soviet Union is Wrong", *Foreign Policy*, July/August.

Bagchi, A. (2010). "Colonialism and the Indian Economy", Delhi: Oxford University Press.

Bai, J., and P. Perron (2003). "Computation and Analysis of Multiple Structural Change Models", *Journal of Applied Econometrics*, 18: 1–22.

Balakrishnan, P. (1995). "The Short-run Behaviour of Prices and Quantities in Indian Industry", in D. Mookherjee, ed., *Indian Industry: Policies and Performance*, Delhi: Oxford University Press.

Balakrishnan, P. (2010). "Economic Growth in India: History and Prospect", Delhi: Oxford University Press.

Balakrishnan, P. (2015). "Kerala and the Rest of India, What We Can Learn from Each Other's Development Experience", *Economic and Political Weekly*, 50: 34–41.

Balakrishnan, P. (2016). "The New Colour of Money", *The Hindu*, 11 November.

Balakrishnan, P. (2019). "Unmoved by Stability: Capital Formation in the Modi Economy", *Economic and Political Weekly*, 54: 33–6.

Balakrishnan, P. (2020). "India Needs a Strong Fiscal Stimulus", *Hindustan Times*, 15 April.

Balakrishnan, P., and A. Goyal (2019). "After Liberalising Reforms: The Importance of Domestic Demand, in A. Goyal, ed., *A Concise Handbook of the Indian Economy in the 21st Century*, New Delhi: Oxford University Press.

Balakrishnan, P. and M. Parameswaran (2007), "Understanding Economic Growth in India: A Prerequisite", *Economic and Political Weekly*, 42: 2915–22.

Balakrishnan, P., and M. Parameswaran (2021). "Modelling Inflation in India", *Journal of Quantitative Economics*, 19: 555–81.

Balakrishnan, P., and S. Namboodhiry (2021). "The Importance of Investing in a Public Health System", *Indian Economic Review*, 56: 233–54.

Balakrishnan, P., M. Das, and M. Parameswaran (2017). "The Internal Dynamic of Indian Economic Growth", *Journal of Asian Economics*, 50: 46–61.

Balakrishnan, P., M. Parameswaran, K. Pushpangadan, and M. Suresh Babu (2006). "Liberalization, Market Power, and Productivity Growth in Indian Industry", *The Journal of Policy Reform*, 9: 55–73.

Balakrishnan, P., R. Golait, and P. Kumar (2008). "Agricultural Growth in India Since 1991", DRG Paper No. 27, Mumbai: Reserve Bank of India.

Balasubramanyan, V.N. (2001). *Conversations with Indian Economists*, Delhi: Orient Longman.

Banerjee, A., and L. Iyer (2005). "The Legacy of Colonial Land Tenure Systems in India", *American Economic Review*, 95: 1190–1213.

Berlin, I. (1969) [1958]. "Two Concepts of Liberty", in idem, *Four Essays on Liberty*, Oxford: Clarendon Press.

Bhagwati, J. (1998). "India's Economic Reforms: Dismantling the Machine for Going Backwards", *Vikalpa*, 23: 5–7.

Bhagwati, J., and P. Desai (1970). *India: Planning for Industrialisation*, Delhi: Oxford University Press.

Blyn, G. (1966). "Agricultural Trends in India, 1891–1947", Philadelphia: University of Pennsylvania Press.

Bourdieu, P. (1986). "The Forms of Capital", in J. Richardson, ed., *Handbook of Theory and Research for the Sociology of Education*, Westport, CT.: Greenwood.

Chakravarty, S. (1987). *Development Planning: The Indian Experience*, Oxford: Clarendon Press.

Chancel, L., and T. Piketty (2019). "Indian Income Inequality, 1922–2015: From British Raj to Billionaire Raj", *Review of Income and Wealth*, 65: S33–S62.

Cumings, B. (1984). "The Origins and Development of the Northeast Asian Political Economy: Industrial Sectors, Product Cycles, and Political Consequences", *International Organization*, 38: 1–40.

Dalrymple, W. (2019). *The Anarchy: The East India Company, Corporate Violence, and the Pillage of an Empire*, London: Bloomsbury Books.

Das, D. (1969). *India from Curzon to Nehru and After*, New Delhi: Rupa.

Das, G. (2000). *India Unbound: From Independence to the Global Information Age*, New Delhi: Penguin Books.

Das, S.K. (2013). *India's Rights Revolution: Has It Worked for the Poor?*, New Delhi: Oxford University Press.

Datt, G., M. Ravallion, and R. Murgai (2019). "Poverty and Growth in India Over Six Decades", *American Journal of Agricultural Economics*, 102: 4–27.

Datta, B. (1978). *Indian Economic Thought: Twentieth Century Perspectives, 1900–1950*, Delhi: Tata McGraw-Hill.

Deaton, A., and J. Dreze (2002). "Poverty and Inequality in India: A Re-Examination", *Economic and Political Weekly*, 37: 3729–48.

DeLong, J.B. (2003). "India Since Independence: An Analytic Growth Narrative", in D. Rodrik, ed., *In Search of Prosperity: Analytic Narratives on Economic Growth*, Princeton: Princeton University Press.

Demirguc-Kunt, A., and L. Serven (2010). "Are All the Sacred Cows Dead?: Implications of the Financial Crisis for Macro- and Financial Policies", http:// documents.worldbank.org/curated/en/332081468154154684/Are-all-the-sacred-cows-dead-implications-of-the-financial-crisis-for-macro-and-financial-policies.

Deokar, B.K., and S.L. Shetty (2014). "Growth in Indian Agriculture: Responding to Policy Initiatives Since 2004–05", *Economic and Political Weekly*, 49: 101–4.

Desai, M. (2007). "Our Economic Growth 1947–2000", *India International Centre Quarterly*, 33: 34–44.

Desai, M. (2017). *The Raisina Model*, New Delhi: Penguin Random House.

Deshpande, S. (1993). "Imagined Economies: Styles of Nation Building in Twentieth Century India", *Journal of Arts and Ideas*, 24–5: 5–35.

Dev, S.M. (2008). "Challenges for Revival of Indian Agriculture", The First Dayanatha Jha Memorial Lecture, New Delhi: Commission for Agricultural Costs and Prices, Government of India.

Dreze, J., and A. Sen (2013). *Uncertain Glory: India and Its Contradictions*, Princeton: Princeton University Press.

Dutt, R.C. (1902). *The Economic History of India*, London: Kegan Paul.

Fischer, S. (1993). "The Role of Macroeconomic Factors in Growth", *Journal of Monetary Economics*, 32: 485–512.

Frankel, F.R. (1971). *India's Green Revolution: Economic Gains and Political Costs*, Princeton: Princeton University Press.

Gandhi, M.K. (1941). *The Constructive Programme: Its Meaning and Place*, Ahmedabad: Navajivan Trust.

Economic Survey (2016, 2017). New Delhi: Ministry of Finance, Government of India.

Government of India (2009). *India 2009: A Reference Annual*, Ministry of Information and Broadcasting, Publications Division.

Government of India (2003). "Literacy in India: Steady March Over the Years", Press Information Bureau Release, 6 September.

Habib, I. (1977). "The Colonialization of the Indian Economy", *Social Scientist*, 3: 23–53.

Hankla, C.R. (2006). "Party Linkages and Economic Policy: An Examination of Indira Gandhi's India", *Business and Politics*, http://www.bepress.com/bap/vol8/iss3/art4.

Heckman, J. (2006). "Skill Formation and the Economics of Investing in Disadvantaged Children", *Science*, 312: 1900–1902.

IMF (2021a). "Fiscal-Policies-Database-in-Response-to-COVID-19", *Fiscal Monitor*, April, https://www.imf.org/en/Topics/imf-and-covid19/, accessed 20 August 2021.

IMF (2021b). *World Economic Outlook*, Washington, D.C.: International Monetary Fund, April.

Johnson, D.G. (2001). "Population, Food and Knowledge", *American Economic Review*, 90: 1–14.

Jukes, M.C. (2005). "The Long-Term Impact of Pre-School Health and Nutrition on Education", *Food and Nutrition Bulletin*, 26: S193–S201.

Kahan, A. (1965). "Russian Scholars and Statesmen on Education as an Investment", in C.A. Anderson and M.J. Bowman, eds, *Education and Economic Development*, Chicago: Aldine.

Kandel, N., S. Chungong, A. Omaar, and J. Xing (2020). "Health Security Capacities in the Context of COVID-19 Outbreak: An Analysis of International Health Regulations Annual Report Data from 182 Countries", *The Lancet*, 395: 1047–53.

Keynes, J.M. (1936). *The General Theory of Employment, Interest and Money*, London: Macmillan.

Khosla, M. (2012). *The Indian Constitution*, New Delhi: Oxford University Press.

Kim, L. (1995). "Absorptive Capacity and Industrial Growth: A Conceptual Framework and Korea's Experience", in B-H Koo and D.H. Perkins, eds, *Social Capability and Long-Term Economic Growth*, New York: St Martin's Press.

Kohli, A. (2006a). "The Politics of Economic Growth in India, 1980–2005, Part I: The 1980s", *Economic and Political Weekly*, 41: 1251–9.

Kohli, A. (2006b). "The Politics of Economic Growth in India, 1980–2005, Part II: The 1990s and Beyond", *Economic and Political Weekly*, 41: 1361–70.

Kotwal, A., B. Ramaswami, and W. Wadhwa (2011). "Economic Liberalization and Indian Economic Growth: What's the Evidence?" *Journal of Economic Literature*, 49: 1152–99.

Krishna, R. (1980). "Assessing India's Economic Development – Part 1", *Mainstream*, 25 October, 28–30.

Krugman, P. (2009). "The Return of Depression Economics and the Crisis of 2008", New York: W.W. Norton and Company.

Lakshmanan, C., and S. Venkatanarayanan (2021). "The Need to Move Away from Clientilism", *The Hindu*, 28 October 2021.

Macpherson, C.B. (1973). *Democratic Theory: Essays in Retrieval*, Oxford: Clarendon Press.

Maddison, A. (1995). "Monitoring the World Economy 1820–1992", Paris, OECD.

Mahalanobis, P.C. (1955). "The Approach of Operational Research to Planning in India", *Sankhya*, 16: 63–110.

Marris, R. (1964). *The Economic Theory of Managerial Capitalism*, London: Macmillan.

Mathews, R. (2015). *The Great Indian Rope Trick*, Gurgaon: Hachette India.

Moore, B. (1966). *Social Origins of Dictatorship and Democracy: Lord and Peasant in the Making of the Modern World*, Boston: Beacon Press.

Mukherjee, A. (2010). "Empire: How Colonial India Made Modern Britain", *Economic and Political Weekly*, 45: 73–82.

MinFin (2021). *Budget at a Glance*, New Delhi: Ministry of Finance, Government of India.

MHFW (2019). *National Health Profile*, New Delhi: Ministry of Health and Family Welfare, Government of India.

MOSPI (2022). "Press Note on First Advance Estimate of National Income 2021–22", New Delhi: Ministry of Statistics and Programme Implementation", Government of India, 2 January.

MOSPI (2021). "Press Note on Estimates of Gross Domestic Product for the Second Quarter of 2021-22", November 30.

MOSPI (2017). "Women and Men in India", New Delhi: Ministry of Statistics and Programme Implementation", Government of India.

MOSPI (2015). "Household Consumer Expenditure across Socio-Economic Groups", NSS 68th Round, New Delhi: Ministry of Statistics and Programme Implementation", Government of India.

MTA (2015). *Statistical Profile of Scheduled Tribes*, New Delhi: Ministry of Tribal Affairs, Government of India.

Naoroji, D. (1901). *Poverty and Un-British Rule in India*, London: Swan Sonnenschein & Co.

Narayana Murthy, N.R. (2004). "The Impact of Economic Reforms on Industry in India: A Case Study of the Software Industry", in K. Basu, ed., *India's Emerging Economy: Performance and Prospects in the 1990s and Beyond*, Cambridge, Mass.: MIT Press.

Nehru, J. (1958a [1947]). "Tryst With Destiny", *Jawaharlal Nehru's Speeches*, vol. 1 (1946–9), New Delhi: Publications Division, Ministry of Information and Broadcasting, Government of India.

Nehru, J. (1958b, [1956]). "The Second Five-Year Plan", *Jawaharlal Nehru's Speeches*, vol. 3 (1953–7), New Delhi: Government of India, Ministry of Information and Broadcasting, Publications Division.

NITI Aayog (2021). *SDG India: Index and Dashboard*, New Delhi.

NSS (2014). *Employment and Unemployment Situation in India*, NSS Office, New Delhi: Government of India.

Nussbaum, M. (2007). "Human Rights and Human Capabilities", *Harvard Human Rights Journal*, 20: 21–4.

Pandey, P. (2018). "You Cannot Expect 8% GDP Growth Without Having Infrastructure", an interview with Sunil Mathur, CEO of Siemens India, *The Hindu*, 1 September.

Patnaik, U., and P. Patnaik (2021). "The Drain of Wealth: Colonialism Before the First World War", *Monthly Review*, 72: 1–22.

Pedersen, J.D. (2000). "Explaining Economic Liberalisation in India: State and Society Perspectives", *World Development* 28: 265–82.

Planning Commission (2014). "Report of the Expert Group to Review the Methodology for Measurement of Poverty", New Delhi.

PLFS (various dates), *Periodic Labour Force Survey*, New Delhi: Ministry of Statistics and Programme Implementation.

Rajamohan, C. (2013). "If Poverty Has to Go, Growth Must Touch 10 Percent and Continue", *Indian Express*, 27 March.

Rangarajan, C., and Mahendra Dev (2017). "Counting the Poor: Measurement and Other Issues", in U. Kapila, ed., *Indian Economy Since Independence*, New Delhi: Academic Publishers.

Rao, V.K.R.V. (1971). *The Nehru Legacy*, Bombay: Popular Prakashan.

Riboud, M., and H. Tan (2009). "Accelerating Growth and Job Creation in South Asia", in S. Ahmed and E. Ghani, eds, *Accelerating Growth and Job Creation*, New Delhi: Oxford University Press.

Rodrik, D., and A. Subramanian (2005). "From 'Hindu Growth' to Productivity Surge: The Mystery of the Indian Growth Transition", *IMF Staff Papers*, 52: 193–222.

Rogoff, K. (2016). *The Curse of Cash*, Princeton, NJ: Princeton University Press.

Romer, P. (2016). "The Trouble with Macro", https:// paulromer.net/wpcontent/uploads/2016/09/WP-Trouble.pdf.

Roy, T. (2000). "De-Industrialisation: Alternative View, *Economic and Political Weekly*, 35: 1442–7.

RBI (2019). *Annual Report*, Mumbai.

RBI (2016). *Handbook of the Indian Economy*, Mumbai.

Sahoo, P., R. Dash, and G. Nataraj (2010). "Infrastructure Development and Economic Growth in China", Discussion Paper 261, Tokyo: Institute of Developing Economies.

Singh, R.K. (2022). "How GST is Killing Small Businesses with Inspector Raj and Suffocating Compliance", https://theprint.in/opinion/how-gst-is-killing-small-businesses-with-inspector-raj-and-suffocating-compliance/861816/; 7 March.

Scott, B.R. (1997). "What Economists Should Know About Economic Growth", *Harvard Business Review*, May–June, 156–64.

Sen, A. (1980). "Equality of What?", in S. McMurrin, ed., *Tanner Lectures on Human Values*, vol. 1, Cambridge: Cambridge University Press.

Sen, A. (1992). *Inequality Reexamined*, New York: Oxford University Press.

Sen, A. (1999). *Development as Freedom*, New York: Oxford University Press.

Sen, A. (2002). "Beyond Liberalisation: Social Opportunity and Human Capability", Lakdawala Lecture, in idem, *Re-imagining India and Other Essays*, Hyderabad: Orient Longman.

Sengupta, M. (2008). "How the State Changed Its Mind: Power, Politics and the Origins of India's Market Reforms", *Economic and Political Weekly*, 43: 35–42.

Shani, O. (2017). *How India Became Democratic*, London: Penguin.
Singh, M. (1995). "Inaugural Address", Delivered at the 54th Annual Conference of the Indian Society of Agricultural Economics, in *Indian Journal of Agricultural Economics*, 50: 1–6.
Singh, T. (2020). *Sixteen Stormy Days: The Story of the First Amendment of the Constitution of India*, London: Penguin.
Sivaraman, B. (1991). *Governance of India in Transition*, New Delhi: Ashish Publishing House.
Sivasubramonian, S. (2005). *The National Income of India in the Twentieth Century*, Delhi: Oxford University Press.
Spear, P. (1964) "Nehru", *Modern Asian Studies*, 1: 15–29.
Srinivasan, T.N. (2005). *Eight Lectures on India's Economic Reforms*, New Delhi: Oxford University Press.
Summers, L. (2016). https://www.firstpost.com/india/demonetisation-resulted-in-chaos-and-loss-of-trust-in-govt-larry-summers-3118042.html, accessed 10 August 2021.
Thapar, R. (2009). "Conversations about History: An Interview with Kalpana Sharma", *The Hindu*, 25 January.
Toyama, K. (2015). *Geek Heresy: Rescuing Social Change from the Cult of Technology*, New York: Public Affairs.
Vickrey, W. (1996). "Fifteen Fatal Fallacies of Financial Fundamentalism: A Disquisition on Demand Side Economics", Columbia University Working Paper Series; http://www.columbia.edu/ dlc/wp/econ/vickrey.html, accessed 28 October 2021.
Visvesvaraya, M. (1936). "Planned Economy for India", Bangalore: The Bangalore Press.
Wade, R. (1990). *Governing the Market: Economic Theory and the Role of Government in East Asian Industrialization*, Princeton: Princeton University Press.
Williamson, J. (2004). "A Short History of the Washington Consensus", Paper Commissioned by Fundación CIDOB for the Conference – "From the Washington Consensus Towards a New Global Governance", Barcelona, Spain, 24–25 September.

Index

Aadhaar 91
"Achche din aane wale hain" 9, 18, 143
agriculture 13, 33–4, 66–82 *passim*, 85, 113, 115, 126–31, 138, 139, 166, 167, 171; capitalism in 85, 225n; crop failure 59; crop yields 23, 35; Farm Laws 171; labourers 128; high-yielding variety 71, 76; minimum support price 71, 76; neglect of 32, 34; procurement policy 76; seed 33, 71, 74; semi-feudal 82; worker movement out of 130; Zamindari abolition 227
agricultural: exports 129; growth 13, 34, 66, 77–82, 113, 121, 126–7, 130, 161, 167, 176n, 232; labourers 128; prices 130, 153; productivity 33, 49n35, 122, 130, 131; research institutions 131; state agricultural departments 70; transformation 75, 84, 131
Ahluwalia, Montek Singh 45
Ambedkar, B.R. 53, 227–8
Ambirajan, S. 14
autarky 95
Ayushman Bharat 100

balance of payments 26–7, 41, 119–21, 148; capital account convertibility 111; controls on capital flows 119; crisis 27, 78, 90, 92, 107, 120; current account deficit 59, 120; external liberalisation 119; stress 121, 131, 139; support 107, 109
Bangalore 36, 88
Berlin, Isaiah 2–5, 21, 207–9
Bhagwati, J., and P. Desai 40–1, 62, 64
Bombay Plan 21, 23
Borlaug, Norman Ernest 74–5
Bose, Subhas Chandra 19
Bourdieu, Pierre 206
business-friendly 61, 67, 157

capability 4, 10, 177, 205–19, 231–8; equalisation of 213; formation 236; and functionings 4–5, 205–7; identification of 209; inequality of 206, 237
capitalism 37, 67, 68, 79, 180; free market 217; managerial 231
caste: development indicators by 224; imprint of 222; inequality 222; lower castes 208n7; political mobilisation 224;

251

reform movement 226;
scheduled castes 222–3,
224n21; system of social stratification 221
central government 101, 124, 174,
181, 184, 188, 196–202
central planning 82
Chakravarty, Sukhamoy 29
Chancel and Piketty 44, 138
Chidambaram, P. 234
China 42–3, 96, 108, 120, 133–4,
199, 214–15, 235
civil liberties 235–6, 238
Cold War 68; politics of 74
collective action 118n, 210
colonialism: Britain 3, 15, 17, 22;
British rule 12, 16–17; ending
of 213; rationale of 137;
stagnation 17, 31, 32, 56, 93
"commanding heights of the
economy" 27, 29, 83
commercial banks 160, 182n;
credit from 159; NPAs of
159
competition 22, 112, 116, 121;
foreign 40; and market structure 110; and productivity 110
computer: impact of 88
Confederation of Indian Industry
(CII) 103
Congress Party 19–20, 59, 61, 65,
70
consumption expenditure of
households 123
co-ordination problem 237
corporate governance: principal-
agent problem 231
corruption 88, 90, 142, 145,
176–9; growth of 173
cotton textile industry 22

COVID-19 119, 171, 189–202,
239; mortality 190–6;
policy response 198–200;
stimulus 142, 161–2, 198–1

Delong, Bradford 82
demand 29, 39, 62, 77, 90,
138–9, 153, 159, 177, 183,
226; aggregate demand 39,
62, 182, 183, 186, 200–1;
derived demand 129; demand
side 138, 187; for food 26;
external 129; external
source of 138; exogenous
drivers of 161; household
demand 122; for goods of mass
consumption 138; loss of 198;
for non-agricultural goods
77–8; for urban products 126;
slow growth of 137; sources
of 130; and supply 186
democracy 5, 13, 15, 21, 41,
48, 59, 173, 178, 215, 218,
221–2, 225–9, 232, 235,
237–8; constitutional 173; and
development 205; government
by discussion 228; history
of 228; liberal democracy
210–11; political 205, 212,
225; social democracy 223–4;
weakening of in India 180;
Westminster model 237
demonetisation 151, 156–7,
162, 167, 171–88 *passim*;
black incomes 174; black
money 173, 175, 178–9, 187;
cash crunch 167; cash hoards
172, 176; consequences of 155;
counterfeit currency 174;
currency 172–3; currency in

circulation 172n27, 177; impact of 155; formalisation of economy 187, 188
deprivation 5, 32, 214, 225, 228–9
Deaton and Dreze 123
Desai, Morarji 105
development: capability approach 209, 232; expansion of freedoms 3, 205, 209–10, 227–8, 235, 238; gender in 220; regional variation of 218. *See also* human development
direct income transfers 152
distributivism 28
Drain Theory, 16

"ease of doing business" 143, 158
East Asia 42, 49n35, 97, 131; late industrialisers of 41
East Asian: experience 42, 132, 136; miracle 135–6; state 135; success in manufacturing 134
East India Company (EIC) 12, 16, 136
ecological: consequences 76; decline 239; emerging challenges 236; factor 131
economic architecture 21, 107, 188–9
economic reforms 8, 83, 94, 99, 108, 112, 120–1, 126–7; of 1991, 6, 9, 10n, 82, 102, 134, 140; economic liberalisation 111; import liberalisation 114; liberalisation of controls on trade and industry 60; overhaul of economic policy regime 94; outcomes of 109–12, 125, 133, 144, 153; politics of 103;

structural reforms 107–9; restructuring of trade and industrial policy 113
education: basic 53; compulsory 213; early childhood 211; higher 47, 55, 124, 217; holistic 54; investing in 53n; low level of spending on 217; outcomes 216; policy 211; public spending 216; role of 48, 50
employment 77, 79, 118, 145, 149, 154–5, 157, 164, 182, 224n20, 233, 234n31; creation 142; generation of 235; issue of 115; pursuit of 129; widespread growth of 115
environmental constraint 118n
epidemic 189–94, 199–201; experience of 190; Spanish flu 189; surveillance and containment 193
export pessimism 129
exports 17, 26, 40–4, 129, 161; and imports 111; competitiveness 121–2 130
external sector 110
equality of opportunity 212–13

famines 13–15
fiscal policy 147, 148, 183, 188; budget deficit 107, 108, 151, 155; fiscal correction 109, 185; fiscal consolidation 146–9, 152, 184–5, 188, 201; fiscal deficit 95, 107, 146, 150, 152, 183–5; fiscal discipline 145, 146, 185; government borrowing 147; public expenditure 47,

91, 145, 146, 181–5, 192–6, 199, 215–17
Fiscal Responsibility and Budgetary Management (FRBM) Act of 2003 146, 152, 185
Fischer, Stanley 147
five-trillion-dollar economy 19, 239
five-year plan 23, 30; First Five-Year Plan 33; Second Five-Year Plan 24–7, 30, 48, 60n, 68
food: aid 68; deficit 69; foodgrains 113; "Grow More Food" campaign 35, 70; inflation 141; production 15, 33, 70, 72–3; real price of 122; self-reliance in 72, 74; share in household expenditure 122; shortages 75, 78, 92, 204; sovereignty 70, 74; stocks 59, 131; subsidy 76; supply 14–15, 26, 46, 70
Food Corporation of India (FCI) 59, 184n38
foreign capital 97, 101, 121; direct and portfolio investments 98; foreign investors 97; inflows 119–21, 165
foreign exchange 26, 27, 33, 68, 69, 104–5: bureaucratic allocation of 40; deficit 59; earnings 89; reserves 59, 120; shortage 119; support 108
Foreign Exchange Regulation Act (FERA) 61
foreign trade policy: elimination of quantitative controls 132; import quotas 97, 98, 106; protectionism 22, 140; quantitative restrictions on trade 111; tariffs 40, 50, 51, 97, 107, 132; trade and industrial policy regime 105, 109
former Soviet Union (FSU) 95–7, 104, 108; disintegration of 96
Frankel, Francine 74

Garibi Hatao 61, 62, 79–82, 232
Gandhi, M.K. 53–4
Gandhi, Indira 8, 59–89 *passim*, 105–6, 109, 144, 203, 232
Gandhi, Rajiv 8–9, 57, 65, 86–92, 105–6, 135–6, 144–5
gender: and development 220; sex-ratio 220–1
General Theory of Employment, Interest and Money 160
global financial crisis (GFC) of 2008 112, 141, 161
globalisation 95, 100–1; challenges posed by 236
goods and services tax (GST) 162–3, 177n, 187, 188
Green Revolution 65, 67–86 *passim*, 131
growth: acceleration of 66–7; engine of 89, 120, 122, 130, 141; inter-sectoral 67; nature of 81, 112; revival of 63–4, 67; Solow model of 159
Gujarat 142, 157, 170, 218–20, 227

health 184, 194–6, 207, 211, 215; allocation for 194; crisis in India 216; of expecting mothers 211; expenditure 195–6, 201; in India 87;

infrastructure 190, 192, 195–6; outcomes 216; personnel 216; public 51n, 192–4, 230; public health system 190–6, 215; public expenditure on 192, 194, 215; security 196
health and education 51–2, 55, 123, 184–5; endowment of 210; in India 215n; India's poor performance on 217; indicators of 219; public provision of 100; reduction in expenditure on 184; share in total expenditure 184; spread of 226
human development 4, 6–7, 9–10, 52, 100, 136, 210–31, 236–9; divergence in 219; in India 214; neglect of 56, 236
human resources 49
hysteresis 160–1

illiteracy 214, 217; among adults 47; assault on 51; elimination of 226
immigration controls 100
imports 22, 26, 40, 111, 116, 120, 139; food 72, 75; income elasticity of 120; influx of 98; quantitative restriction on 98
import-substituting industrialisation 40, 96–7
inclusive growth 115, 118, 233
Indian Constitution 71; amendment of 60n; Directive Principles 230n, 231; Fundamental Rights 230n, 231
industry 22, 30, 35, 40, 61, 79, 87, 89, 101, 103, 106, 126, 137, 164, 169, 204; capacity

expansion 101; delicensing 110–11; deregulation 146; globally competitive software 88; heavy industries 48, 78; industrial policy 37, 99, 101–2, 105, 109, 113, 145; legal barrier to exit 105; licensing 101, 107, 110; private investment in 63; protection of domestic industry 110, 113, 186; and services 127; and trade sectors 132
Industrial Disputes Act 1947 85: amendment of 85; chapter VB of 85
Industrial Policy Statement of 1991 101, 107
inequality: income 44, 96; basic capability 206; absolute level of 138; caste 222; gender 221, 224; between social groups 223
infrastructure 30, 34, 117, 118n, 134, 135, 140, 143, 168–70, 184, for digital payments 179; health 190, 192–3, 195–6; lending to 159; in public health sector 193; publicly provided 121; physical 117, 130, 169, 193; public investment in 42, 135; spending on 187
International Monetary Fund (IMF) 64, 102, 106–9, 119, 147, 199, 200
investment: capital formation 65, 93, 157–62, 166, 169–70, 185, 235; collapse of private corporate 203; licensing 98, 110; long-term expectations 160, 203; in machine manufacturing sector 29; outlay 24,

26; planning 38; as a share of
national income 38

Jaitley, Arun 145–6, 148, 188
Johnson, Lyndon 68

Kaldor, Nicholas 132
Kalecki, Michal, 68
Kerala 49n35, 176, 218–27;
ending of landlordism 226;
"Kerala Model of
Development" 221
Keynes, J.M. 18, 160; Keynesian
demand-constrained equilibrium
198; Keynesian Revolution in
economic theory 128–9
Kidwai, Rafi Ahmed 22, 52, 69
Kim, Linsu 49
knowledge 3, 23, 33, 79, 131; of
agriculture 25; scientific 73;
stock of 211
Korea 22, 43, 48–9, 69
Kotwal, Ramaswami, and
Wadhwa 64
Krishna, Raj 34
Krishnamurti, B.V. 48

labour: coercive allocation of 96;
cost 128; landless rural 128;
manual 128; productivity
of 50, 128, 187; suppression
of 226
labour law: tightening of 105
land: productive capacity of
118; reforms 49n35, 226,
227; revenue 12, 13, 15;
tenure 13
"liberalisation, privatisation,
globalisation" (LPG) 99
license-quota raj 10n

life expectancy 214, 218
literacy 47, 87, 134, 217, 226;
adult 214, 216; and child
mortality 223; and infant
mortality 224; low levels of
229; rate of 50, 222; spread
of 55
lockdown 156, 197–8, 200–1;
clampdown on movement
and economic activity 197;
hardship and mental stress for
migrant labourers 197; loss of
livelihood 198; loss of output
during 198; nationwide 197;
stringency 197

Macpherson, C.B. 209–10, 235
macroeconomic: consequences
of 39; environment 147,
154–5, 159; framework 147–8;
fundamentalism in policy-
making 180–1; indicators 86;
management 119; policy
148–50; reforms 107–8;
stability 149–54, 159;
stimulus 142; truisms 150
Maddison, A. 16
Mahalanobis, P.C. 2, 24–33, 36,
48, 138; model 25–7, 30, 33,
37, 43
"Make in India" 97, 162–7,
169–70
malnutrition 211
Malthus 14–15; Malthusian
ideology 14
manufacturing: dynamic enclaves
within 115; dynamism in 66;
East Asian success in 134; global
hub for 164; investment in 29,
63, 67; organised 97; sector 29,

72, 132, 134, 137–8, 167, 170; share of 133, 138, 168–9
manufactures 78, 139; British 44; export of 27; growth of demand for 130; high quality 132
market forces 95, 98, 109
market reforms 102, 109, 113, 124
Mathai, John 23
"maximin principle" 223
"minimum government, maximum governance" 143
Modi, Narendra 9, 23, 97, 142–9, 157, 160–1, 164, 166, 170, 172, 181, 185, 202–3
Modi government 8, 110n, 146–203 *passim*, 205
Modinomics 180
"monetary policy" 150, 153–4, 182–3, central bank 149–54, 182; central objective of 149; inflation targeting 149, 153–4, 182; "multiple indicators' approach 149; modern monetary policy framework 188
Monopolies and Restrictive Trade Practices (MRTP) Act, 1961
Moore, Barrington 51, 225
Mukherjee, Pranab 108

Naoroji, Dadabhai 16
National Rural Employment Guarantee Scheme (NREGA) 100, 124
National Democratic Alliance (NDA) 28, 146
nationalisation 29, 61
Nehru era 7, 31–49 *passim*, 55–9, 69, 79, 83, 106, 138; economic policies of 8, 83
Nehru, Jawaharlal 2, 5, 19, 20,

22–30, 33–7, 44, 46, 51–3, 60n, 68–9, 82–3, 144, 204, 213; long tenure of 92; after the passing of 57
Nehru-Mahalanobis Strategy 28–40, 44, 55, 72, 134
natural resource availability 130
NITI Aayog 144, 218, 220
non-performing assets (NPAs) 159–60, 168

Panchayati Raj 54
pandemic 58, 112, 123, 129, 200, 216; COVID-19, 119, 171, 189–202 *passim*, 239; second wave of 197
paternalism 234
planning: decentralised 54
Planning Commission 22, 23, 35, 48, 144
"policy paralysis" 142
policy regime 39, 97–8, 101, 113n16, 137; change initiated in 1991, 99; character of 111; economic 7, 8, 60, 76, 83; external 98; in India 40, 102; liberalisation of 127; overhaul of 94, 164; reform of 133; shift in 57; trade and industrial 105, 109
population growth 13–15, 31, 45
poverty: eradication of 53, 80, 232; extreme 19, 139, 214, 226; multidimensional 218; official estimates of 124; rural 45, 126; strategies for elimination of 127; trends in 45, 90; urban 126–7
positive freedom 3–6, 10, 61, 207–9
private investment 18, 38–9,

86, 90, 110, 135, 145, 159, 162, 181–3, 186, 189, 198, 202, 232; climate for 160; corporate 63; crowding in 161; in industry 63; rate of growth of credit for 127; response of 157; revival in 201
private sector 21, 26, 29, 32, 35, 37–9, 42, 46, 79, 83, 90, 97, 145, 157, 162, 169, 175, 181, 202, 203; animal spirits of the 65; capital formation in 157; enterprises 35; investment response of 62, 89; organised 65; output of 38; reducing government control over 121; regulatory powers over 23; suppression of 38
pro-business 85, 202
property rights: strengthening of 146
public distribution system 15, 71, 76, 185, 198
public goods 117–19, 212, 234n31; absence of 237; equal access to 222; in Europe's welfare states 147; externalities associated with 212
public investment 29, 30, 34–9, 42, 65, 78–9, 89, 127, 138, 141, 161, 162, 202; allocation of 134; high rate of 235; ideological approach to 170n24; increase in 186; in infrastructure 135; upsurge in 161
public–private-partnership (PPP) 72
public sector 29, 30, 32, 35–8, 79, 83, 99, 116, 176; banks 160;

capital formation in 158; enterprises 35–7, 42, 109; inefficiencies in functioning of 184; management institutes 6; performance of 35; privileging of 106; role of 35; savings of 35; state-wise data on health infrastructure in 192
pre-modern society 225

quality of life 115–18

Rao, Narasimha 144
Rao, V.K.R.V. 34
regional imbalance in development 96
Ricardo, David 122
Right to Information (RTI) Act 178
Rodrik, D., and A. Subramanian 64–7, 77, 85, 106, 157
rural: areas 48, 190; economy 13, 49n35; hierarchy 51; incomes 126; landless labour 128; population 45; poor 127; poverty 45, 126; prosperity 77; social structure 49n35; and urban 126, 222

Sarva Shiksha Abhiyan 100n
self-reliance: in food 72, 74
Sen, Amartya 3–5, 13, 205–10
Shastri, Lal Bahadur 59, 73
Singh, Manmohan 91, 141, 144
Singh, V.P. 89, 105
Sivasubramonian, S. 16, 31
schooling 47, 134, 217; expenditure on elementary 82; primary

55; public 82, 212; secondary school enrolment 216; superior level of 133; uniformity of 206, 237
skills 134, 140, 212; skilling 128, 171; upgrading of 233
small and medium enterprises (SME) sector 63
Smith, Adam 39, 136
social cohesion 212–13, 237
socialism 61, 65, 67, 232; Fabian 82; Nehruvian 83
socialist 46, 72, 82, 96, 217
"socialistic pattern of society" 27, 83
social transformation 10, 213, 226
software services: exporters 121; industry 89
standard of living 75
Subramaniam, C. 73
subsidies 50, 51, 108, 184–5; non-merit 184
surgical strike: against black money hoards 179, 187. *See* demonetisation

taxation: cascading of taxes 187; extortionate tax rate 232; income tax department 177, 178; income tax rates 61; tax authorities 173–4; tax evasion 173; tax reform 89, 145; tax revenue 163, 187; value added tax 187
Tamilnadu 71, 219–35; "Dravidian movement" 227
technical progress 159
technology 79, 87, 190, 236; information 187n; Indian

Institutes of Technology (IITs) 46; introduction of 87; state-of-the-art 106; transfer of 79
technological: consciousness 87; innovation 87
telecommunications 87, 106, 116–17; public sector monopoly in 106; revolution 88
trade barriers 105
"twin balance-sheet problem" 160
Twitter 45, 73

unemployment 142, 155–7, 202, 234n31; discouraged workers 157
United Progressive Alliance (UPA) 28, 141
Uttar Pradesh 71, 218–20

Vajpayee, A.B. 141, 146
Visvesvaraya, M. 20

Wade, Robert 42, 135
wages 77, 132
Washington Consensus 102, 145, 147, 185; important tenet of 183
water: drinking 87; and electricity 118n18; management 87; overuse of 76; supply 71, 76
welfare 228n; economic 230; Europe's welfare states 147, 234n31; impact 106; initiatives 235; leakage in delivery of schemes 91; of man 51; private 92, 231; programmes 207; provision 101; schemes 235; social 231; state 3, 235;

welfarism 234–5; well-being 4, 115, 208
West Bengal 218–20,
Williamson, John 145
women: anaemia among 220; crimes against 220–1; empowerment 220; female labour force participation rate 221, 224; female literacy rate 220; literacy of 47n, 227; marginalisation in India 221; suppression of agency 5
World Bank 45, 64, 107, 158, 170, 214, 216, 220n15
World Health Organisation (WHO) 194n
World Trade Organisation (WTO) 98, 111

Xiaoping, Deng 42